AF473906

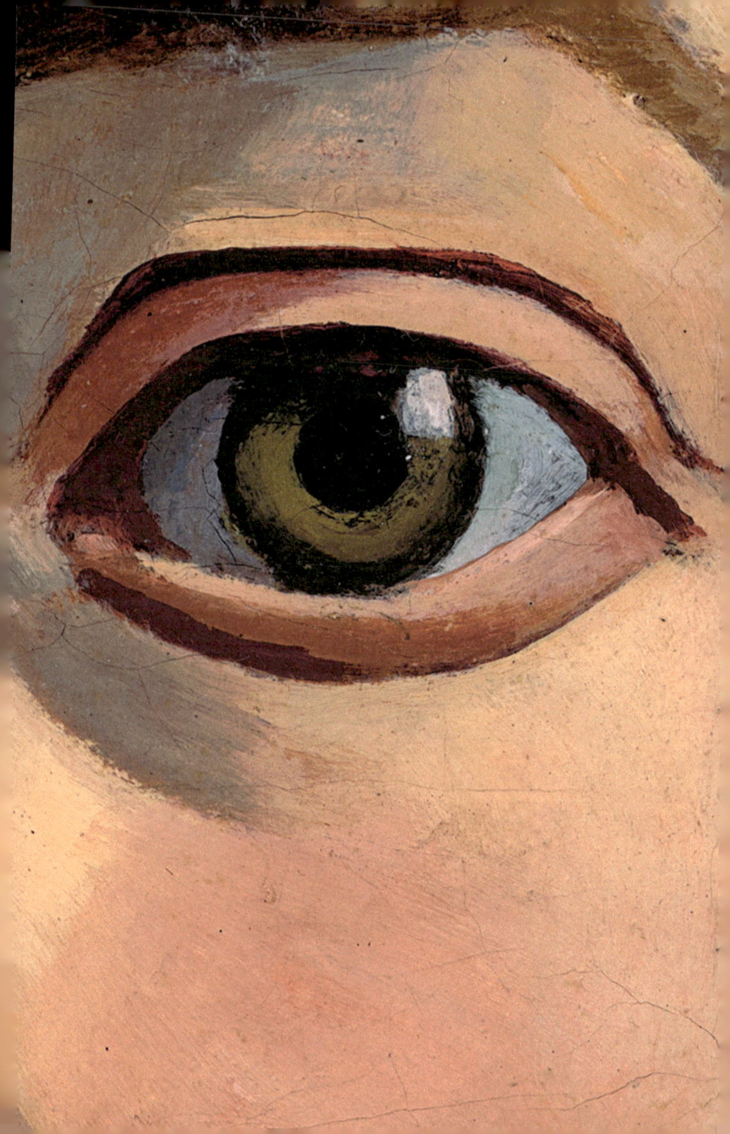

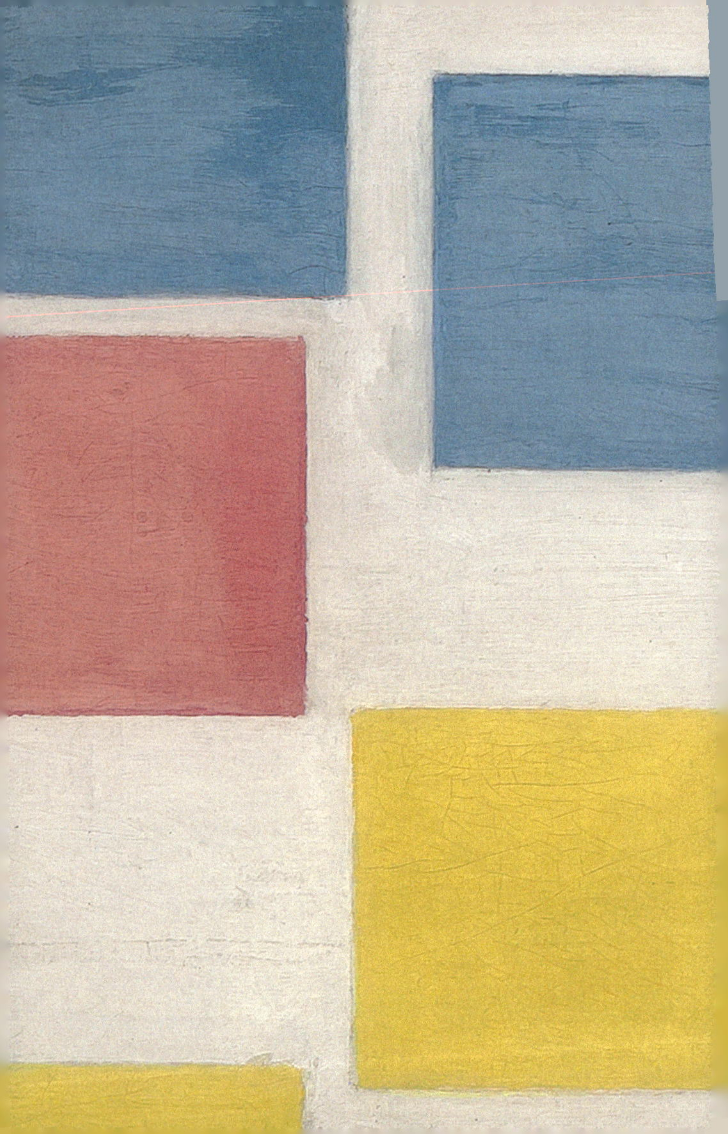

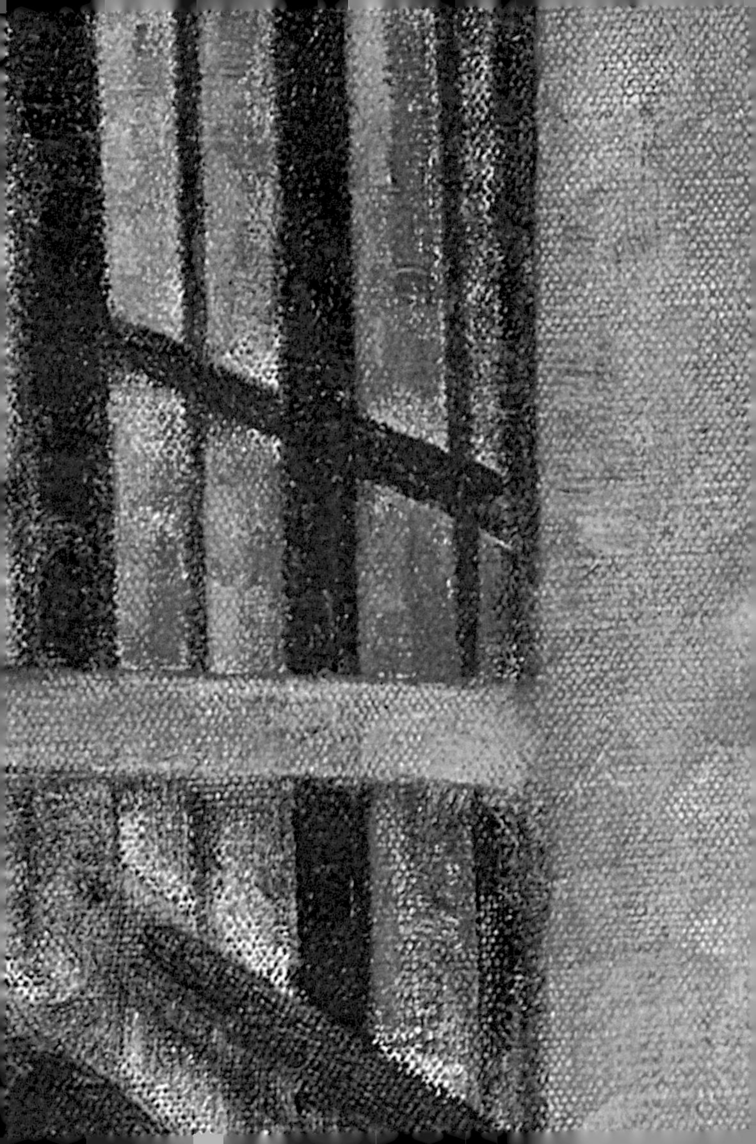

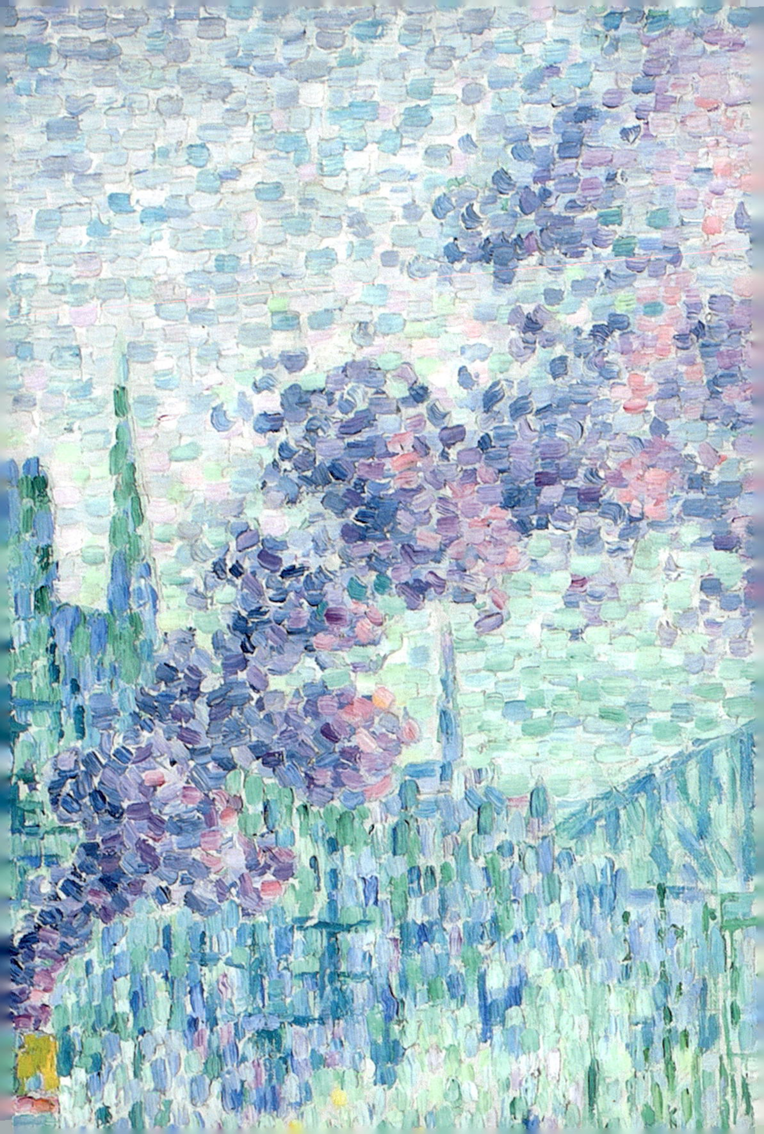

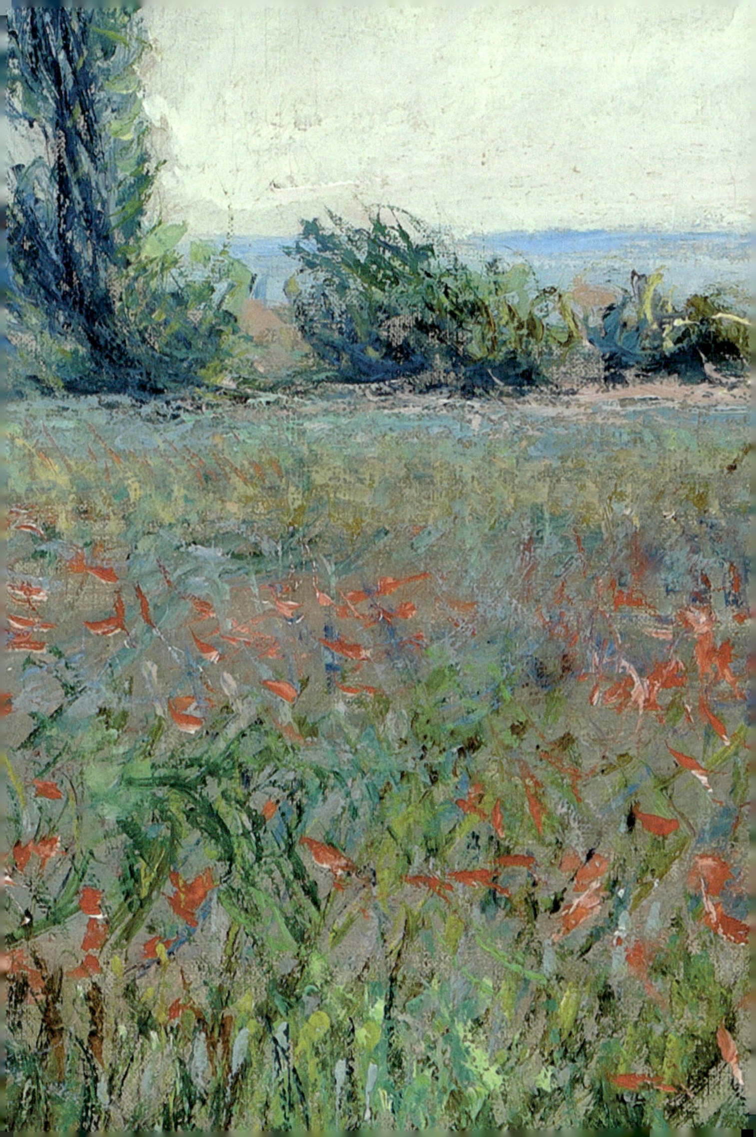

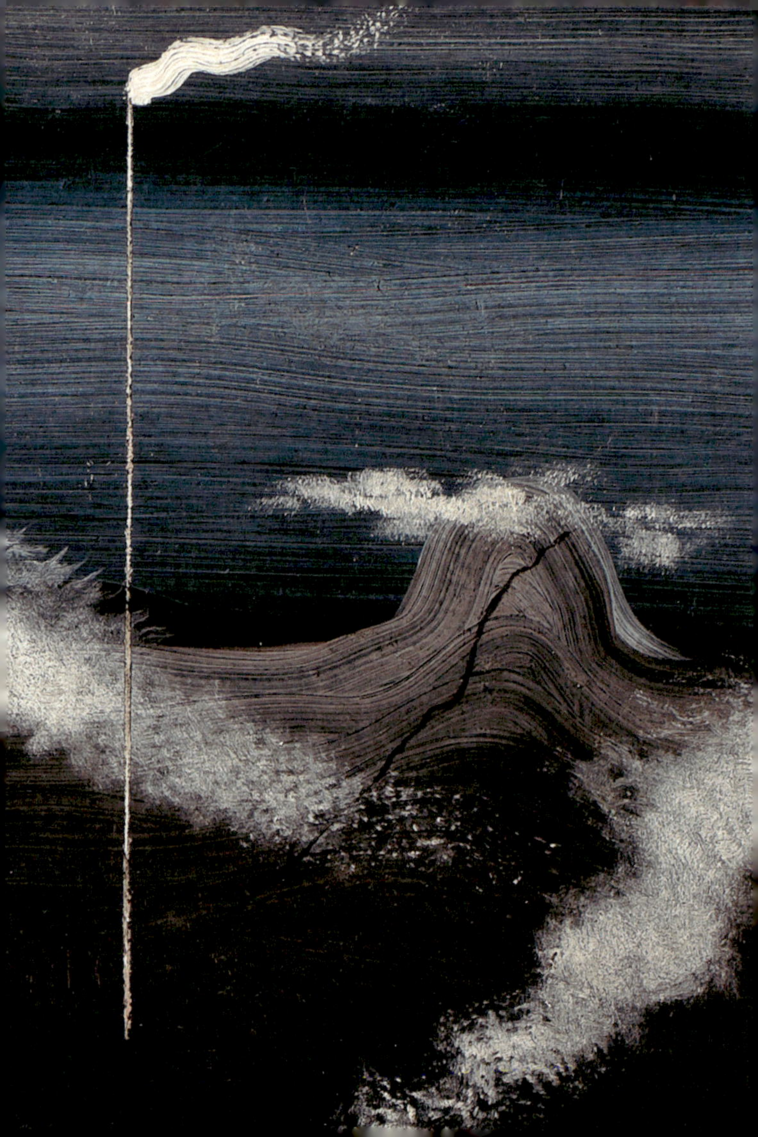

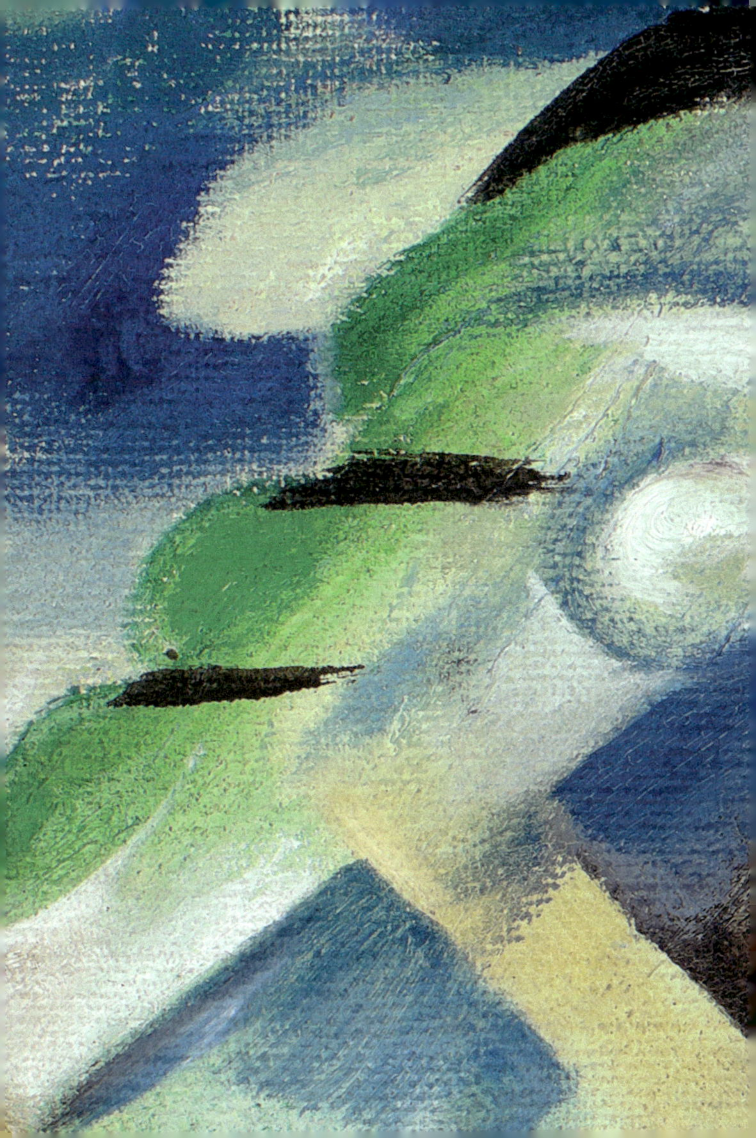

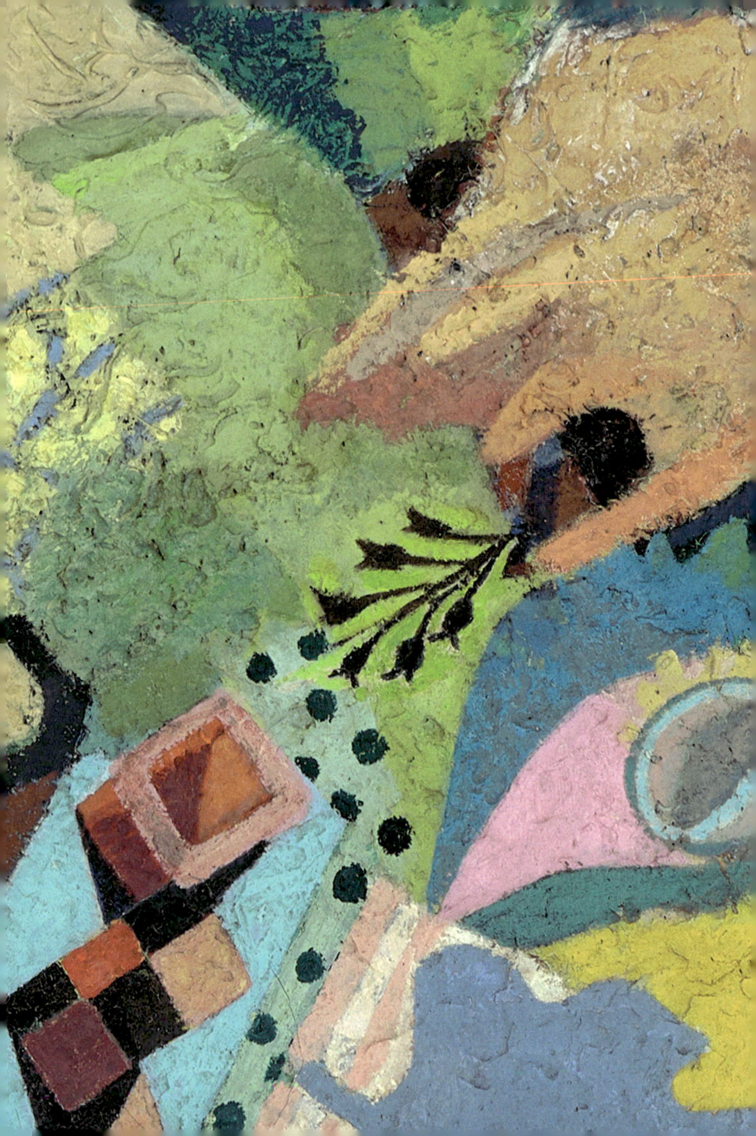

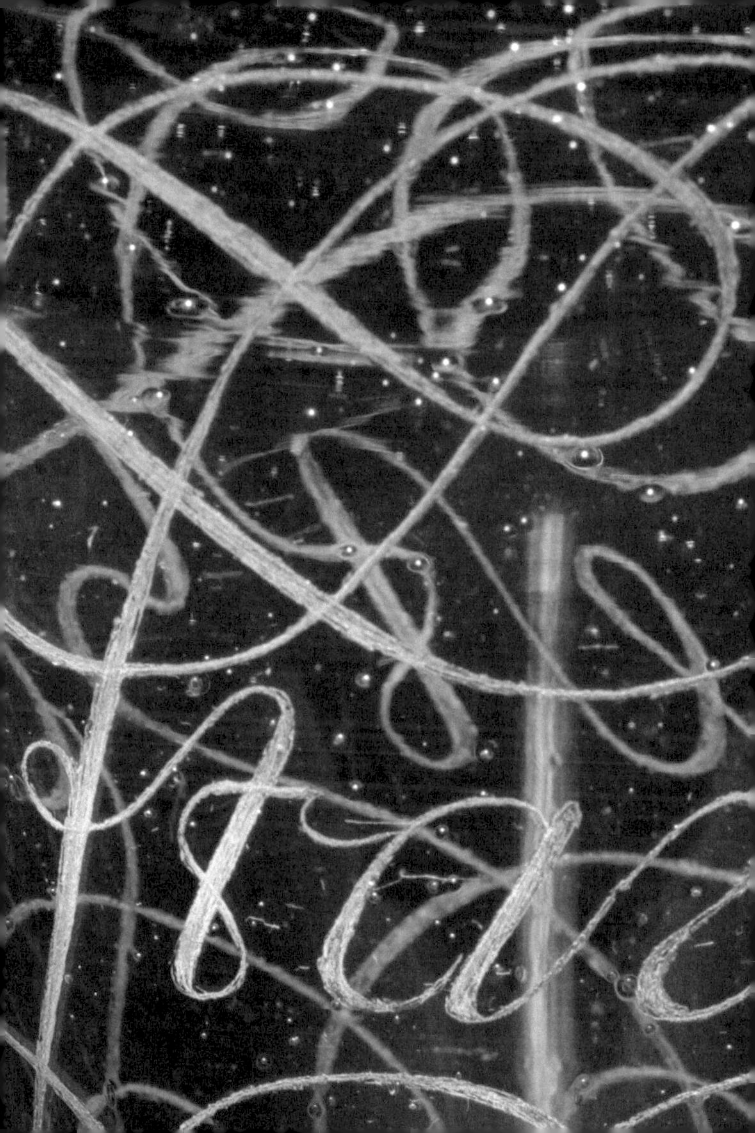

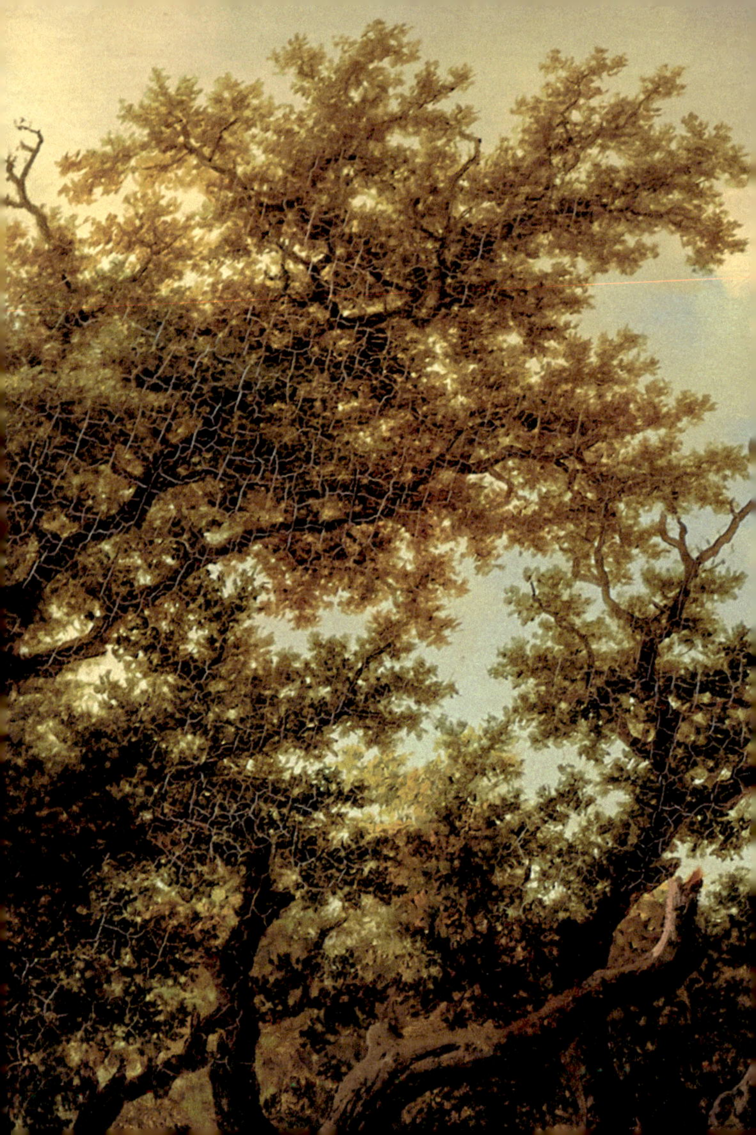

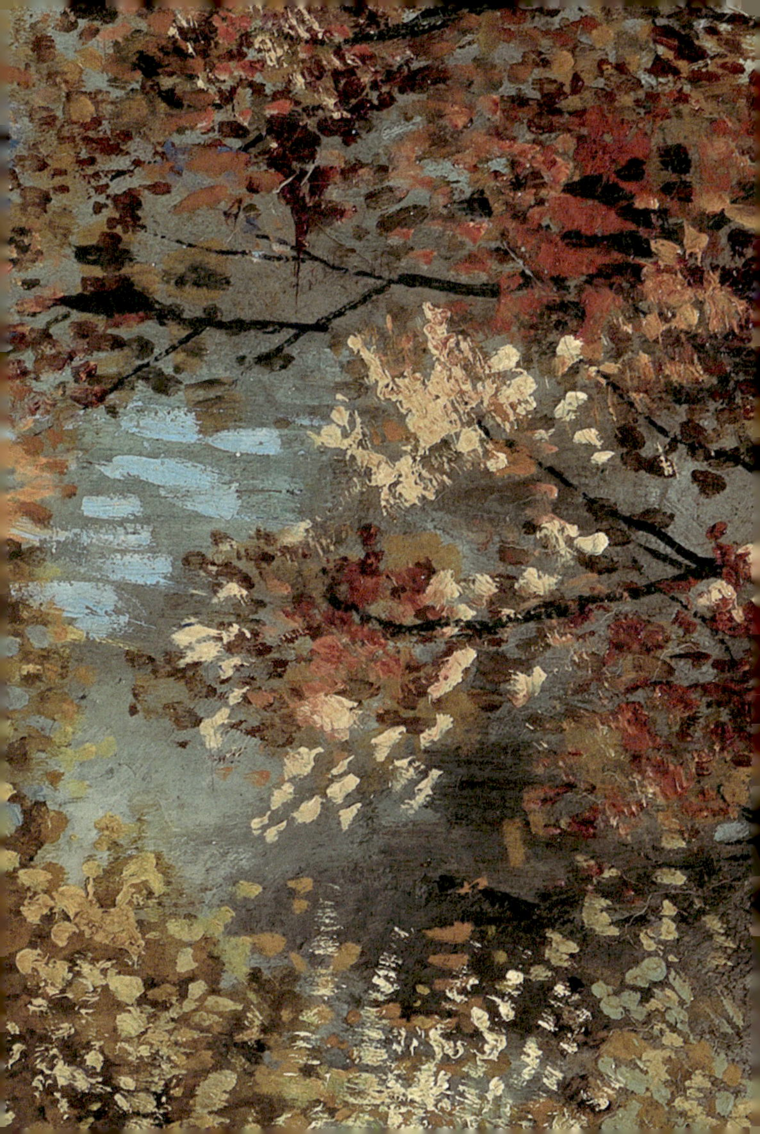

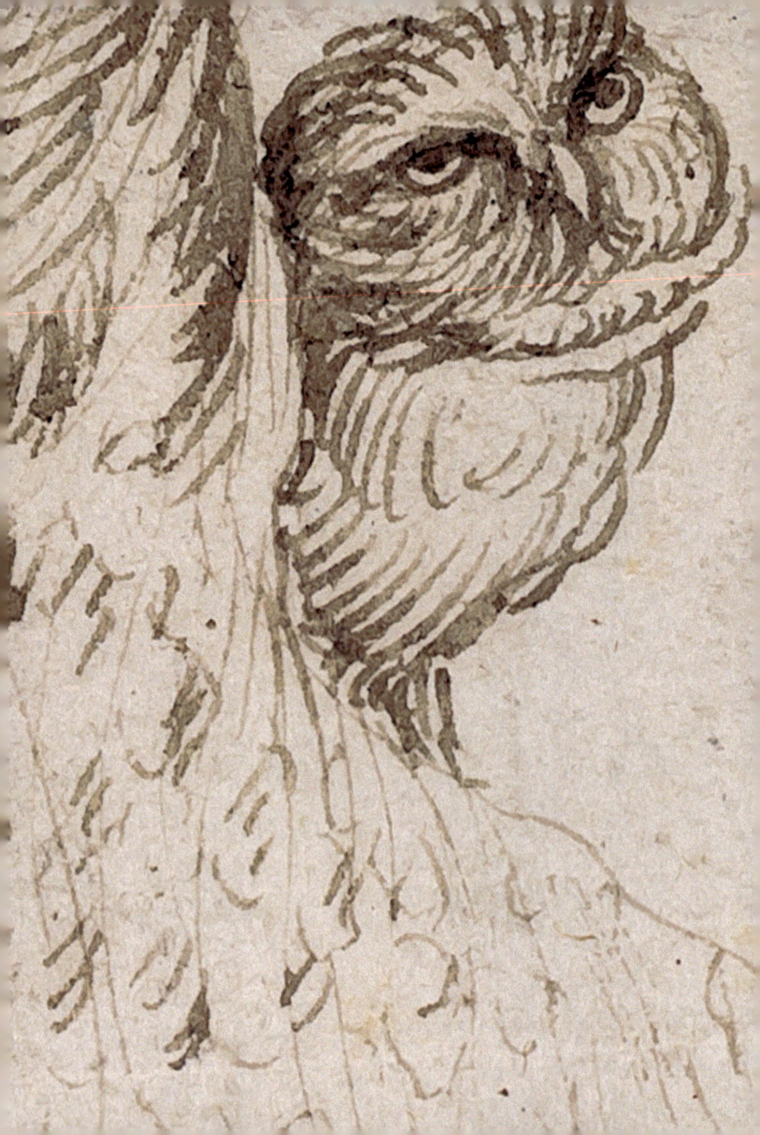

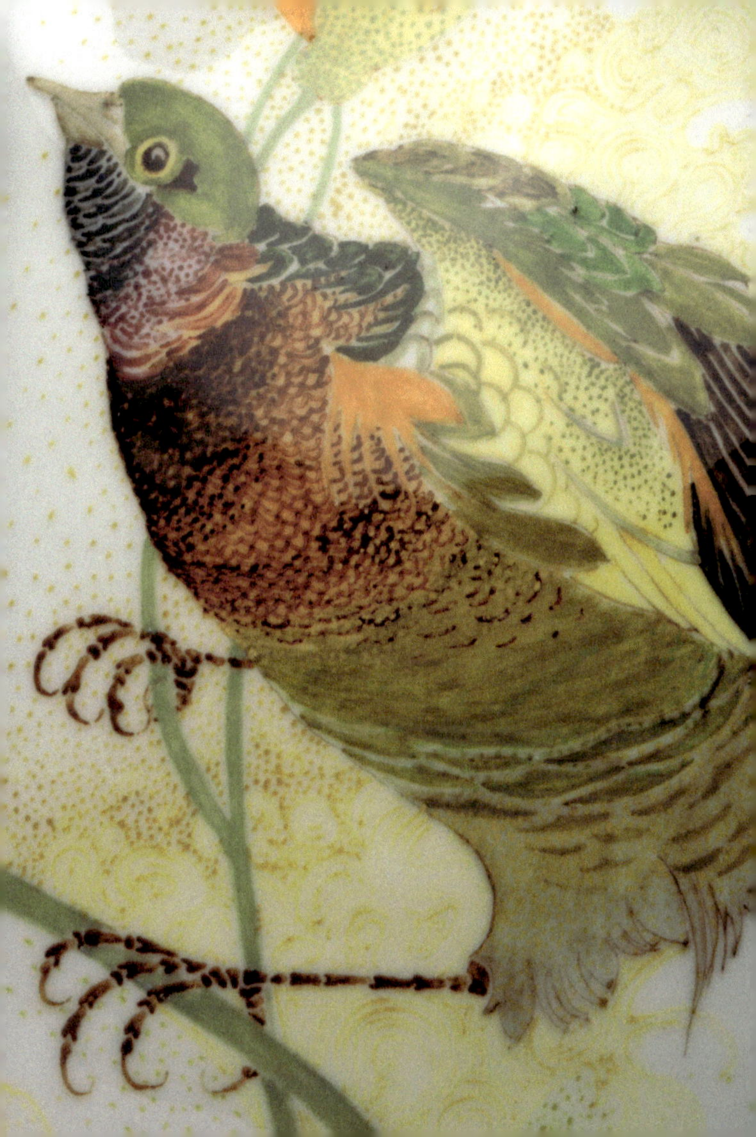

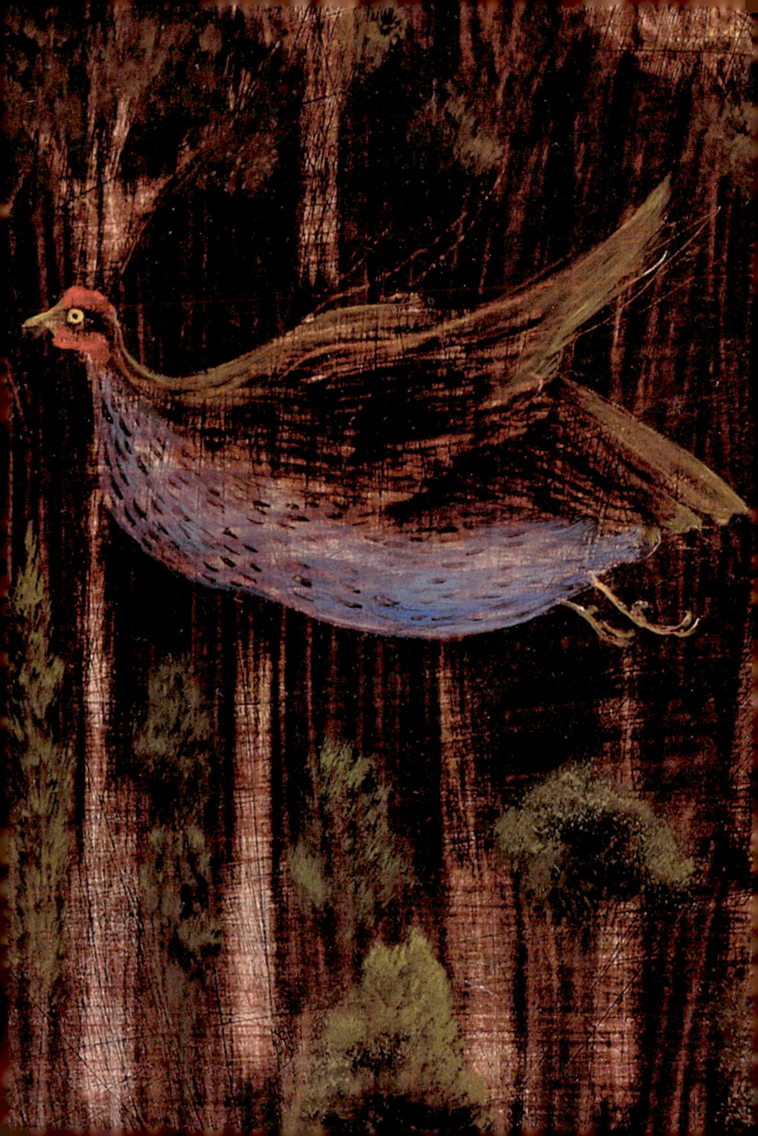

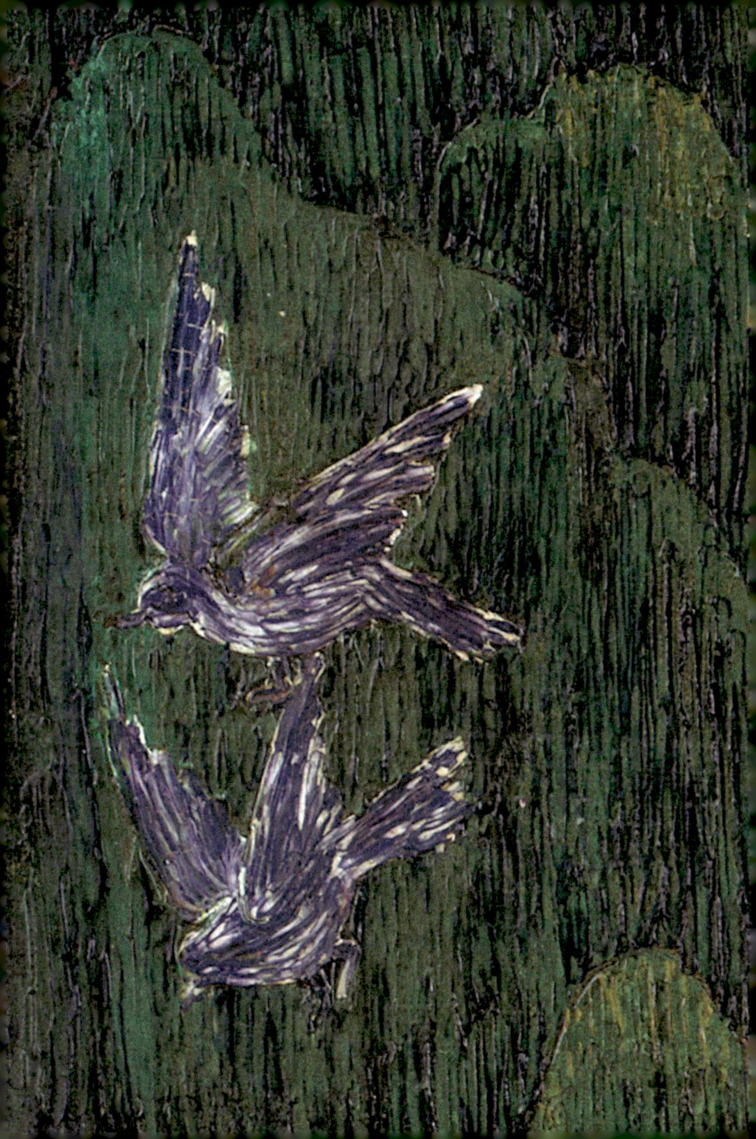

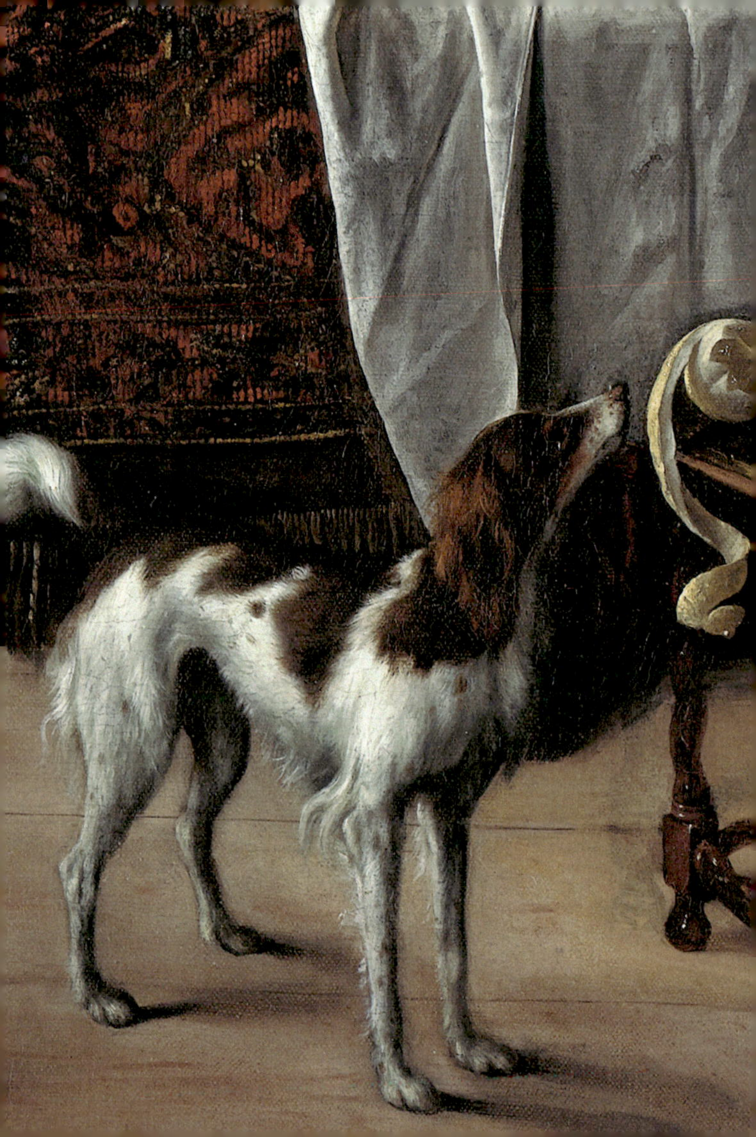

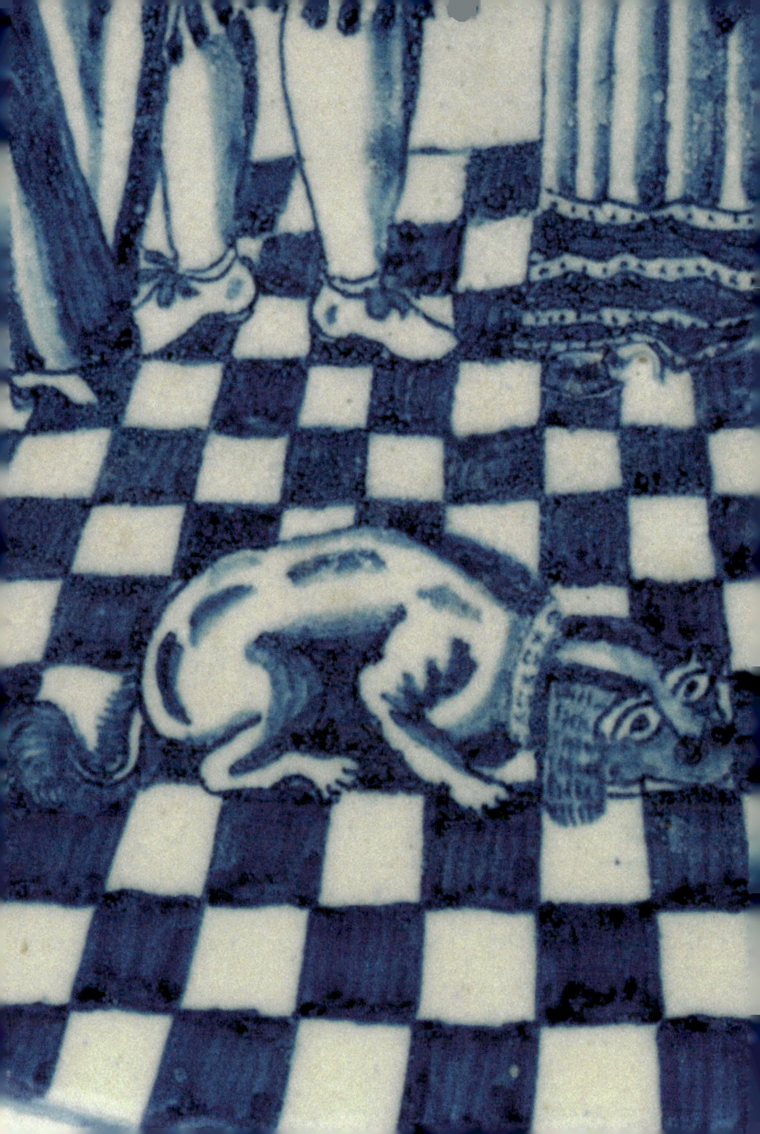

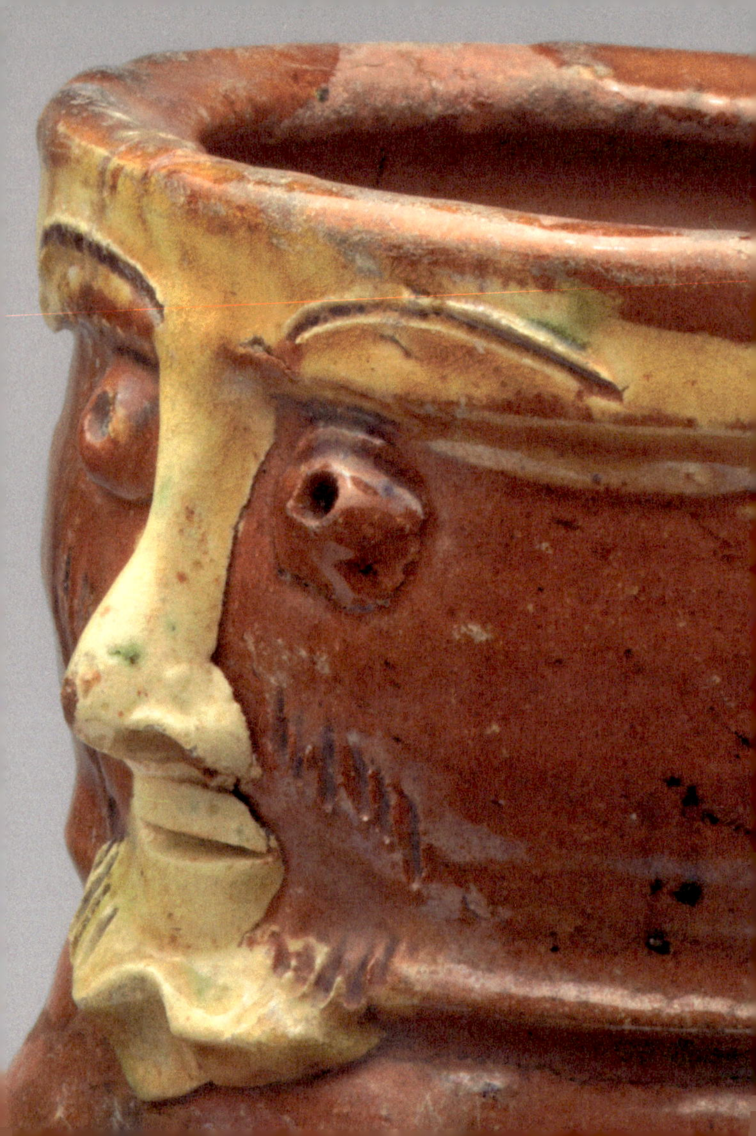

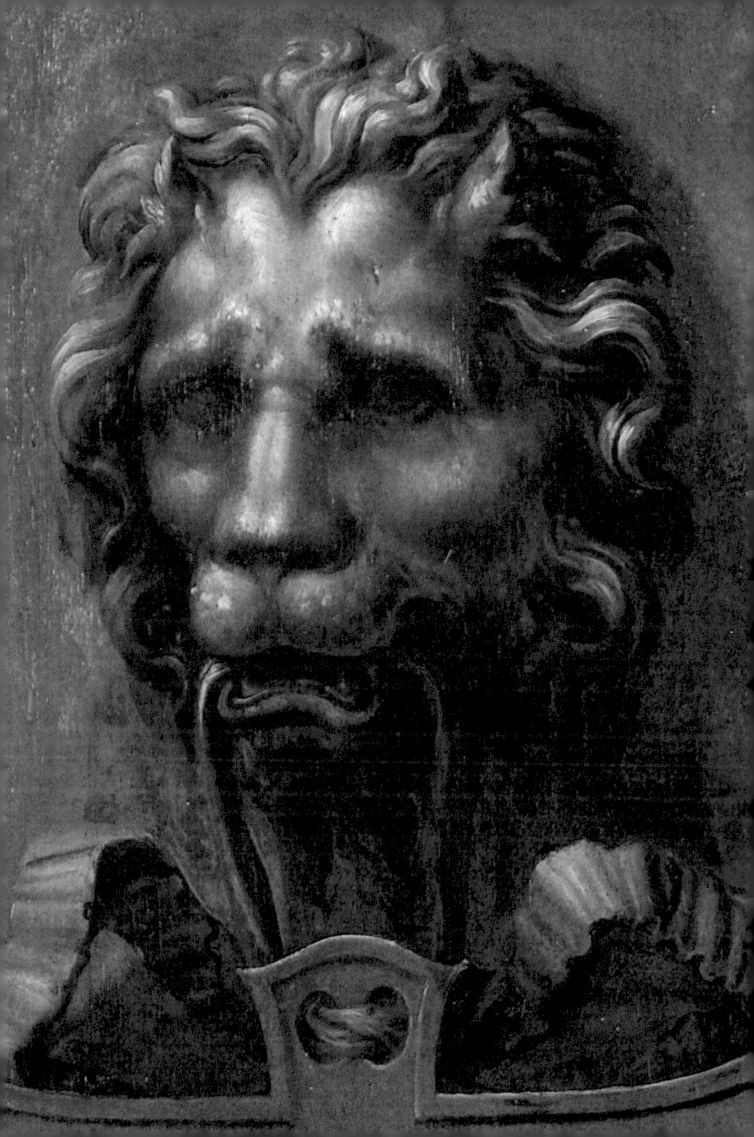

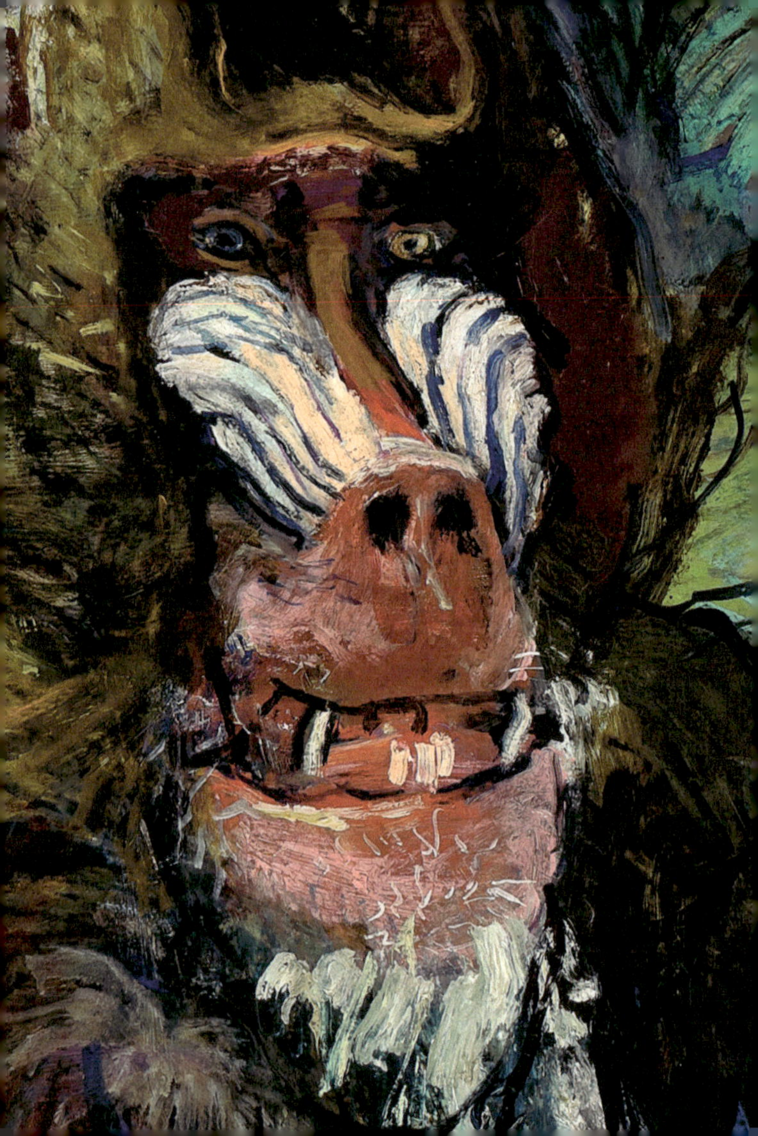

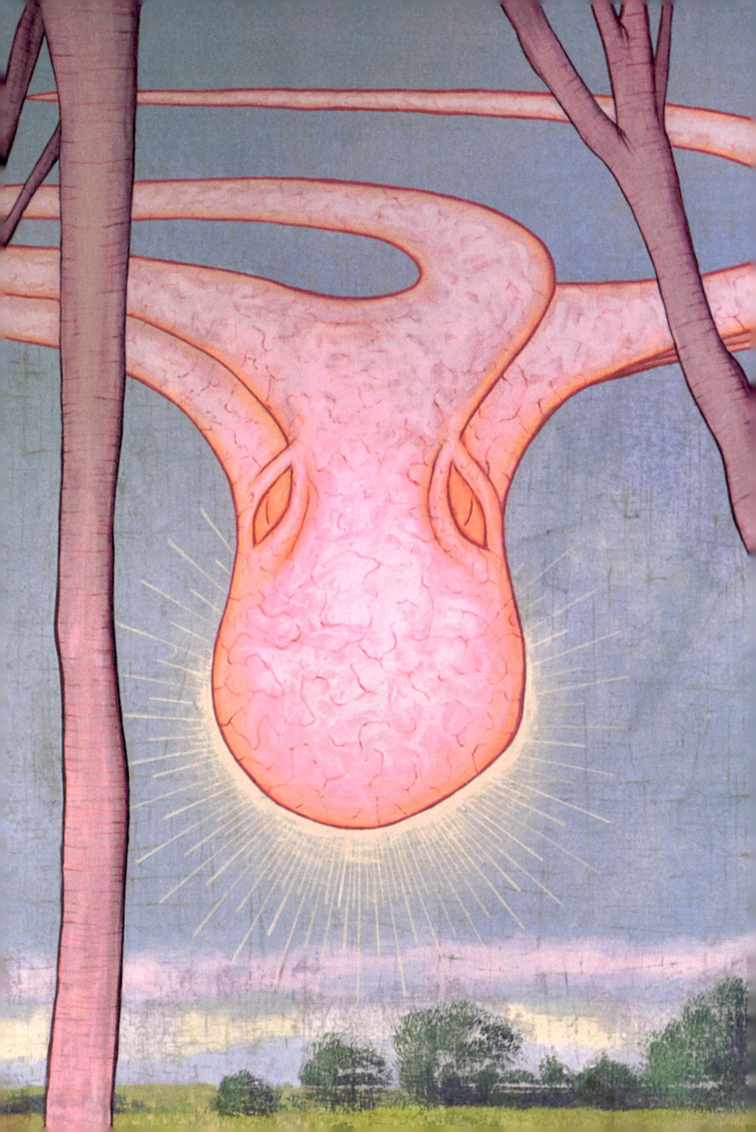

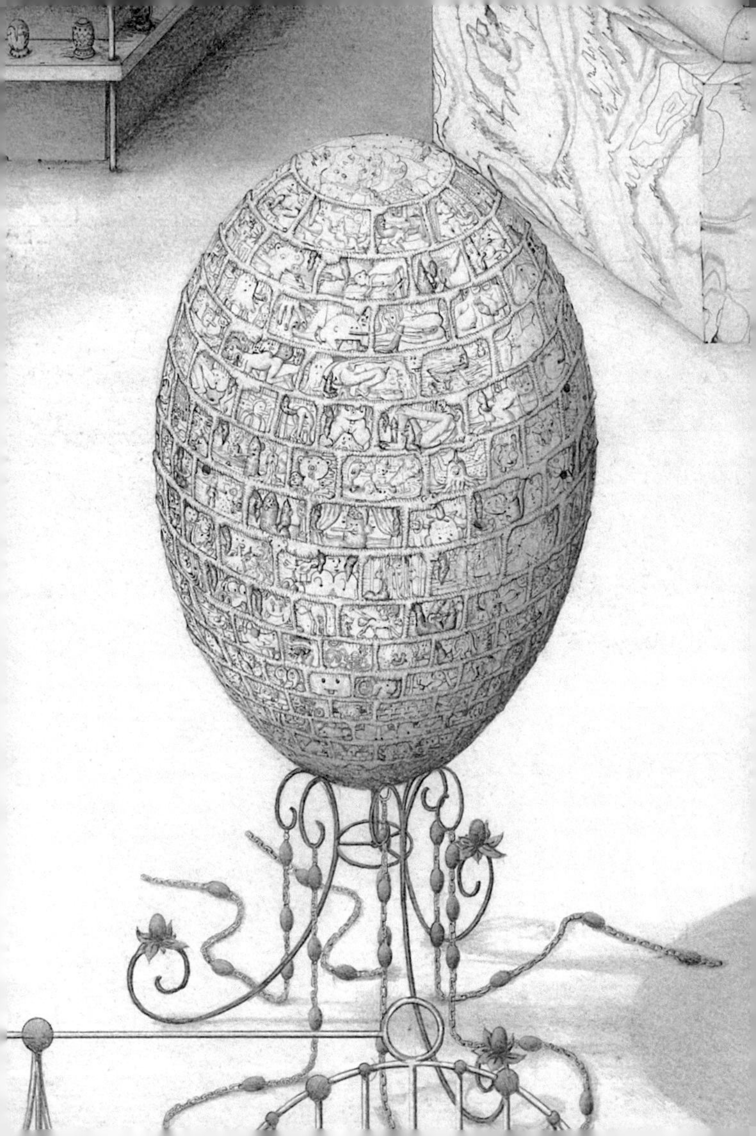

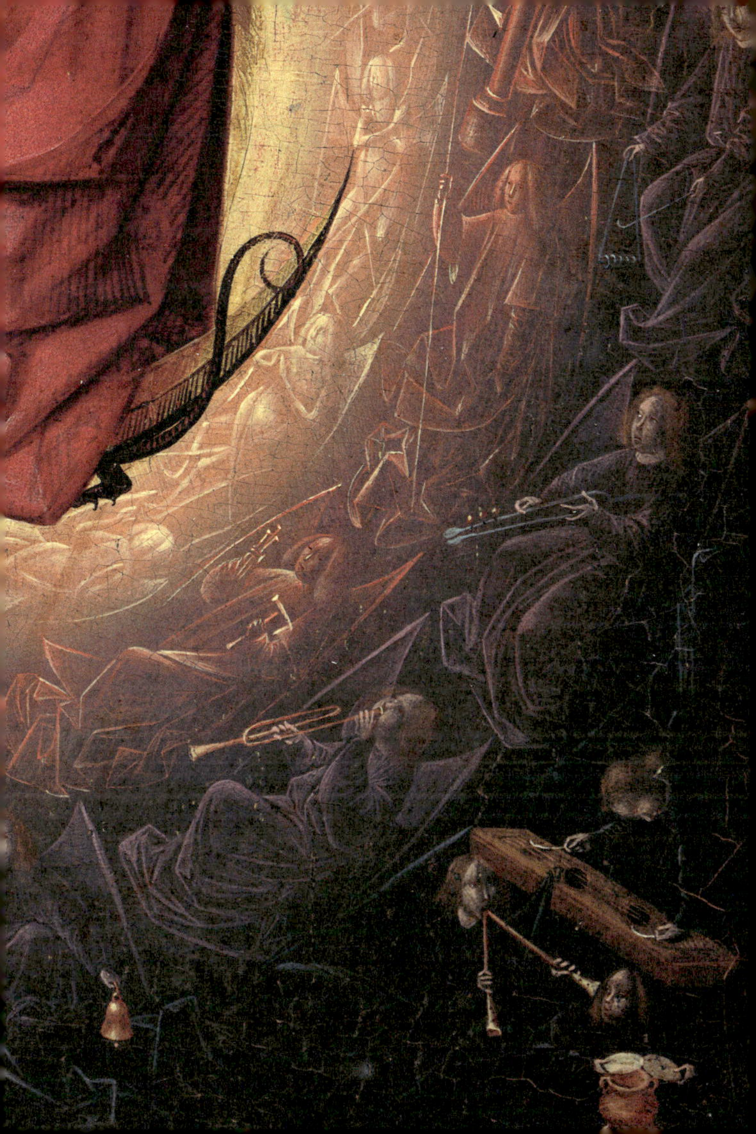

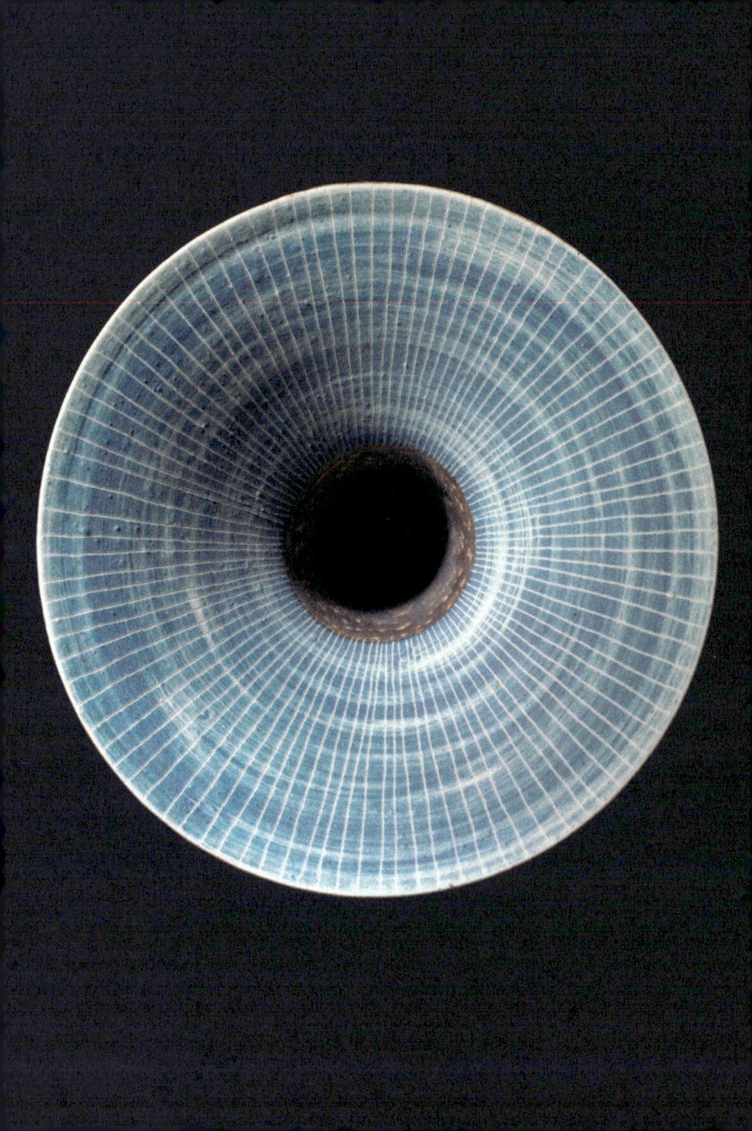

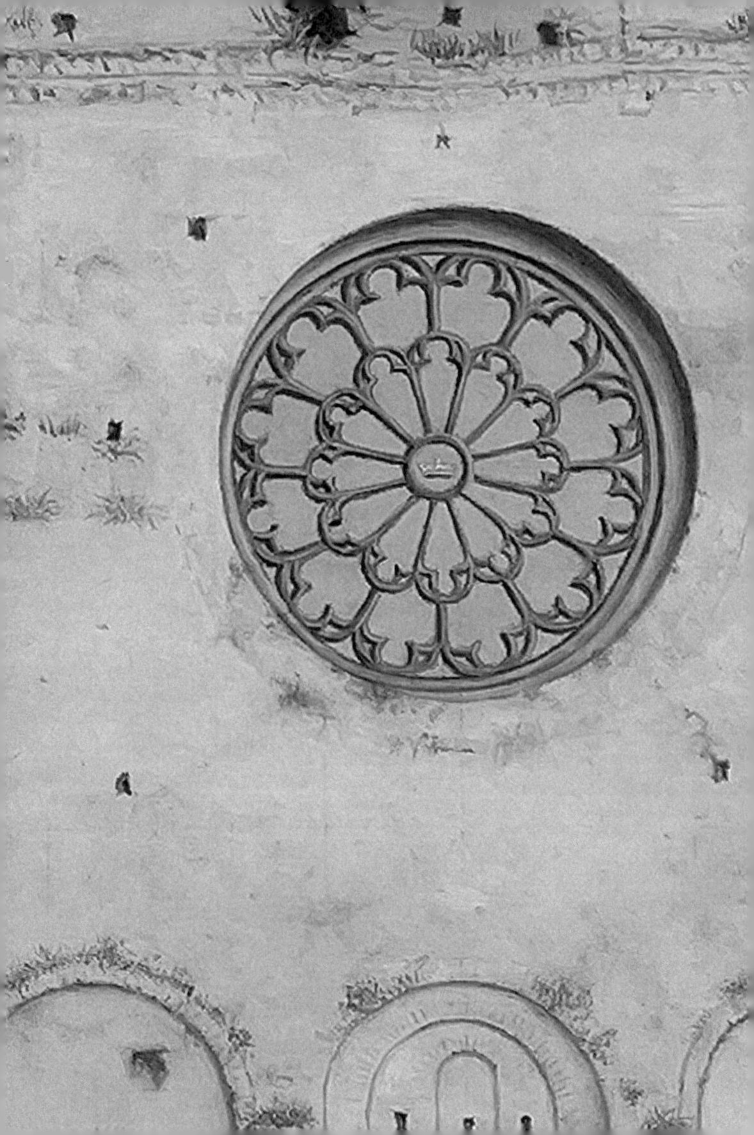

Highlights of the Museum Boijmans Van Beuningen Collection

Best *of* Boijmans

Foreword

Circles, eyes, lines, leaves or birds. How do you view such a wide-ranging collection as Museum Boijmans Van Beuningen's? Do you see it as a succession of movements and styles or as expressions of skill and an artist's eye? Do you look at the way hands are depicted, like rhythmic arcs of connection in the portrait Max Beckmann made of the art dealer Helmut Lütjens's family, at hands putting on a pair of earrings or a string of pearls, or the Devil's hands gripping the legs of the dead? On the first and last pages, designer Tessa van der Waals shows how you can discover parallels between very diverse works by zooming in on details. In colour, shape or subject, in style or atmosphere.

In this little book you will find a selection of more than a hundred and fifty masterpieces from the museum's collection. A difficult task, because we want to offer a representative overview of the collection focusing on all the disciplines, from works on paper to modern art installations, at the same time highlighting the diversity of the makers. We chose works because they are a proof of a famous print series, a masterly representation of architecture in design, the first work by an artist in the Dutch national collection, or a penetrating self-portrait. We chose pictorial quality or the ability to move the viewer, innovative design and technical ingenuity, but equally well the pure simplicity of an oil and vinegar set. Sometimes the works come with a statement by the artist, sometimes with a surprising fact about the provenance or the function of an object. Did you know, for example, that the plaster cast of *Eve* by Auguste Rodin was purchased directly from the artist following an exhibition that toured

Belgium and the Netherlands in 1899? That Museum Boijmans Van Beuningen was the first public art institution to have a painting by Vincent van Gogh in its collection? Or that 20,562 litres of water are needed for Olafur Eliasson's installation *Notion Motion*?
You will meander through many centuries of art history almost without realising. We hope that it will touch you and inspire you just as much as it does us.

Sandra Kisters
Head of Collections and Research
Museum Boijmans Van Beuningen

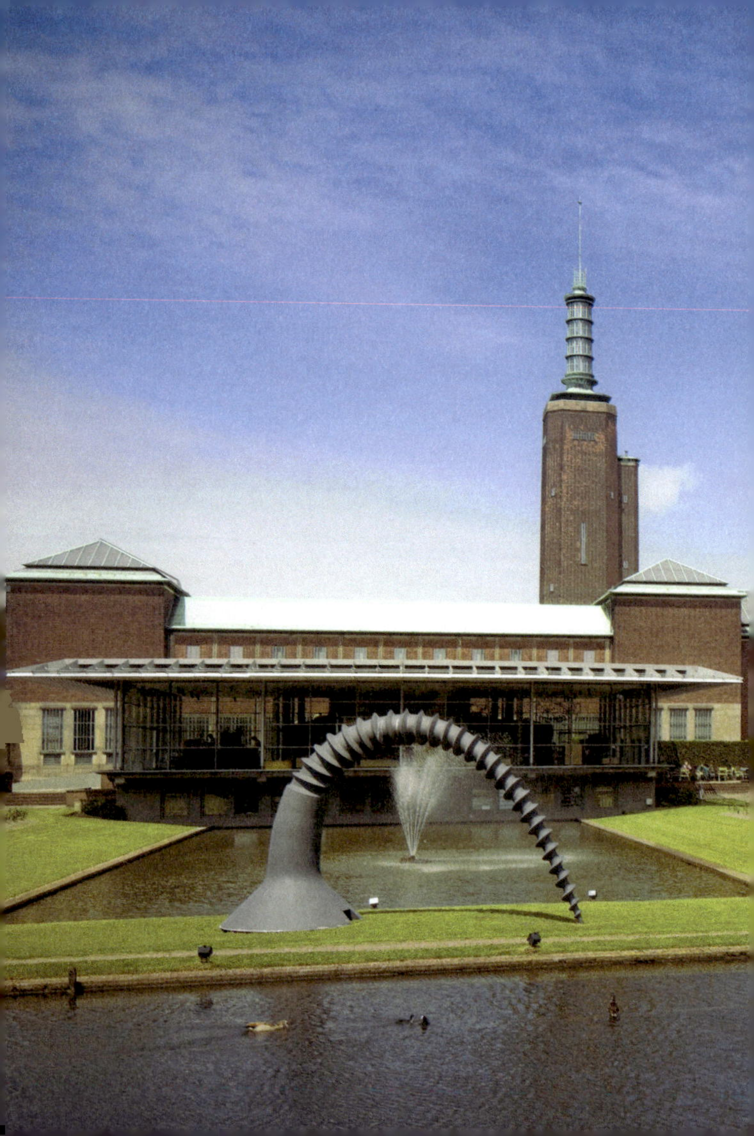

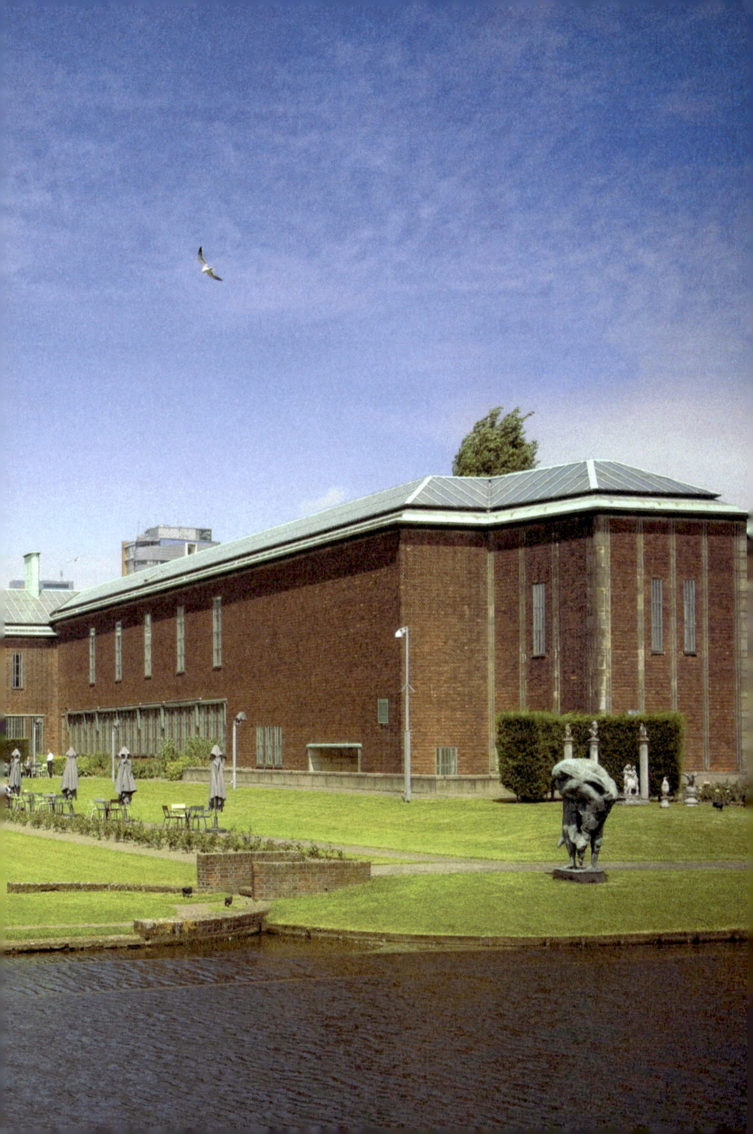

Museum Boijmans Van Beuningen

A Collectors' Museum

In the 170 years and counting since Museum Boijmans Van Beuningen was established, we have built up a rich, eclectic collection of art and design from the early Middle Ages to the present day. It is the wide- ranging nature of the collection that defines this museum in the international port of Rotterdam. Early Dutch and Flemish art is the starting point, with Old Masters like Jheronimus Bosch, Pieter Bruegel the Elder, Rembrandt van Rijn and Peter Paul Rubens. Classical modern art is represented with works by Claude Monet, Vincent van Gogh, Wassily Kandinsky, Piet Mondrian and many more. The museum owns an outstanding collection of Surrealist art, including famous works by Salvador Dalí, René Magritte, Max Ernst and Leonora Carrington. The museum also keeps pace with the latest developments in contemporary art, reflected in an international collection of present-day masterpieces. The Print Room holds thousands of sheets that provide an almost encyclopaedic overview of western drawing and printmaking; only a few highlights can be shown in this book. The works in the large Department of Applied Art and Design include valuable decorative objects and innovative contemporary design as well as everyday utensils from the late Middle Ages to the present day. The museum's exhibitions and displays seek to establish connections between the different disciplines and periods, presenting the collection as unity in diversity.

Private collectors have been crucial to building the museum's collection from the outset, and it takes its name from two of them. The museum, which opened to the public in 1849, is based on the collection of the Utrecht lawyer Frans Boijmans (1767-1847). The collection amassed by the Rotterdam port baron Daniel George (D.G.) van Beuningen (1877-1955) was acquired in 1958. The arrival of works of art from his collection, like Pieter Bruegel's *Tower of Babel* (p. 221) and Van Gogh's *Portrait of Armand Roulin* (p. 206), was such an extraordinary event that it was reflected

in the name of the museum: Museum Boymans became Museum Boijmans Van Beuningen.
There are dozens more collectors whose collections have come to the museum in their entirety or in part. Their often very different interests and collecting fields have all had an impact on the museum's character. The gift and legacy of the Rotterdam patron, scientist and globe-trotter Elie van Rijckevorsel (1845-1928) encompassed European glass, Japanese and Chinese porcelain, colonial furniture from the Dutch East Indies and a few European paintings. The museum has no civic guard portraits, large altarpieces or official portraits – they tend to be housed in museums that developed out of public or royal collections. Museum Boijmans Van Beuningen's trademark is its broad scope, which makes an encounter with the collection an exciting journey through the history of western art.
After a rather hesitant start in the nineteenth century, the museum went from strength to strength in the first decades of the twentieth. Rotterdam rapidly grew into a major port, and its economic

success spawned a generation of trade and shipping magnates who patronized the arts. Around 1925, the city had a number of wealthy private collectors, who supported the museum financially in making purchases, gifted important works of art and quite often bequeathed all or part of their collection to the museum.
D.G. van Beuningen was the most important collector among the Rotterdam notables. His greatest loves were the Flemish and Dutch primitives, and he was one of the first people in the Netherlands to collect them. He owned, for instance, Jan van Eyck's *Three Marys at the Tomb* (p. 259), the Norfolk Triptych painted by an anonymous artist in Maastricht or Liège around 1420 (pp. 216-217) and Geertgen tot Sint Jans's magnificent *Glorification of the Virgin* (p. 107). His tastes were broad, however, and his collection also contained seventeenth-century Flemish paintings, such as the Achilles series by Rubens (p. 75), Italian artists like Titian (p. 198) and modern French painters like Monet (p. 125). In 1940, Van Beuningen donated the greater part of the famous Koenigs collection, at a

stroke making the museum's drawings collection one of the finest in the world.

The Rotterdam businessman Willem van der Vorm was another collector who was of considerable significance to the museum. He made financial contributions to a number of acquisitions and since 1972 the museum has had his entire collection on long-term loan. Van der Vorm chiefly collected paintings by Dutch and Flemish Old Masters, among them Anthony van Dyck's *St Jerome* (p. 79), and by French nineteenth-century artists. The Willem van der Vorm Foundation, which was set up posthumously, continues to enhance the collection with acquisitions, such as Paul Cézanne's *Landscape near Aix met with the Tour de César* (p. 247).

The collection of prints and drawings is also indebted to a number of important collectors, among them J.C.J. Bierens de Haan and A.J. Domela Nieuwenhuis. Bierens de Haan was an erudite collector, who decided to make his extensive print collection over to the museum at an early stage, and took this into account as he put it together. He was particularly interested in sixteenth-century Dutch and Flemish printmaking. He used his intuition and knowledge to add to this area of study superb impressions of prints by often as yet unknown artists.

By the end of the nineteen-fifties, Museum Boijmans Van Beuningen had grown into one of the leading museums in the Netherlands and acquired an international reputation. The works of art that had come to the museum from private collectors became a factor in determining the purchasing policy. The international character of Van Beuningen's collection, for instance, was an added incentive to buy works by German, French and Italian artists. In parallel with this, there was an ambition to bring old and modern art together in one museum. Work by contemporary artists was acquired in the first half of the twentieth century. These were often top-flight pieces, such as the *Poplar Avenue* (p. 127) – the earliest painting by Van Gogh to enter a public art collection, gifted to the museum in 1903 – and the first Mondrian painting in a public collection, which was donated in 1928 (p. 156). In the nineteen-thirties the museum acquired masterpieces by Kandinsky (p. 195), Franz Marc (p. 194), Lyonel Feininger and Jacoba van Heemskerck from the estate of Marie Tak van Poortvliet, and Kokoschka's provocative *Mandrill* (p. 196) was purchased in 1950. In the nineteen-sixties, the focus on modern and contemporary art was sharpened with the acquisition of, among other things, an important suite of paintings by Kandinsky, and since then the collection has been augmented with numerous acquisitions in this area. Surrealism became a significant focus with the acquisition of key works by Dalí (pp. 76-77) and Magritte (p. 80) from the collection of the English patron, Edward James. There were also notable purchases of contemporary art, like the 1960 abstract painting *Grey, Orange on Maroon, No. 8* by Mark Rothko (p. 109). In the nineteen-eighties, large-scale installations and sculptures by icons like Bruce Nauman (pp. 162-163), Joseph Beuys (p. 160) and Claes Oldenburg (p. 226) were acquired. At the same time, the museum turned its attention to German painting with works by Anselm Kiefer (p. 231) and others. The rise of photography and video art saw new areas of collection within contemporary art, with work by artists such as Cindy Sherman (p. 64) and Bas Jan Ader (p. 265).

The museum also built up a reputation for leading exhibitions. In 1935 the opening of a museum building constructed especially for the collection – the Van der Steur Building in Museumpark – made it possible to stage temporary exhibitions. One of the first was *Jheronimus Bosch: Northern Netherlandish Primitives*. The exhibition took place in 1936, a few years after the spectacular acquisition of Jheronimus Bosch's *Pedlar* (p. 51), and attracted the unprecedented number of almost 55,000 visitors. This total was far surpassed in 1956 by a Rembrandt exhibition staged jointly with Amsterdam's Rijksmuseum and shown in both locations. 282,000 visitors came to Rotterdam, and almost as many formed long queues in the winter of 1970 to see the first retrospective exhibition of Dalí in Europe.

A new wing, designed by the architect Alexander Bodon, was added to the museum in 1972. This made it possible to show large-scale modern artworks, with installations created especially for the space by Walter de Maria (p. 154), Olafur Eliasson (p. 240) and others. Since then, the space has been the setting for many very diverse exhibitions – from *Gods and Pharaohs* (1979) and *The Gold of the Thracians* (1984) to, more recently, *The Road to Van Eyck* (2012), *Mad About Surrealism* (2017) and *Netherlands ⇆ Bauhaus* (2019), as well as solo exhibitions by contemporary artists like Pipilotti Rist and Ugo Rondinone. The museum regularly collaborates with other international museums, as it did in 2018 for the major exhibition *Pure Rubens* with the Prado in Madrid, and loans out hundreds of works for exhibitions in the Netherlands and beyond every year.

A collection is never complete – and Museum Boijmans Van Beuningen's is no exception. With the support and involvement of present-day patrons and collectors, the collection – now more than 154,000 objects – continues to grow. The majority, some ninety percent, belongs to the city of Rotterdam, ten percent is the property of the Museum Boijmans Van Beuningen Foundation. As

a result of this growth, new additions were made to the building in 1991 and at the start of this century. Despite this, large parts of the collection have to be kept in the repository. The museum wants to open up this hidden collection to visitors not just virtually – new works are added every day to the large online collection – but physically too. A public depot opened immediately adjacent to the museum in 2021. In Depot Boijmans Van Beuningen the whole collection is accessible, with guided tours in the storerooms, restorations carried out under the public's watchful eye and presentations about putting together and managing an art collection. Visitors can also wander through the building alone, climb the Piranesi-like stairs in the thirty-metre-high atrium, take a peek into the depot spaces or admire the displays in the large atrium vitrines. The design of this bowl-shaped, reflecting building was created by Rotterdam architects MVRDV.
At the same time, the museum is due for restoration and refurbishment. The striking building with the tall tower in the heart of Rotterdam is now eighty-eight years old. Over the next few years, the monumental

buildings erected in 1935 and 1972 will be renovated and refurbished, and new architecture developed by Mecanoo architects will reflect and embrace the twenty-first century. There will be more space for collection displays, better routing through the different parts of the buildings, and of course space for beloved works of art that have become a permanent part of the building, such as Maurizio Cattelan's sculpture (p. 60) and Yayoi Kusama's mirror room (pp. 120-121). Supported by Rotterdam's exceptional art collection and with magnificent museum buildings and depot, Museum Boijmans Van Beuningen will remain an inspiring meeting place for art, artists and the public long into the future.

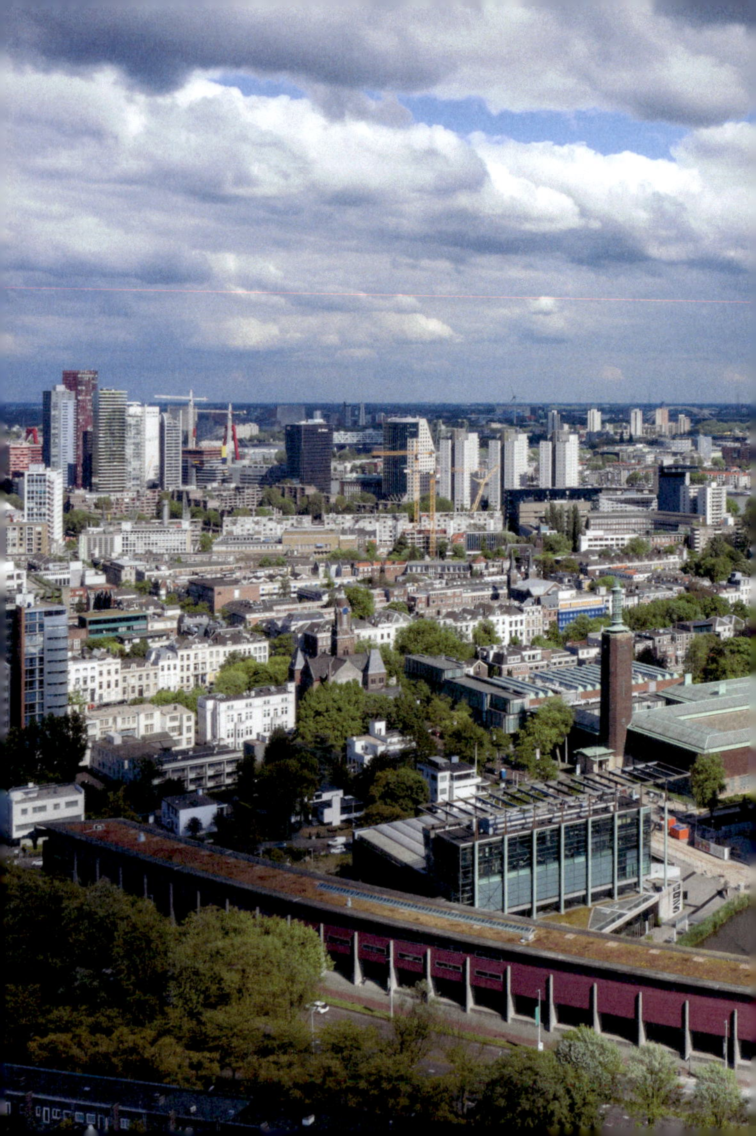

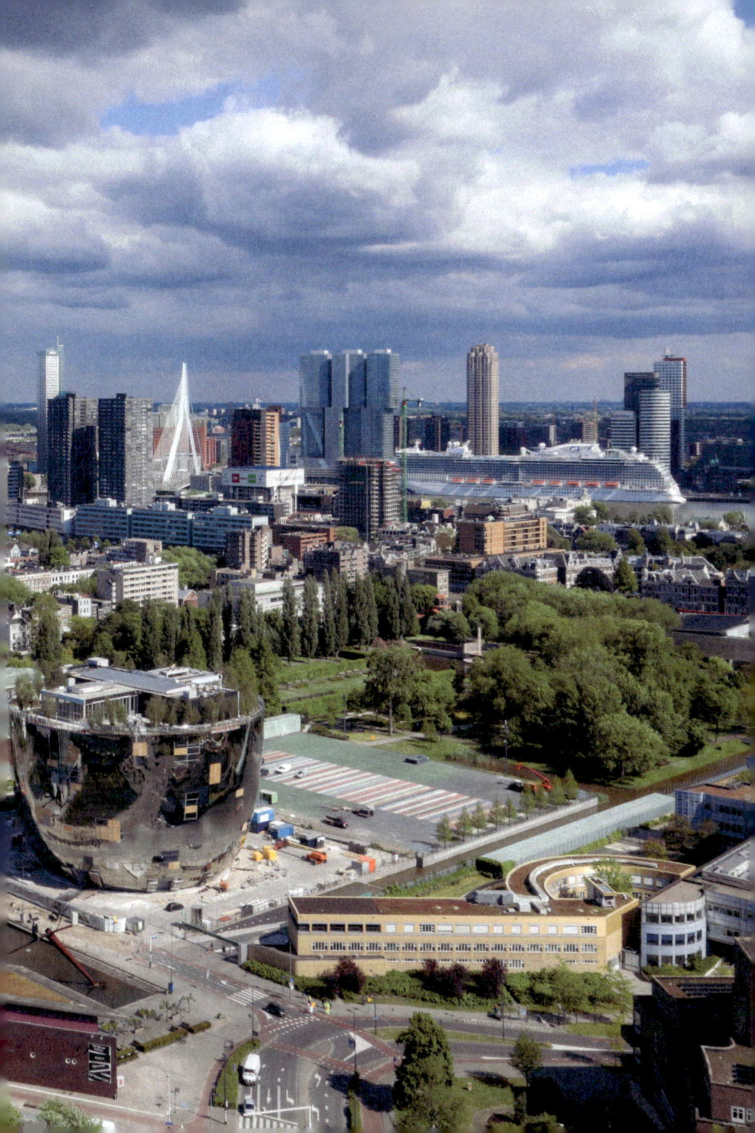

Highlights of the Museum Boijmans Van Beuningen Collection

Best *of* Boijmans

Jheronimus Bosch, *The Pedlar*, c. 1500

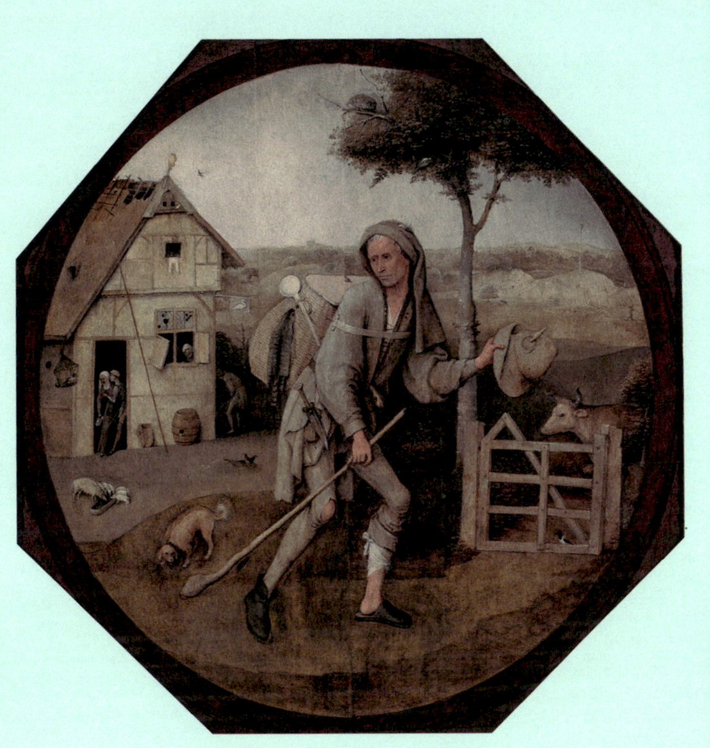

This painting was purchased in 1931 as a stand-alone work. Much later, after scientific examination, it was found that it had once been sawn. It was originally the exterior of the shutters of a triptych.

Jheronimus Bosch, *The Pedlar* (detail), c. 1500

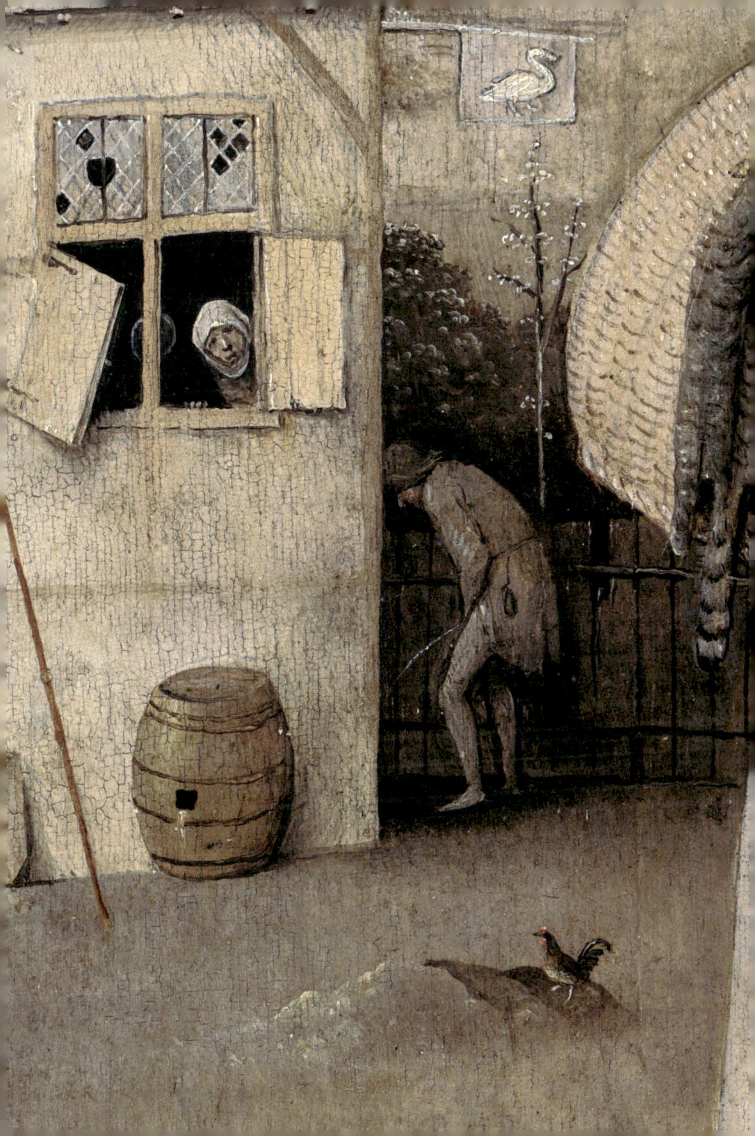

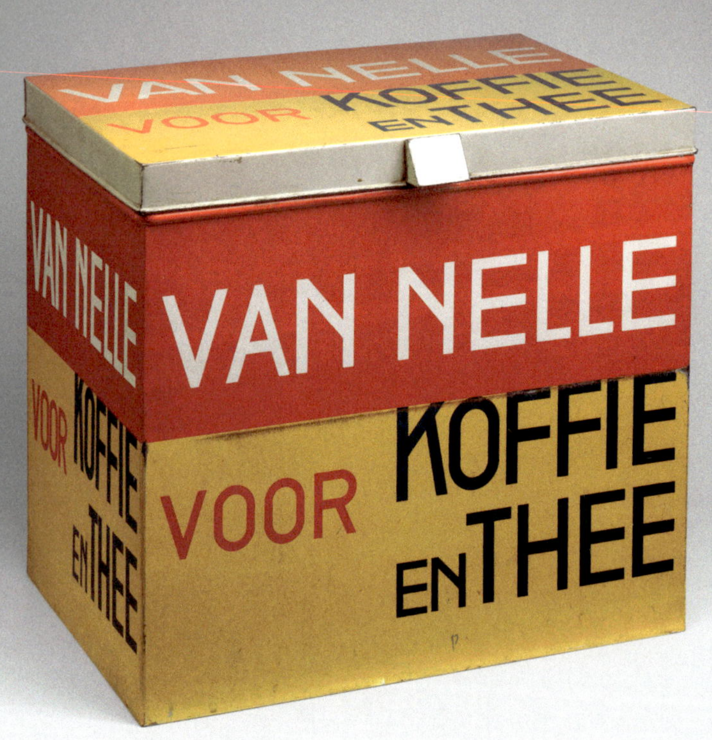
VAN NELLE
VOOR KOFFIE EN THEE
VAN NELLE
VOOR KOFFIE EN THEE
VAN NELLE
VOOR KOFFIE EN THEE

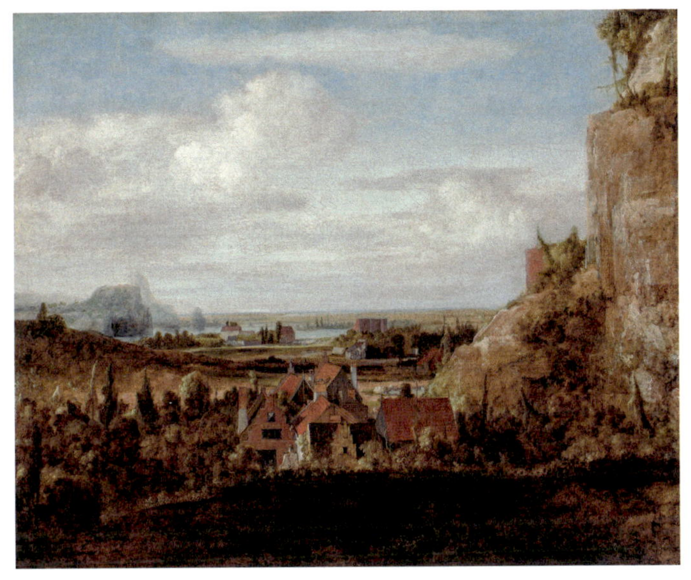

Hercules Segers, *River Valley with a Group of Houses*, c. 1625

◂ Jacob (Jac.) Jongert, *Van Nelle for Coffee and Tea*, 1930

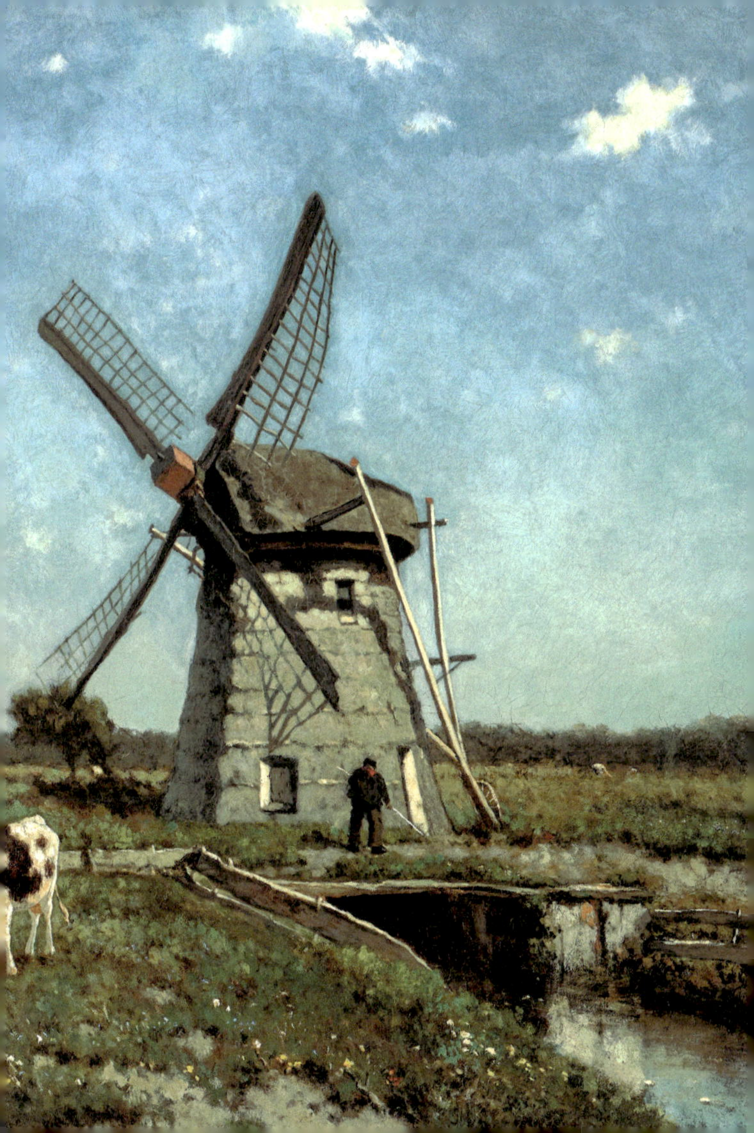

...

and no one knows what he's waiting for
not even that child

that's what we see – that
something can't be written

RUTGER KOPLAND

extract from
Geluk is gevaarlijk. Een keuze uit gedichten, 1999

Rembrandt van Rijn, *Titus at His Desk*, 1655

◂ Johannes Hendrik Weissenbruch, *Landscape with a Windmill near Schiedam*, 1873

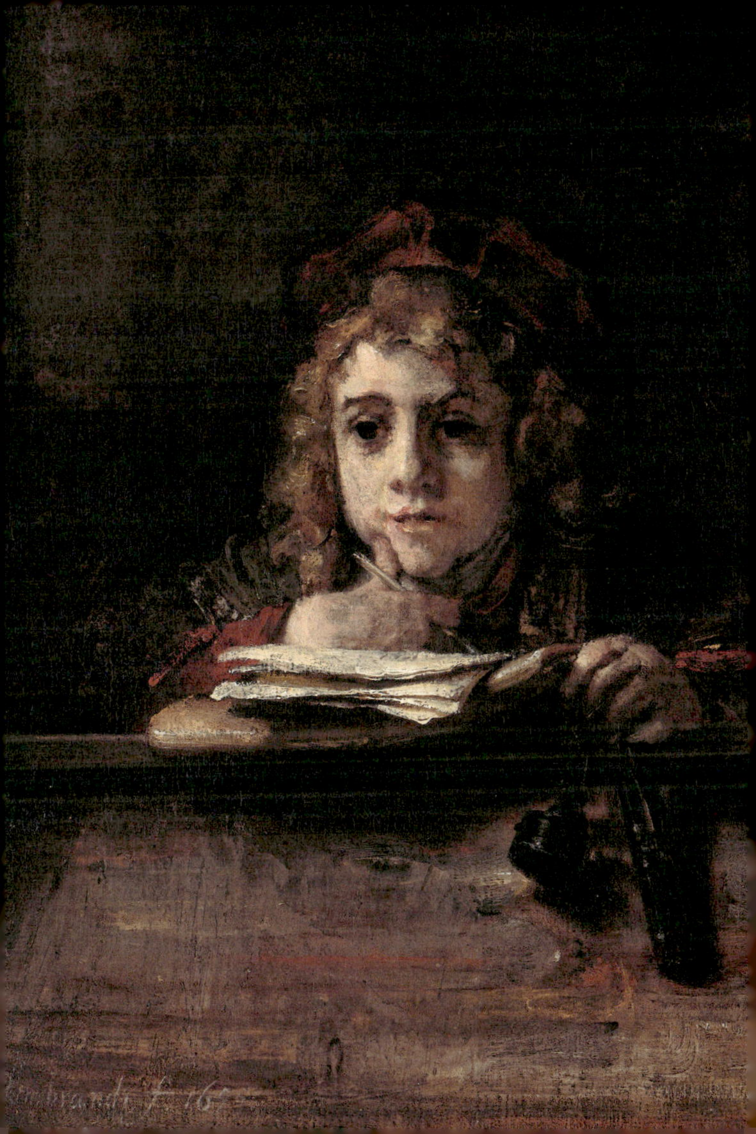

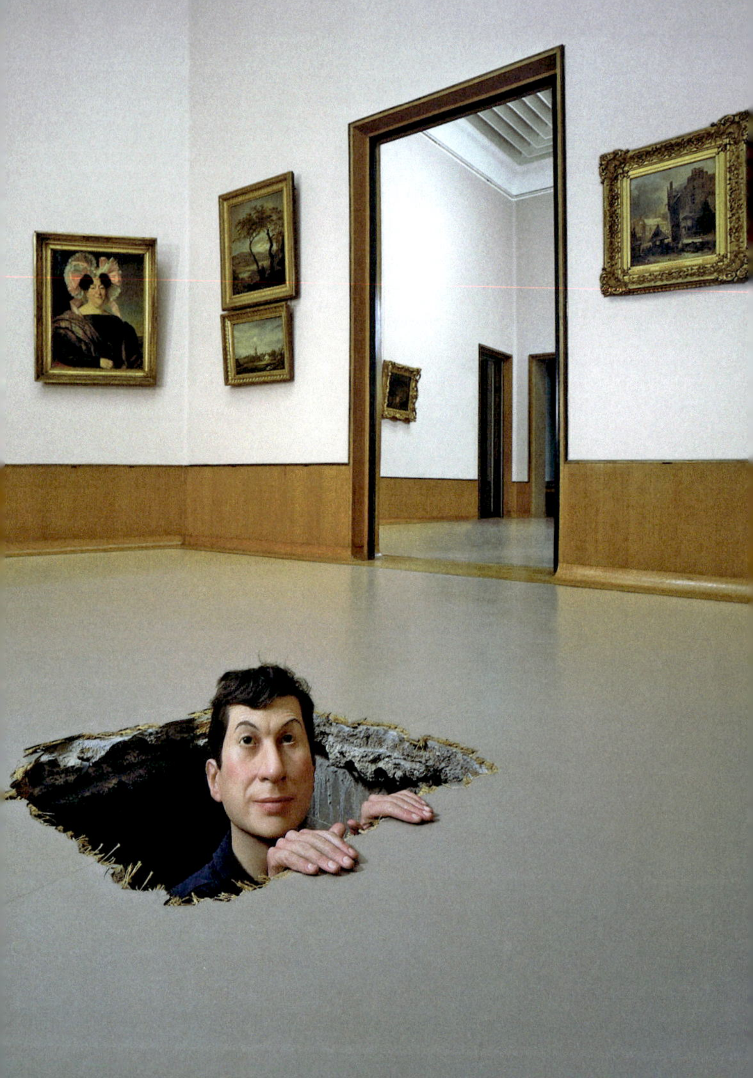

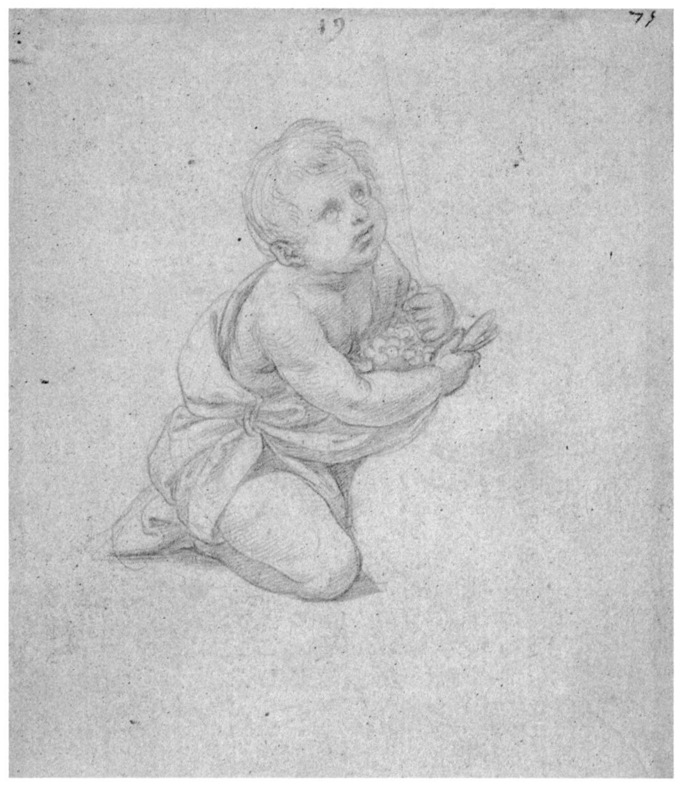

Raphael, *Study for the Kneeling Infant St John in 'The Alba Madonna'*, c. 1509-1510

◂ Maurizio Cattelan, *Untitled*, 2001

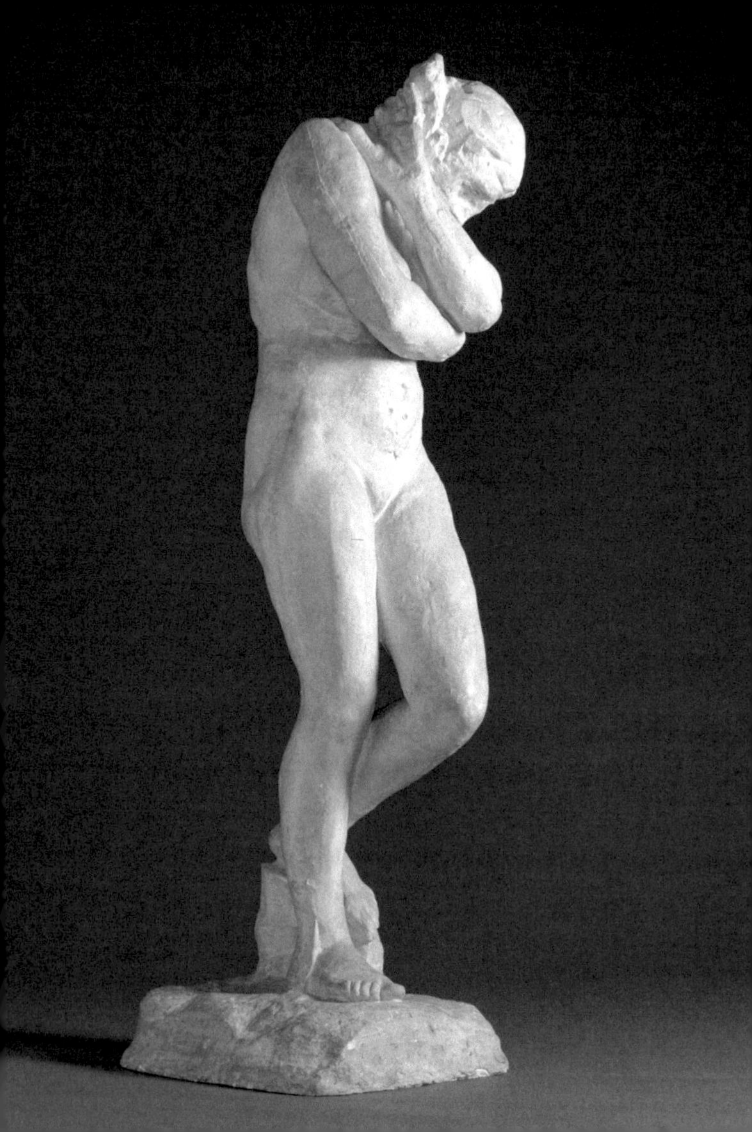

In 1901 Museum Boymans ordered this plaster model straight from the sculptor's workshop following the touring exhibition of his oeuvre in the Netherlands and Belgium in 1899.

Auguste Rodin, *Eve after the Fall*, 1881

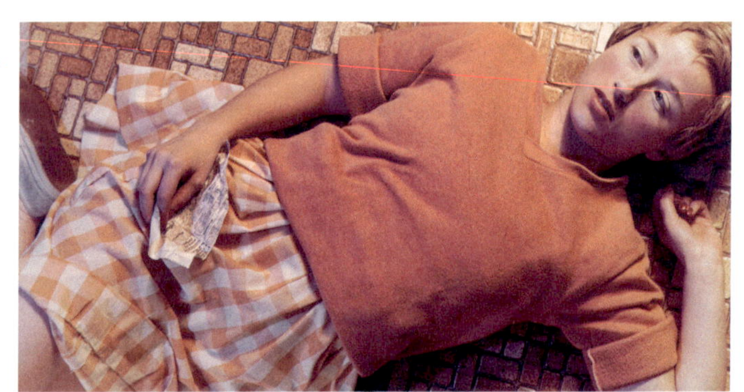

Cindy Sherman, *Untitled 96*, 1981

Francisco Goya, *Content with Her Lot*, c. 1810-1820 ▸

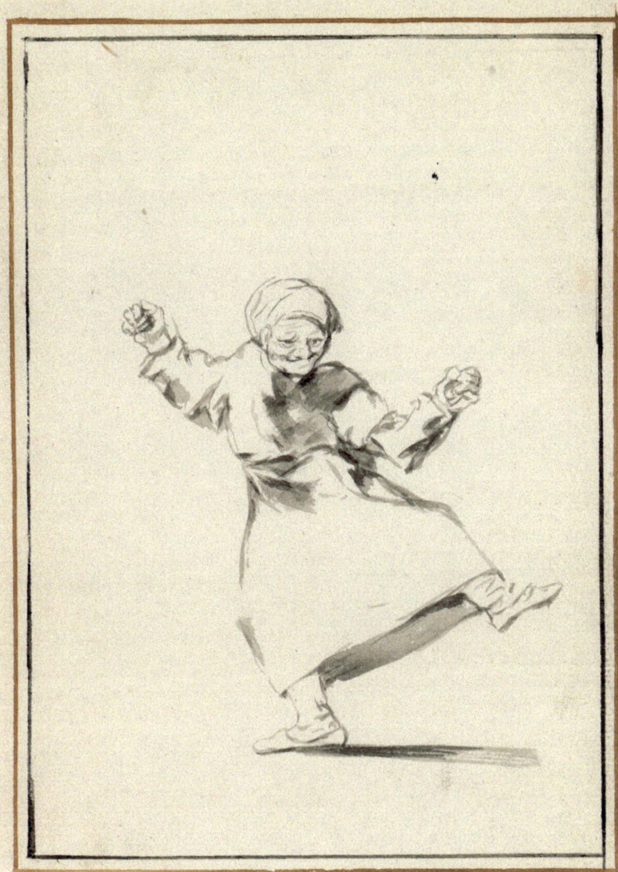
2

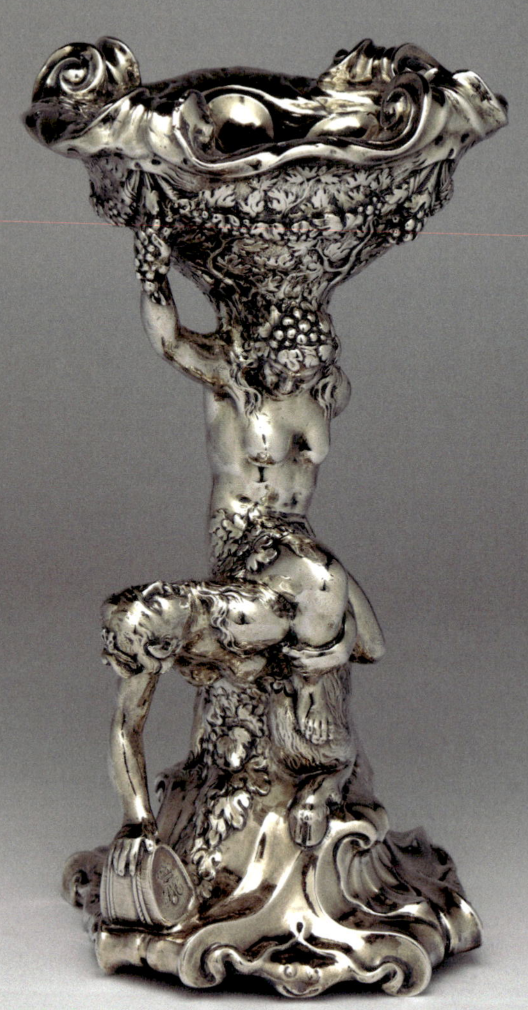

In the seventeenth century salt was so expensive that the extremely wealthy put it into silver sculptures on dinner tables.

Adam van Vianen, salt, 1622

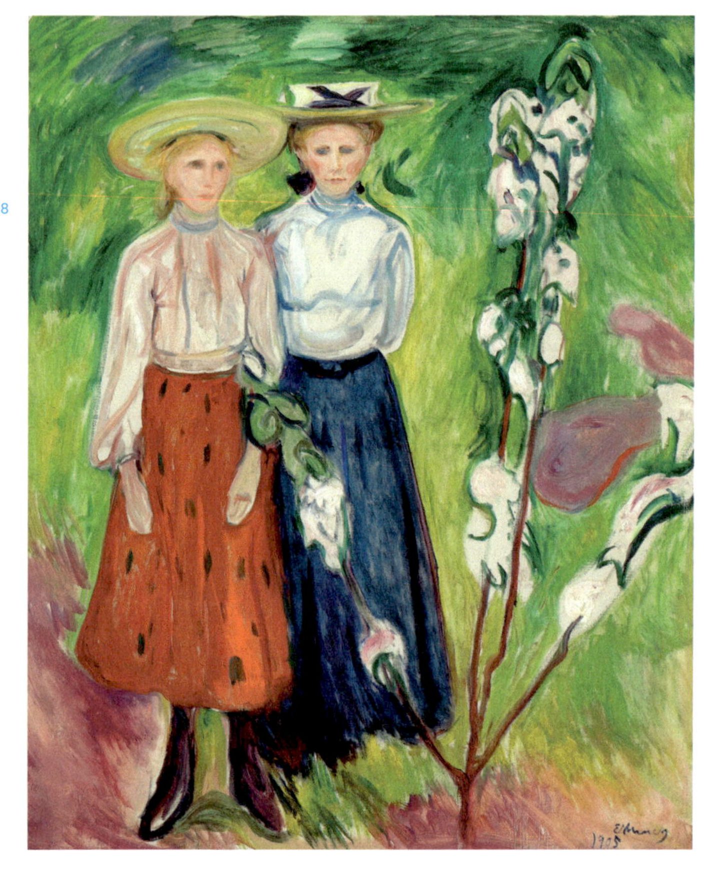

Edvard Munch, *Two Girls beside an Apple Tree in Blossom*, 1905

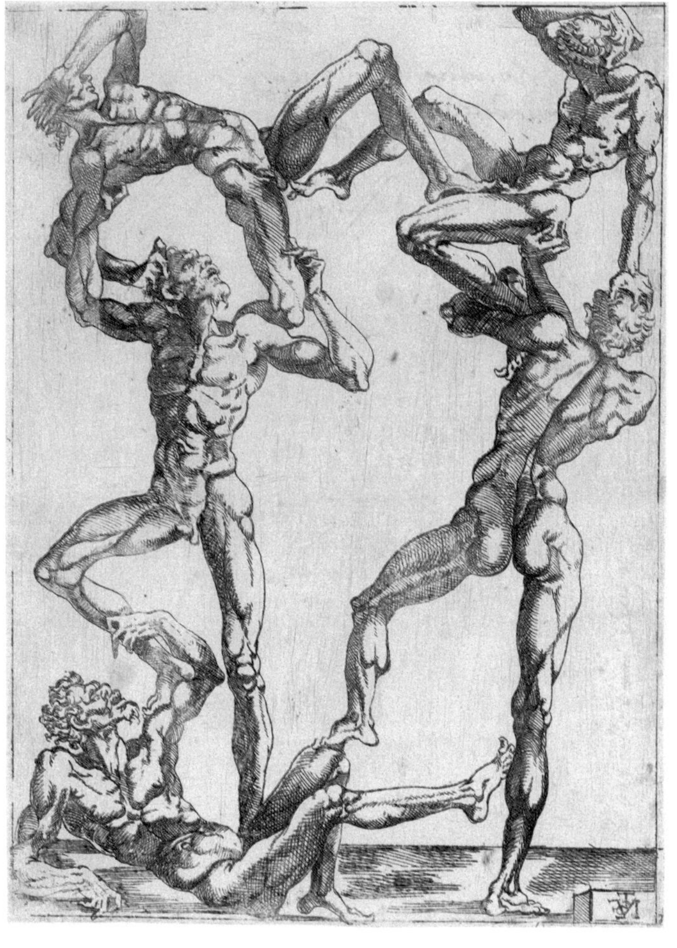

Juste de Juste, *Pyramid of Five Men*, c. 1543

This little bronze dancer, modelled after the fourteen-year-old ballet student Marie van Goethem, wears a real hair ribbon and a muslin tutu.

Edgar Degas, *Little Fourteen-Year-Old Dancer*, 1880-1881 (1922)

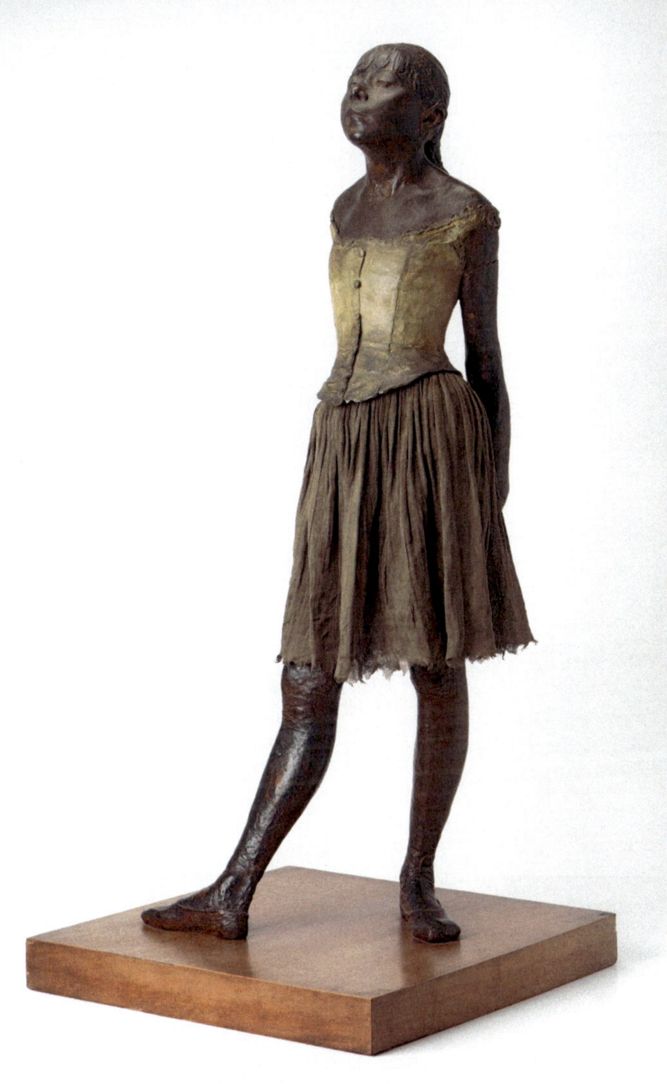

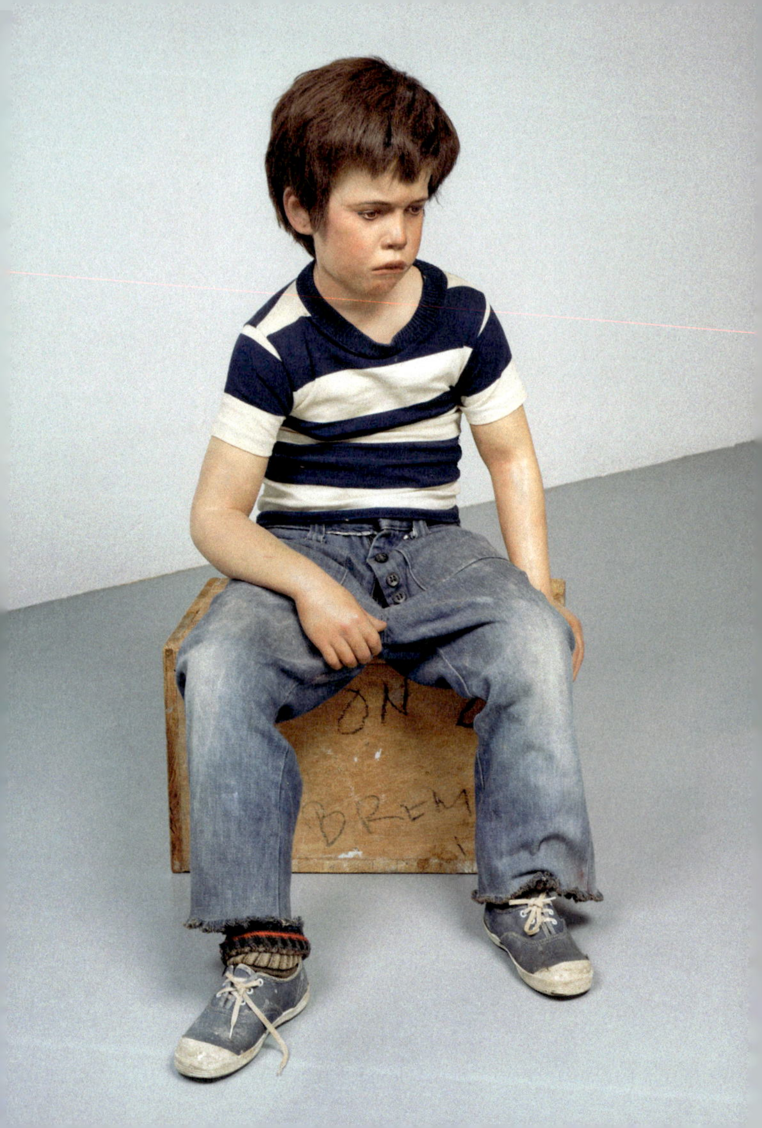
ON
BREM

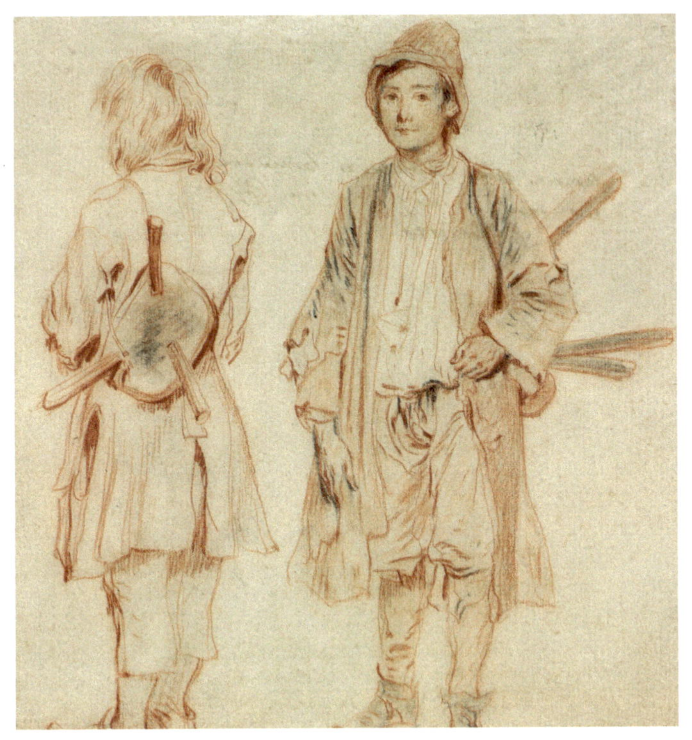

Jean Antoine Watteau, *Study of two Young Cobblers*, c. 1715-1716

◂ Duane Hanson, *Seated Child*, 1974

Peter Paul Rubens, *Achilles Educated by the Centaur Chiron*, 1630-1635

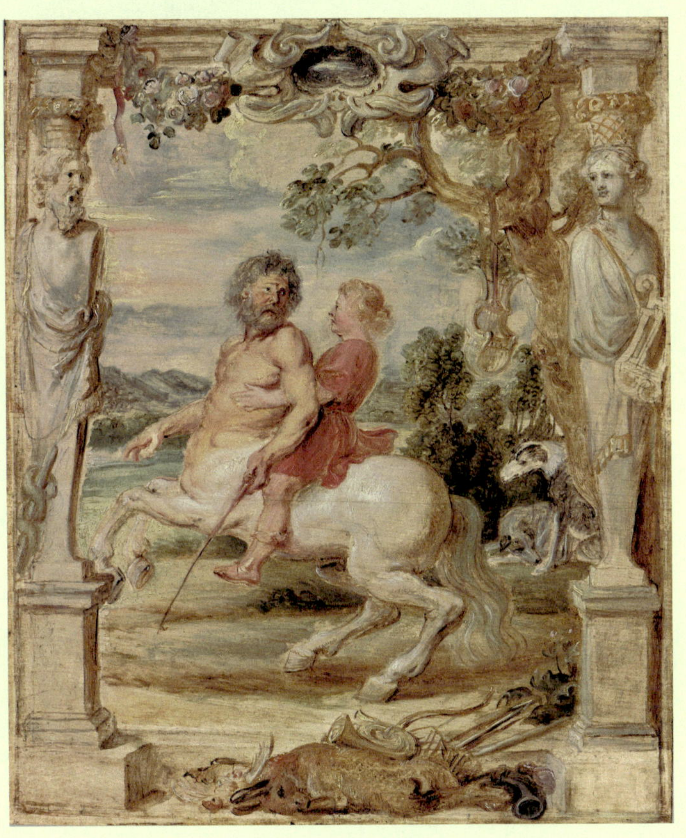

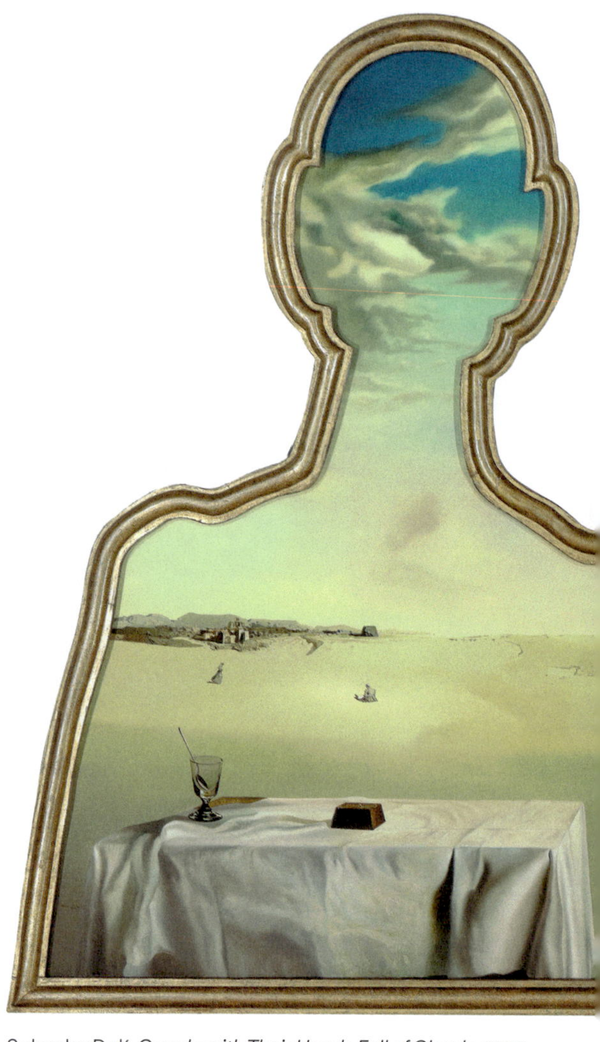

Salvador Dalí, *Couple with Their Heads Full of Clouds*, 1936

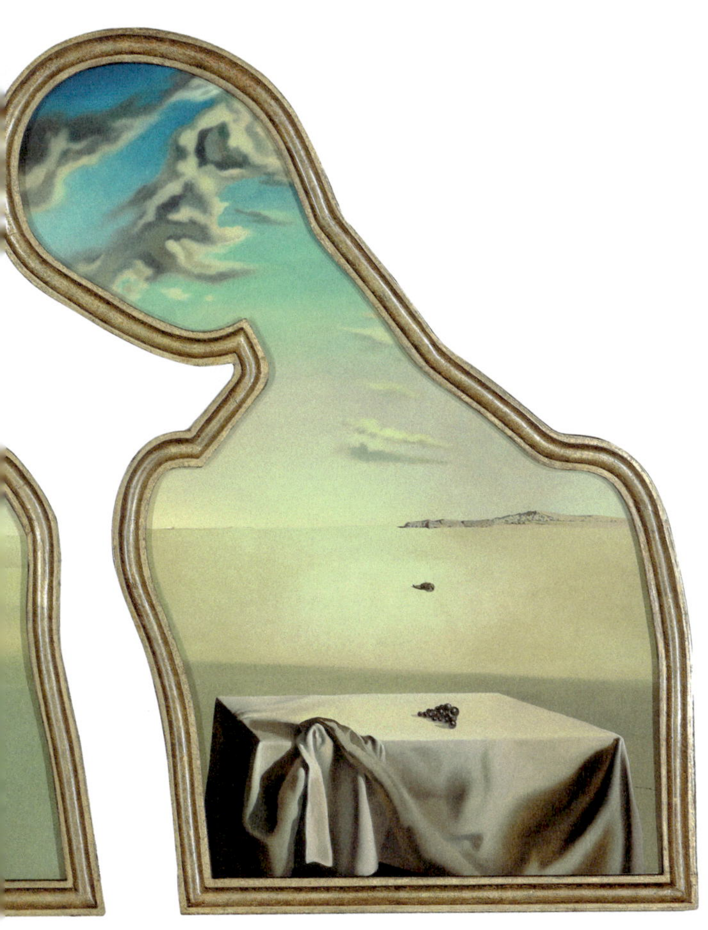

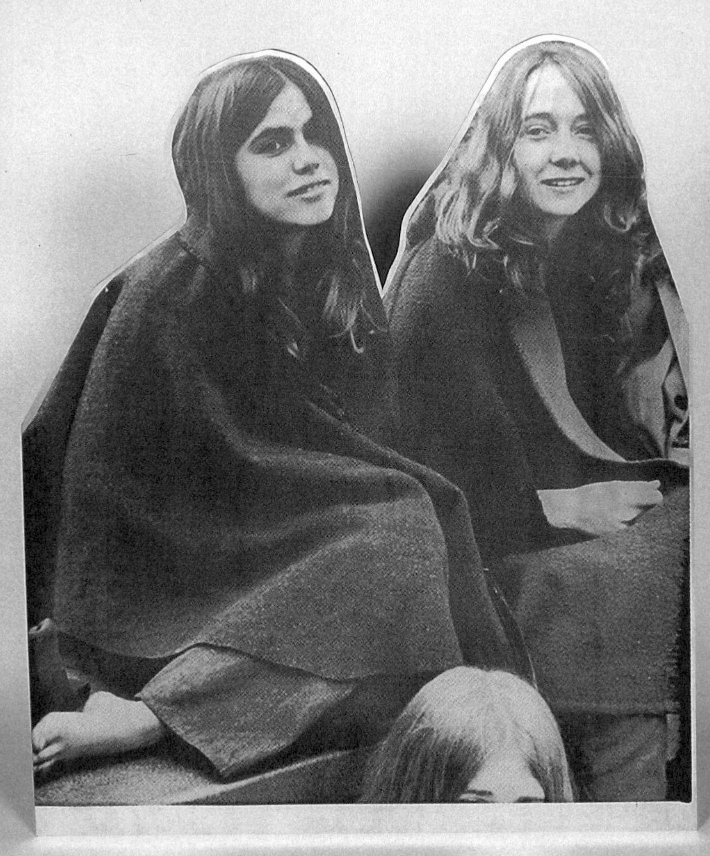

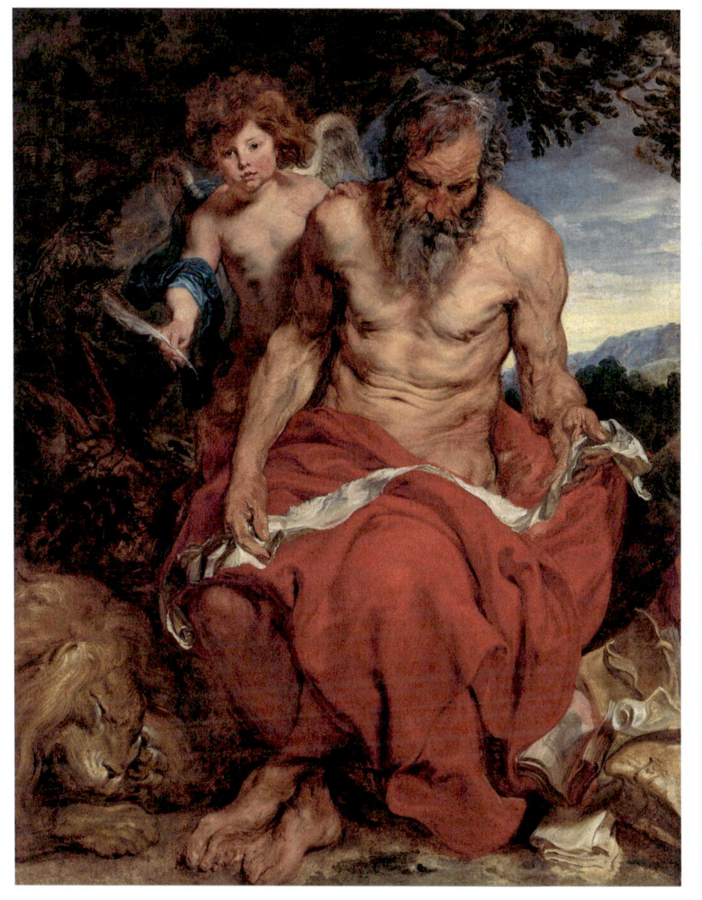

Anthony van Dyck, *Saint Jerome*, 1618-1620

◂ Cady Noland, *Manson Girls 'Sit-In'*, 1993-1994

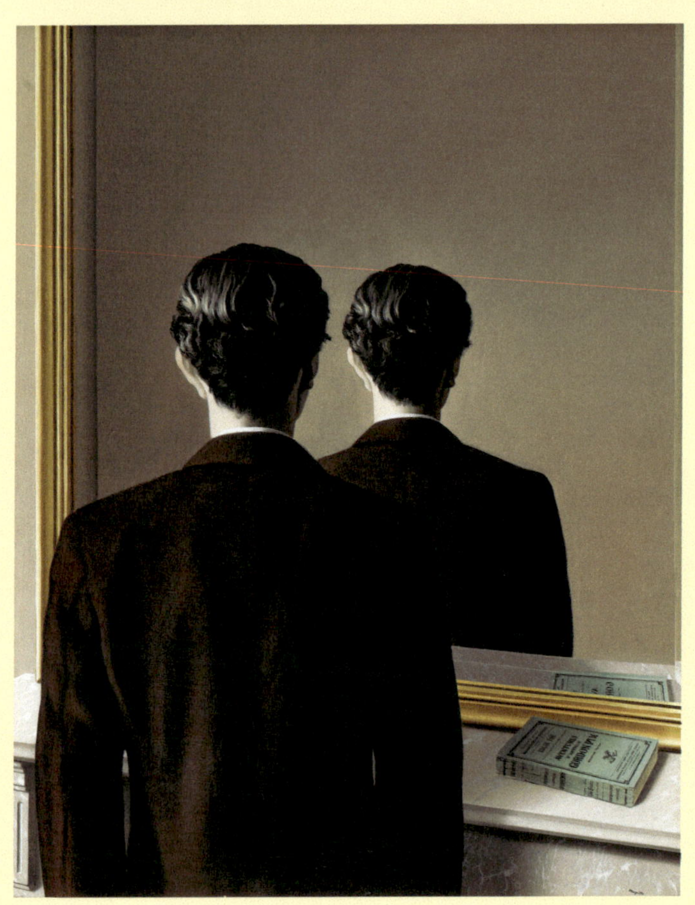

Here René Magritte portrayed his most important patron: the eccentric British collector Edward James from whom the museum acquired no fewer than fourteen surrealist masterpieces in 1977 and 1979.

René Magritte, *Not To Be Reproduced*, 1937

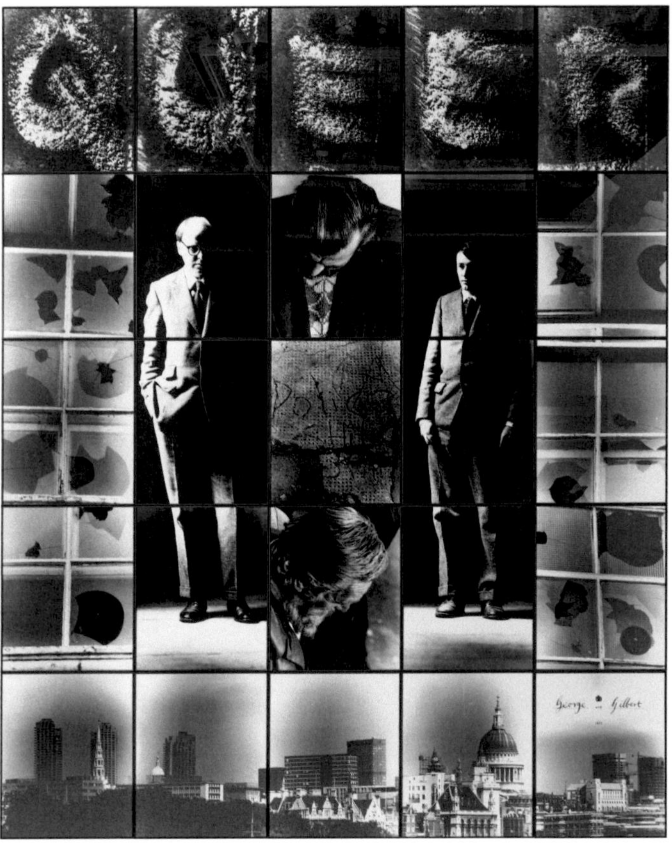

Gilbert & George, *Queer*, 1977

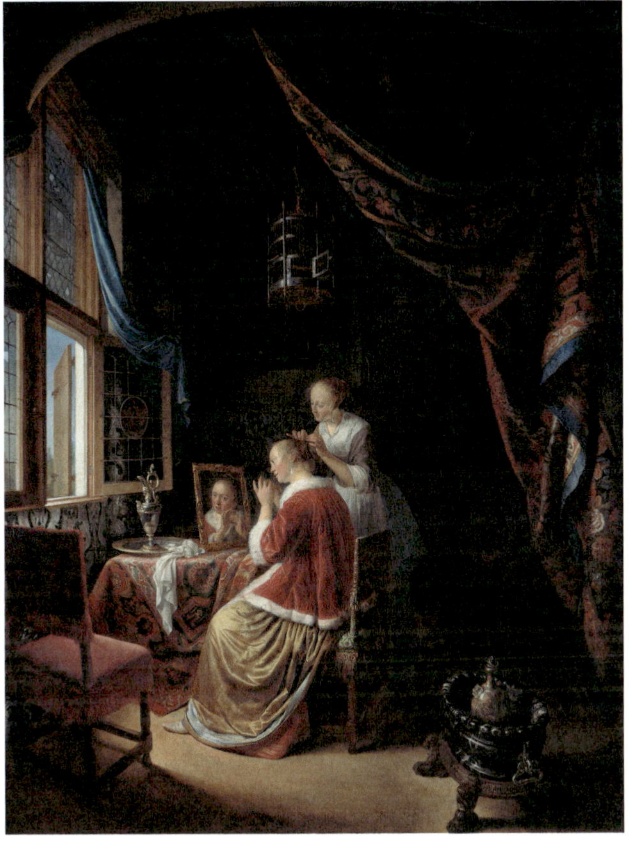

Gerard Dou, *A Young Woman at Her Toilet*, 1667

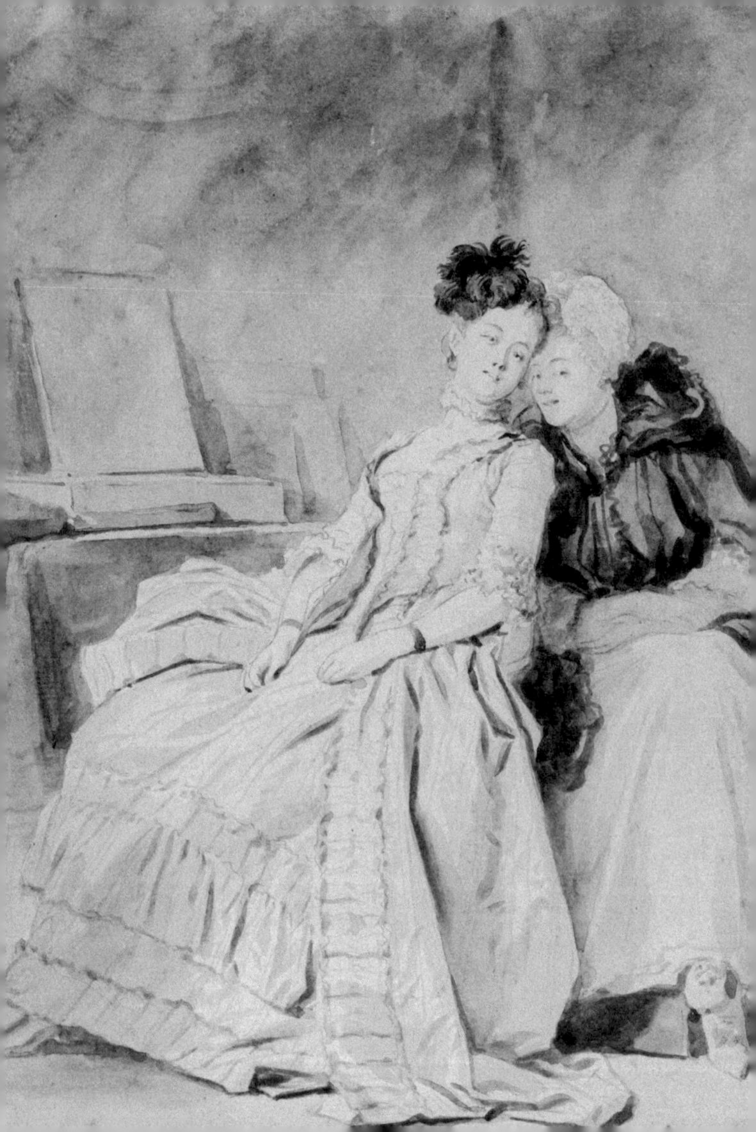

Fragonard had a studio and an apartment in the Louvre, which at that time was not a museum. This drawing, probably a portrait of his wife and her younger sister, must have been made there.

Jean-Honoré Fragonard, *The Intimate Conversation (La Confidence)*, c. 1778-1780

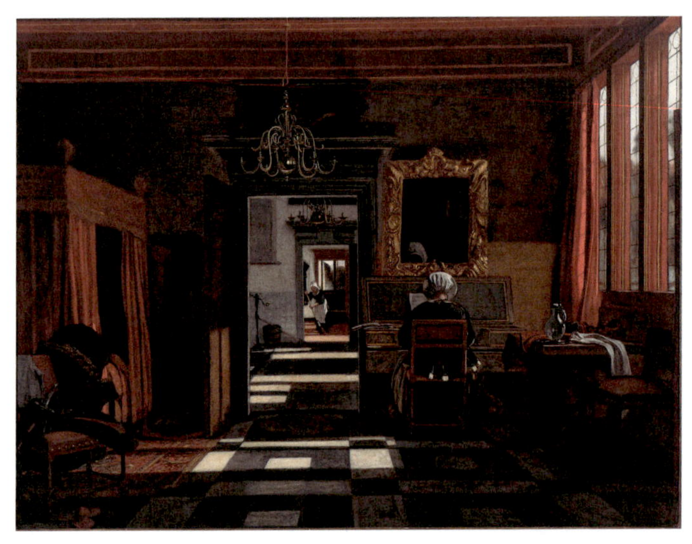

Emanuel de Witte, *Interior with a Woman at the Virginal*, 1665-1670
George Hendrik Breitner, *The Earring*, 1893 ►

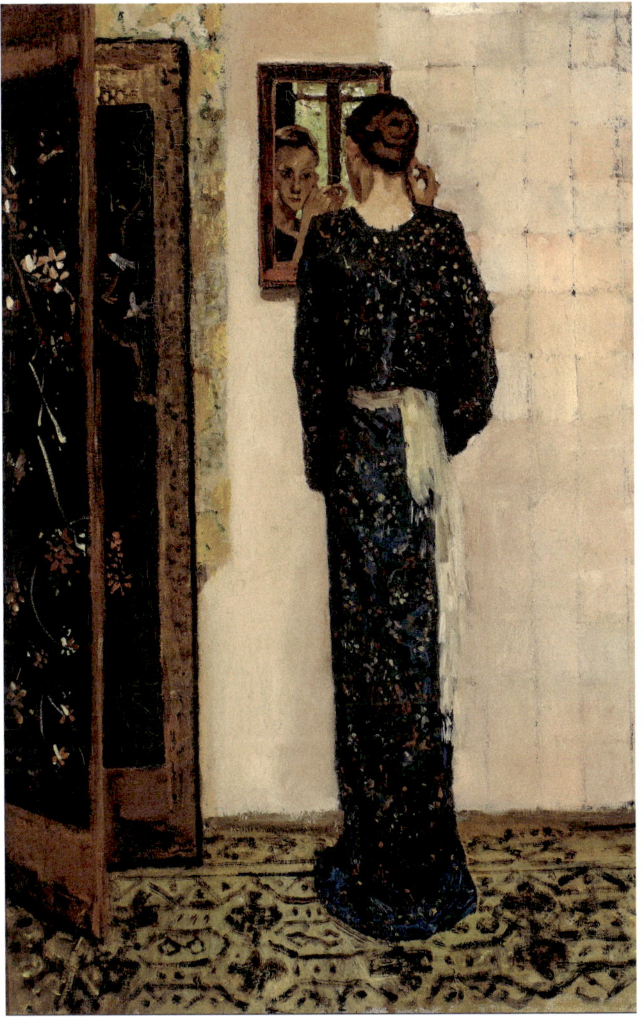

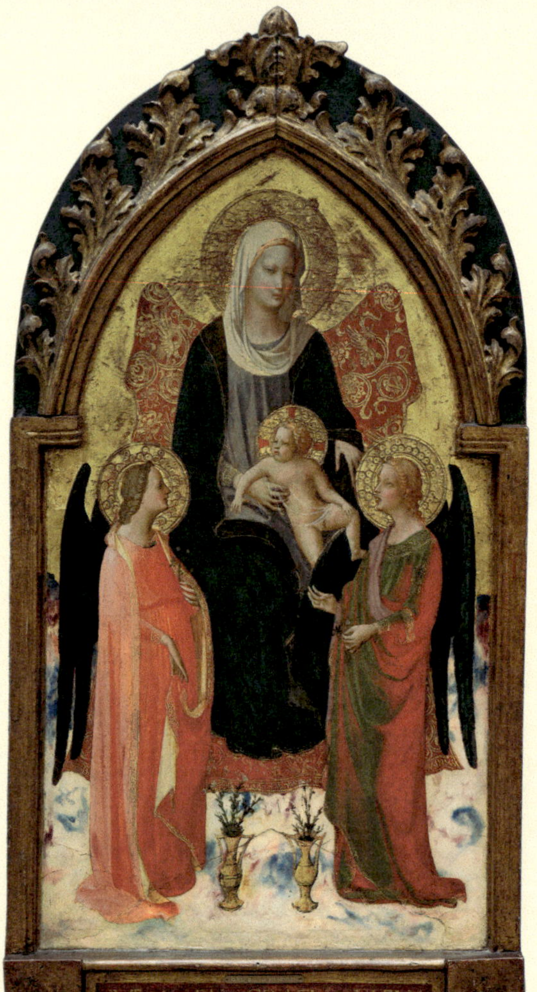
AVE MARIA GRAZIA PLENA

This panel is a fine example of art-historical re-evaluation. During the last hundred years it has been attributed to various early Italian artists, but now it is generally regarded as an early work by the famous Florentine master.

Fra Angelico, *Madonna and Child with Two Angels*, c. 1420

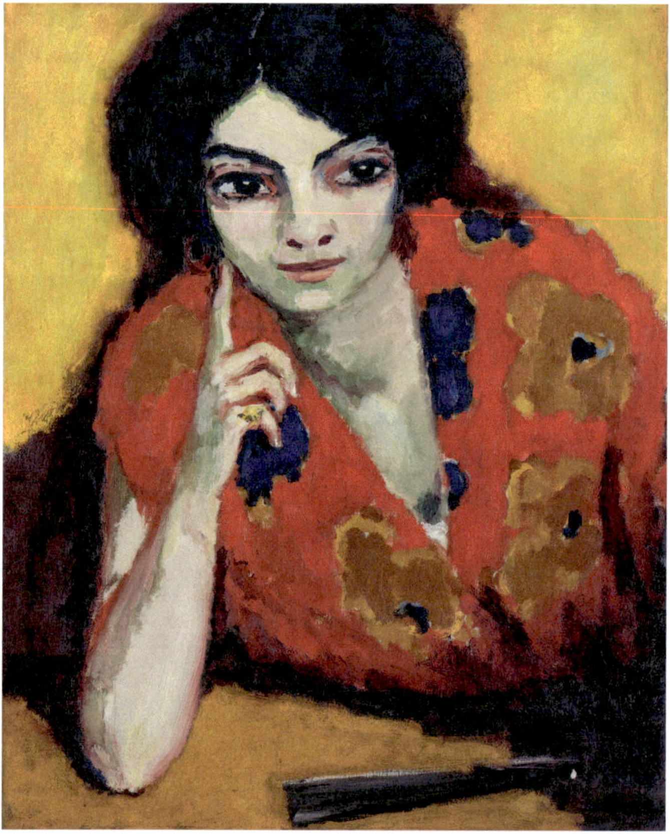

Kees van Dongen, *The Finger on the Cheek*, c. 1910

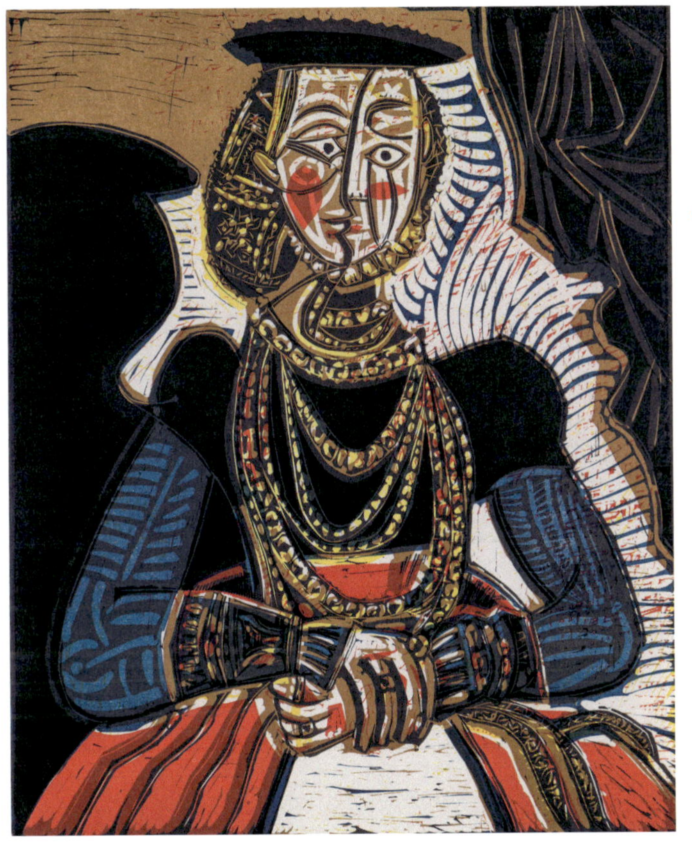

Pablo Picasso, *Portrait of a Young Woman after Cranach the Younger*, 1958

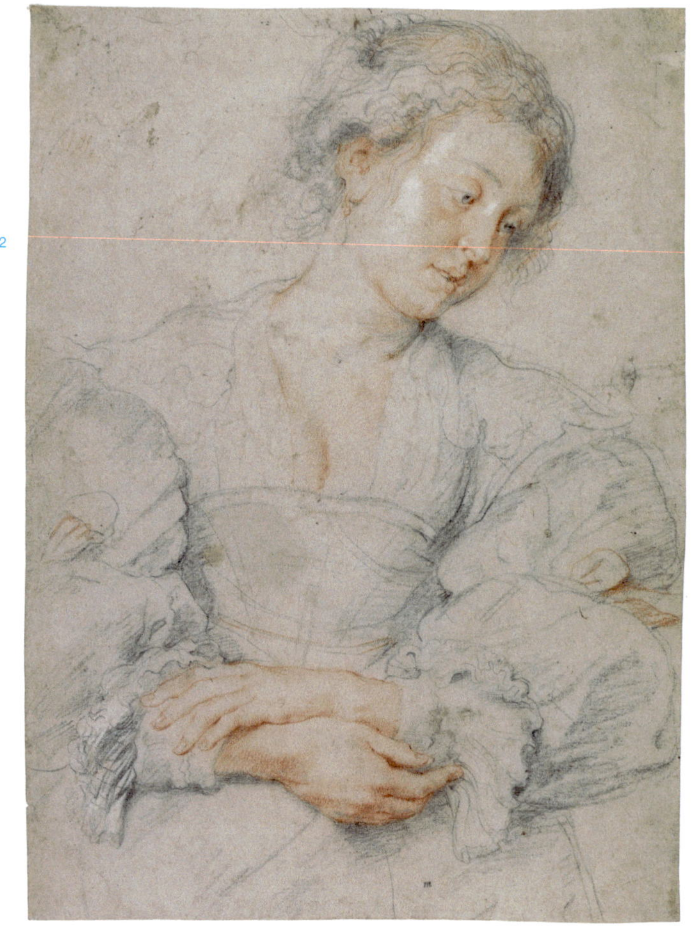

Peter Paul Rubens, *Young Woman with Folded Hands*, c. 1629-1630

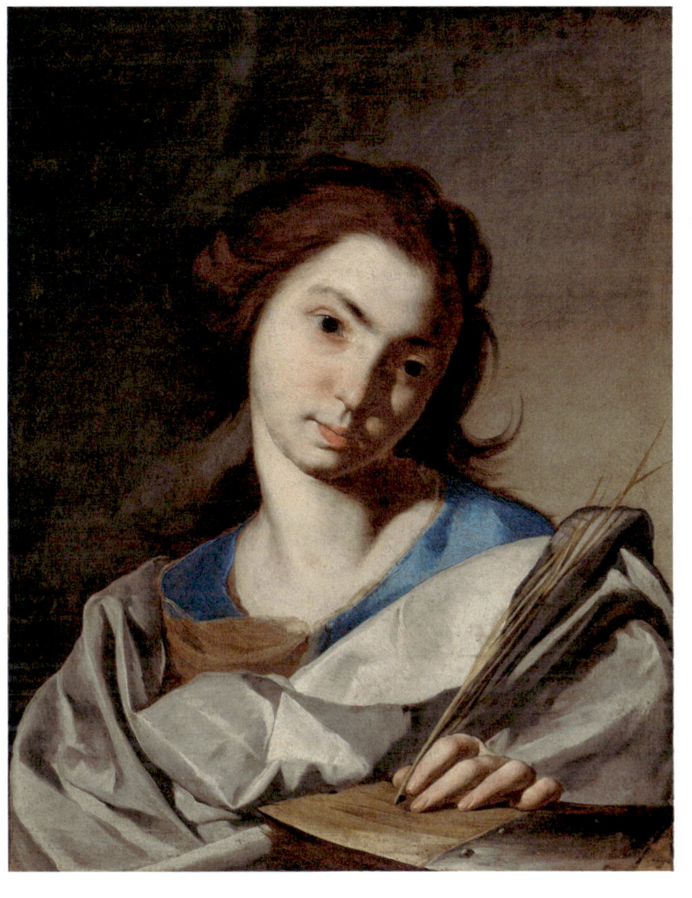

Bernardo Cavallino, *Saint Catherine of Alexandria*, 1645-1655

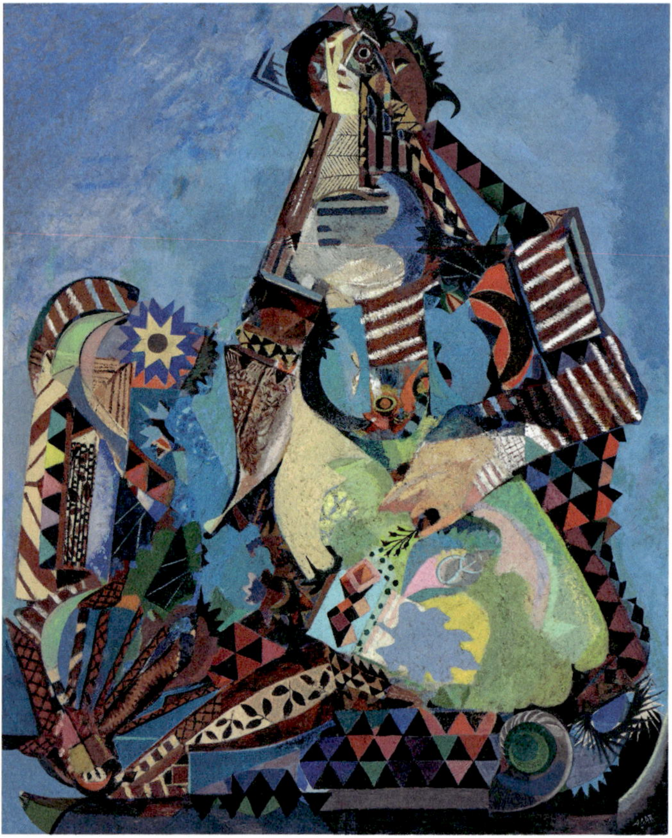

Eileen Agar, *Seated Figure*, 1956

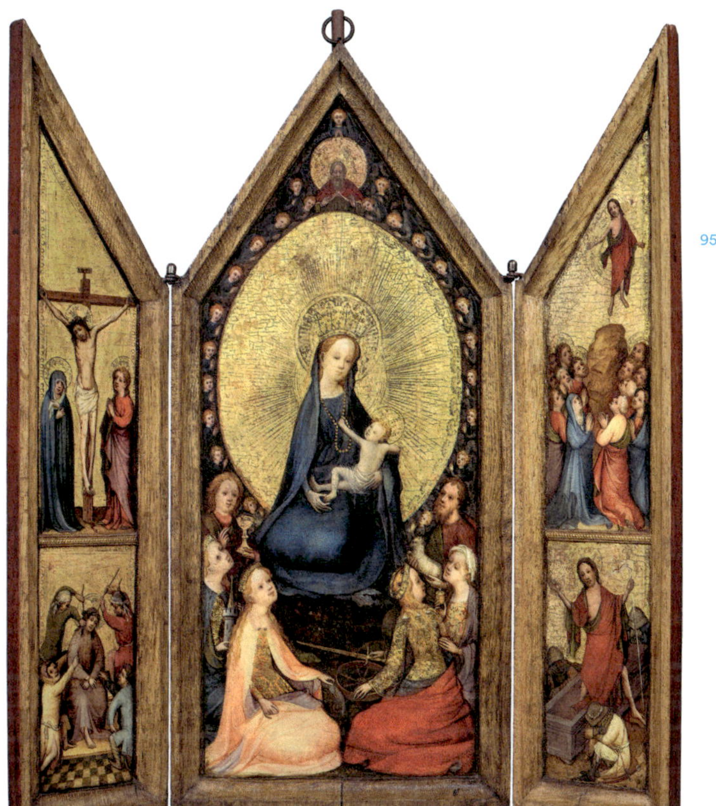

Master of St Veronica, *Triptych of the Virgin and Child enthroned*, c. 1410

In the early nineteen-forties, Leonora Carrington settled in Mexico, once described by André Breton as the most surrealistic country in the world. It was where she painted this work, which came to the museum in 2019.

Leonora Carrington, *Again, the Gemini are in the Orchard*, 1947

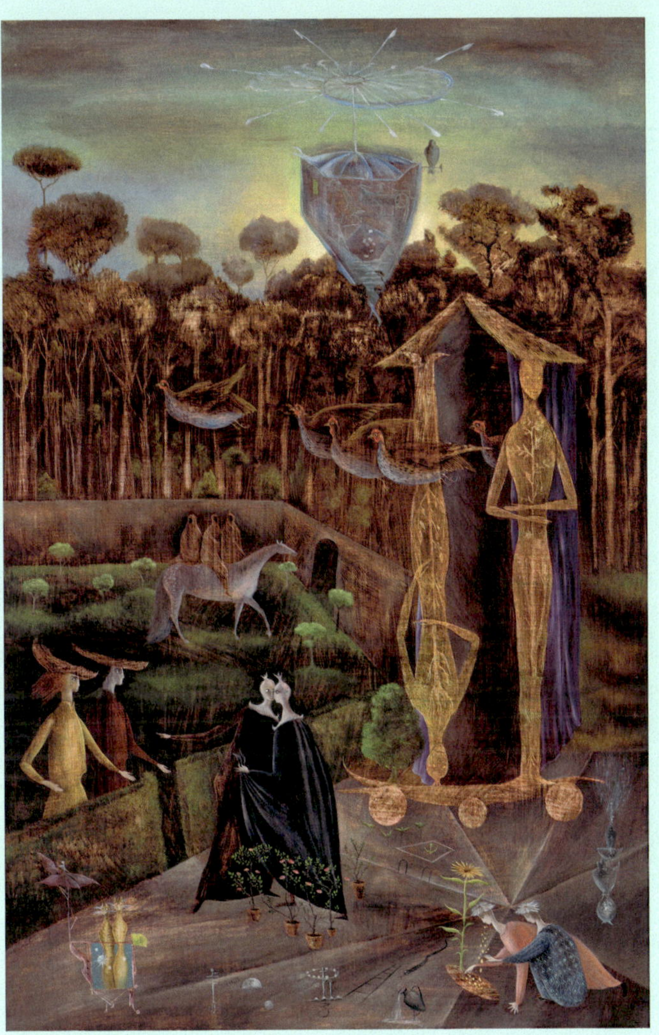

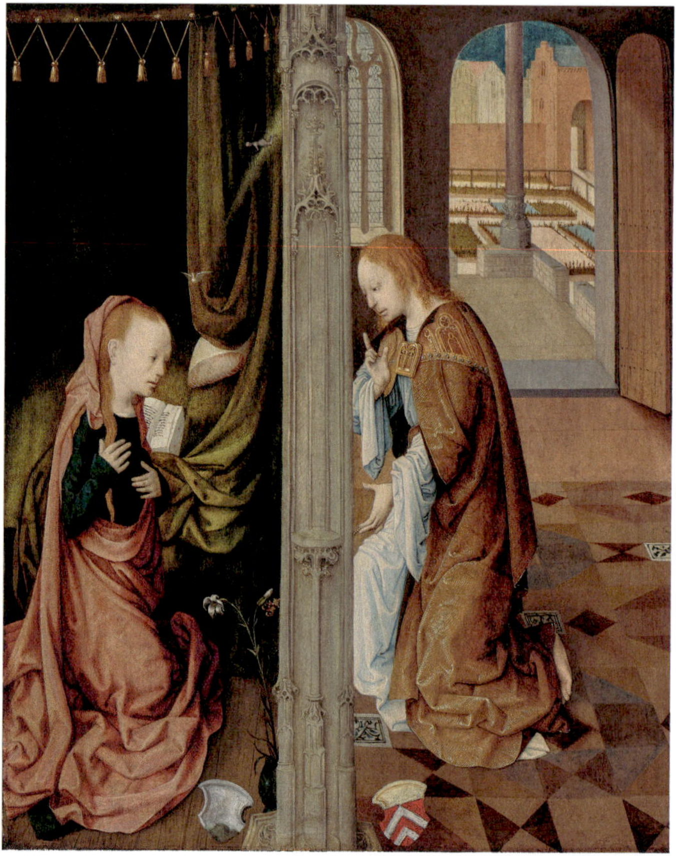

Master of the Virgo inter Virgines, *The Annunciation*, 1470-1500
Mark Manders, *Dry Clay Head on Concrete Floor*, 2016 ▸

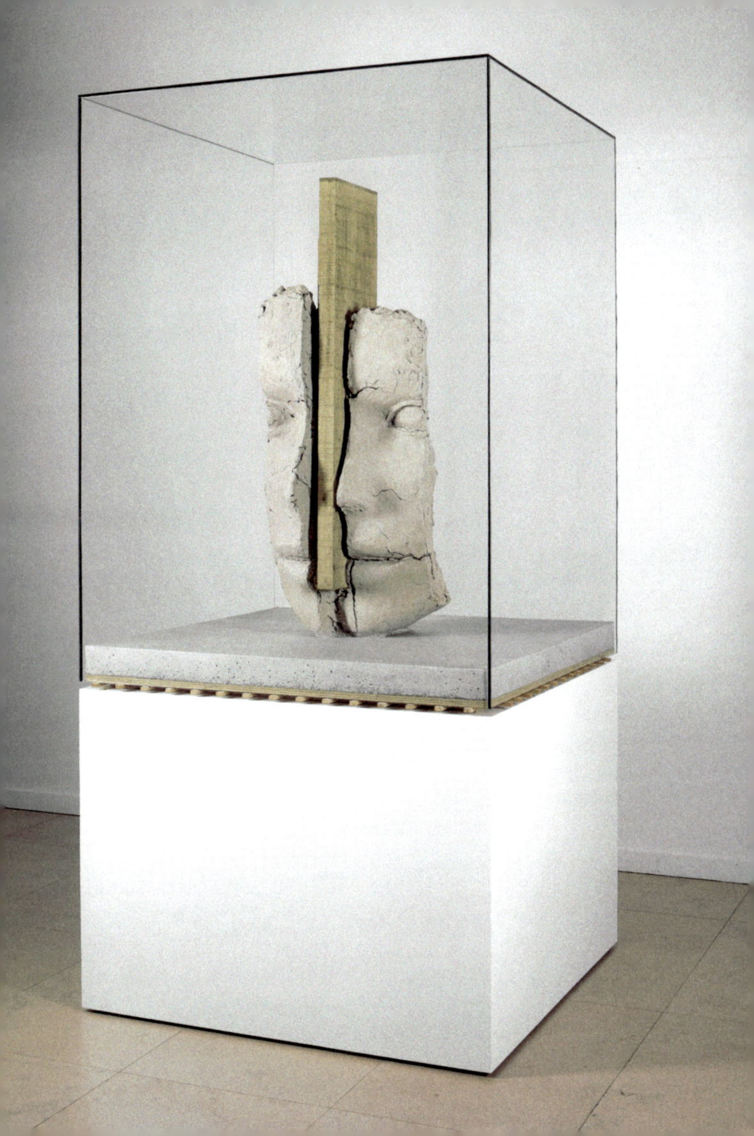

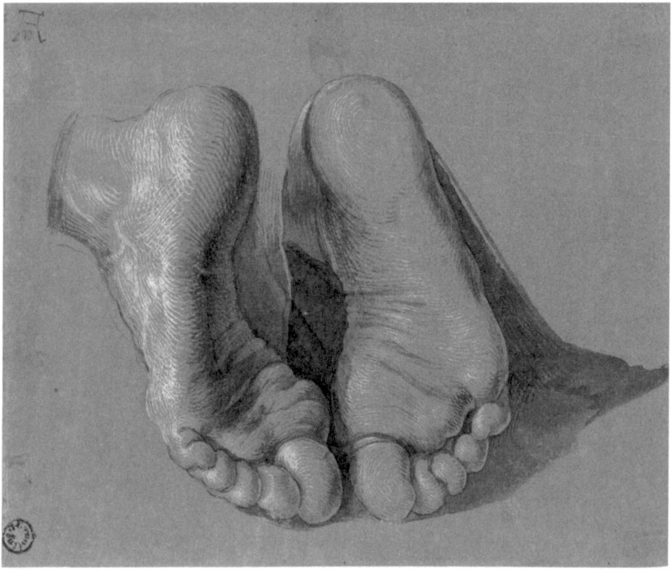

Albrecht Dürer, *Study of Two Feet for the Apostle Paul in the Heller Altarpiece*, c. 1508

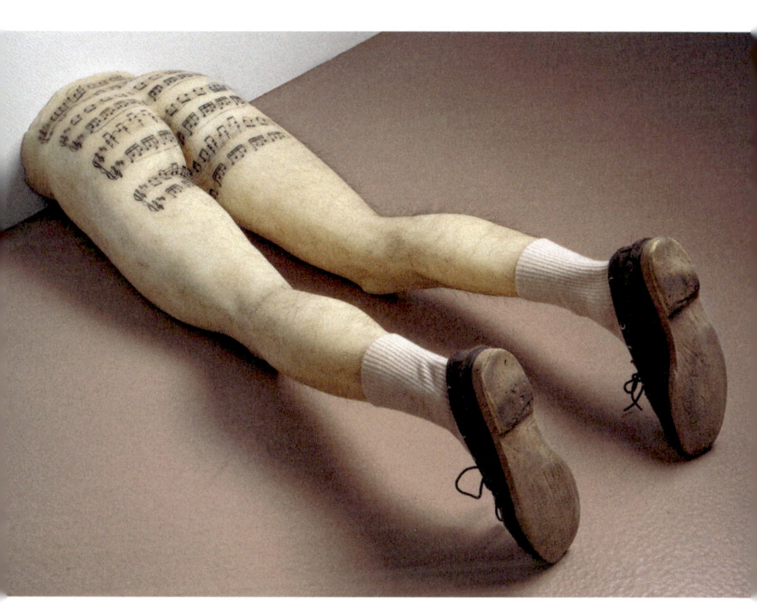

Robert Gober, *Untitled*, 1990

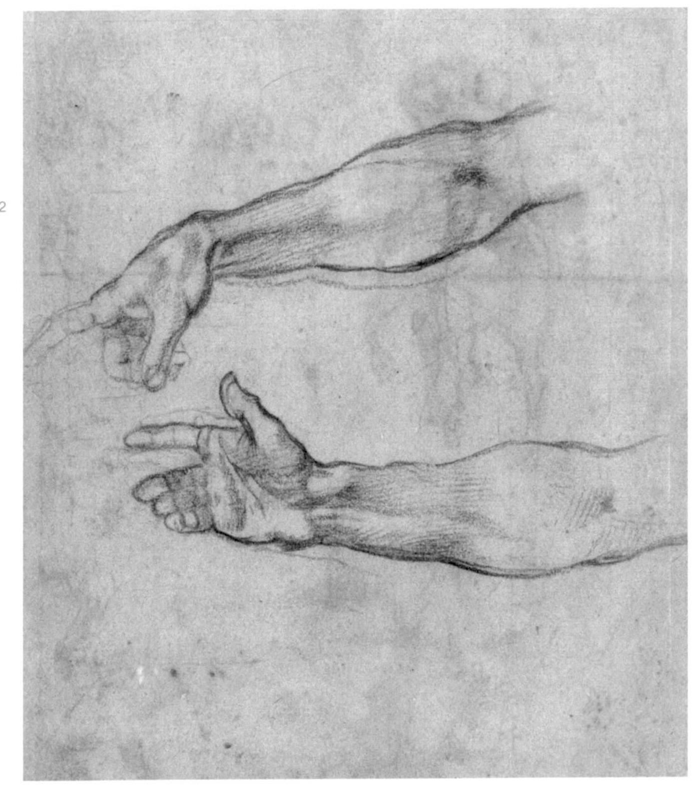

Michelangelo Buonarroti, *Studies of an Outstretched Right Forearm for the Fresco 'The Drunkenness of Noah' in the Sistine Chapel*, c. 1508-1509

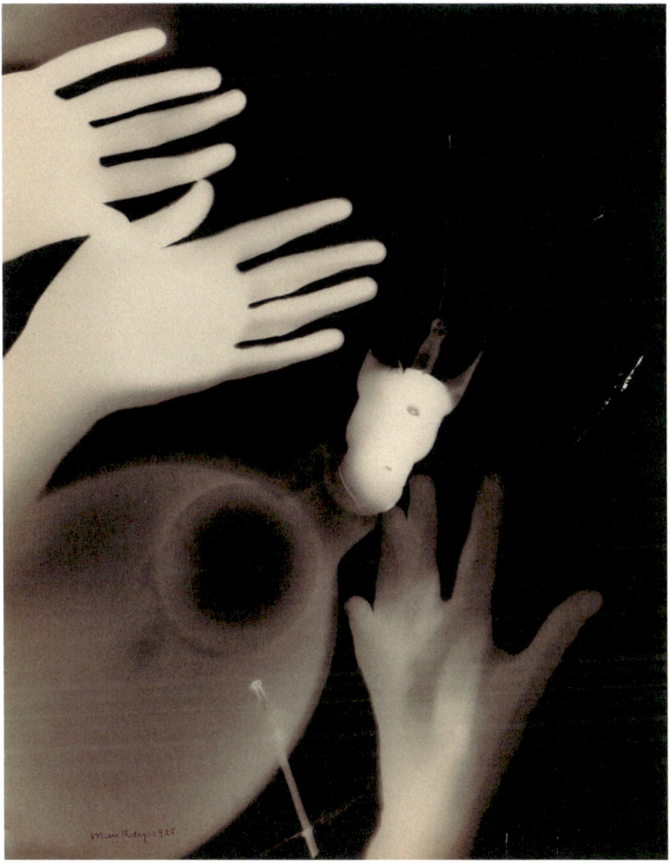

Man Ray, *Rayograph*, 1925

‘The womb, a fantastic thing, the source of life and the object of desire. As soon as the plug goes into the socket [the artwork] becomes a living machine, or a *machine à habiter*.’

JOEP VAN LIESHOUT

Atelier Van Lieshout, *Wombhouse*, 2004

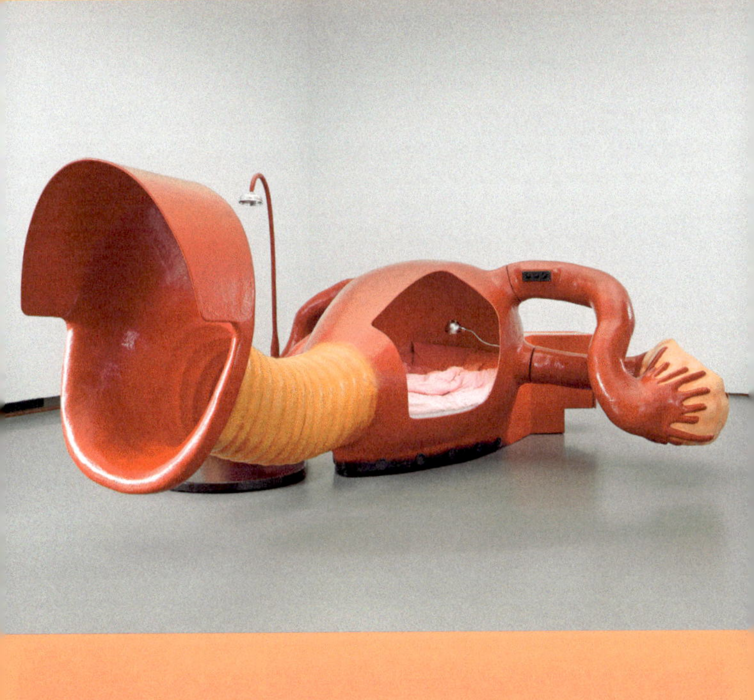

‘I do not know of a work of art in which a non-material, irrational thought is expressed so effectively by means of material attributes.’

GERARD REVE, *letter to the museum*, 1 April 1982

Geertgen tot Sint Jans, *The Glorification of the Virgin*, 1490-1495

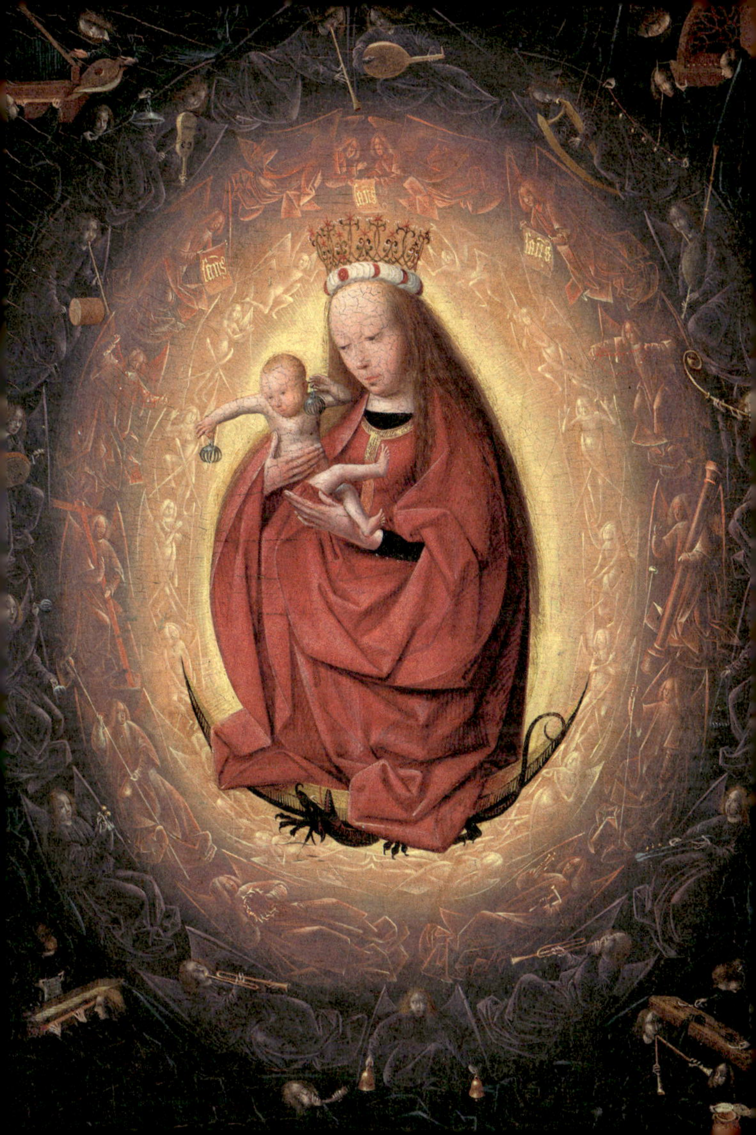

Mark Rothko, *Grey, Orange on Maroon, No. 8*, 1960

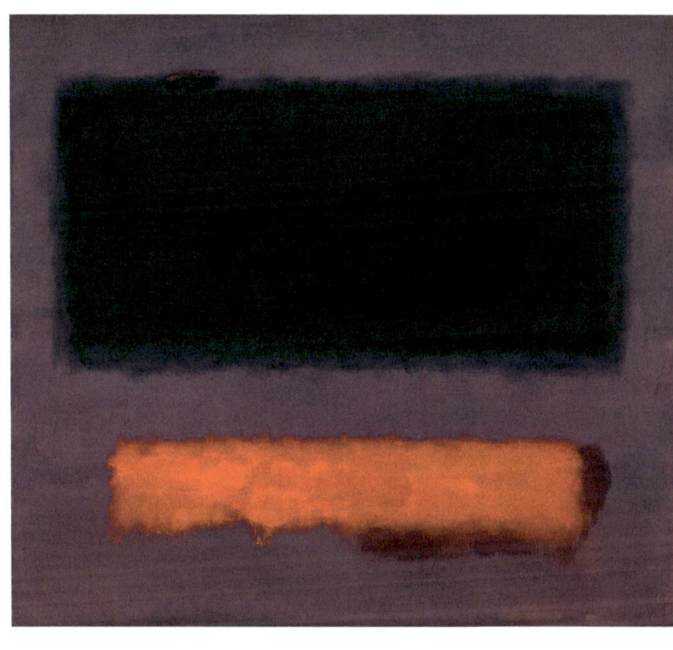

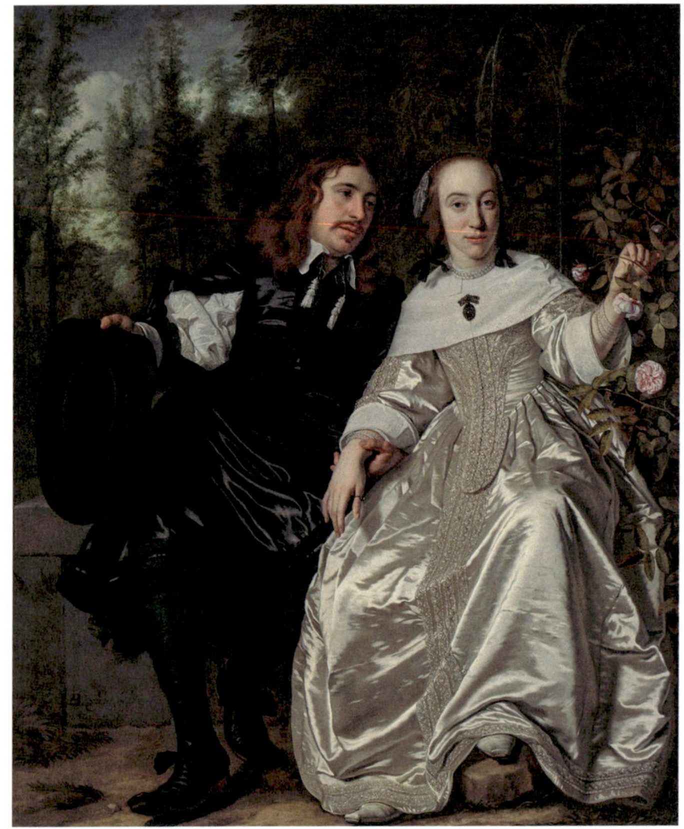

Bartholomeus van der Helst, *Abraham del Court and His Wife Maria de Kaersgieter*, 1654

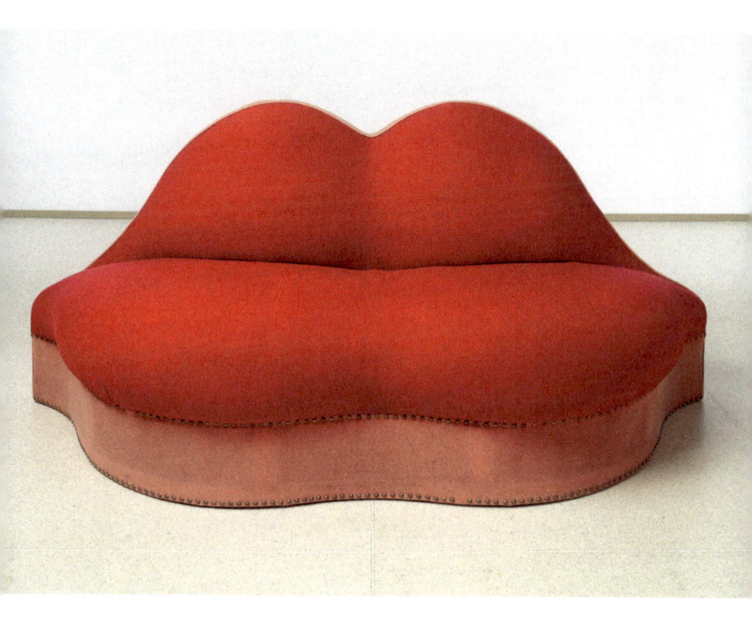

Salvador Dalí, *Mae West Lips Sofa*, 1938

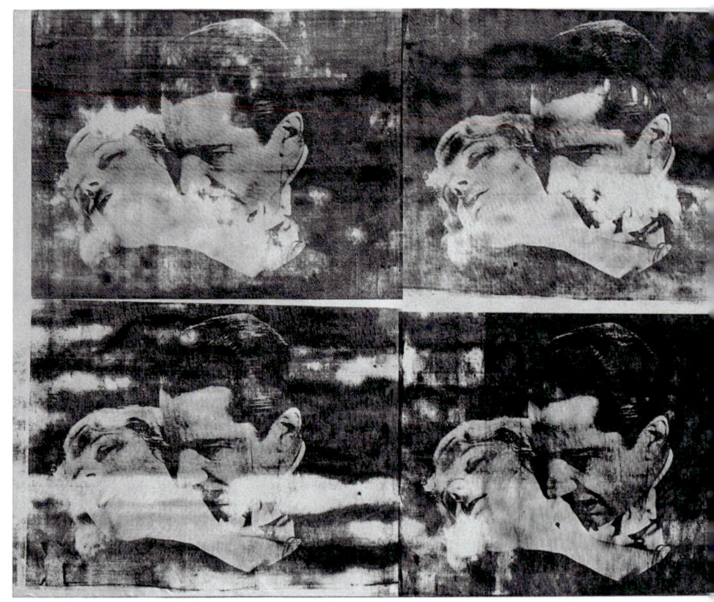

Andy Warhol, *The Kiss (Bela Lugosi)*, 1963

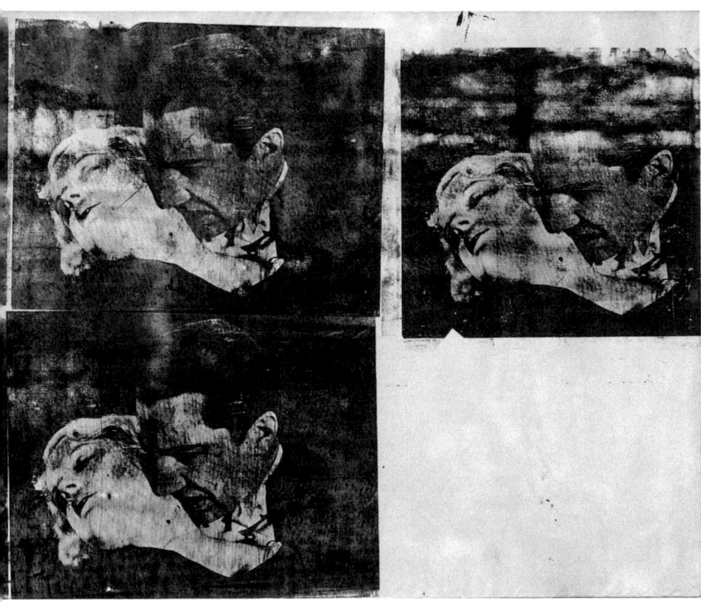

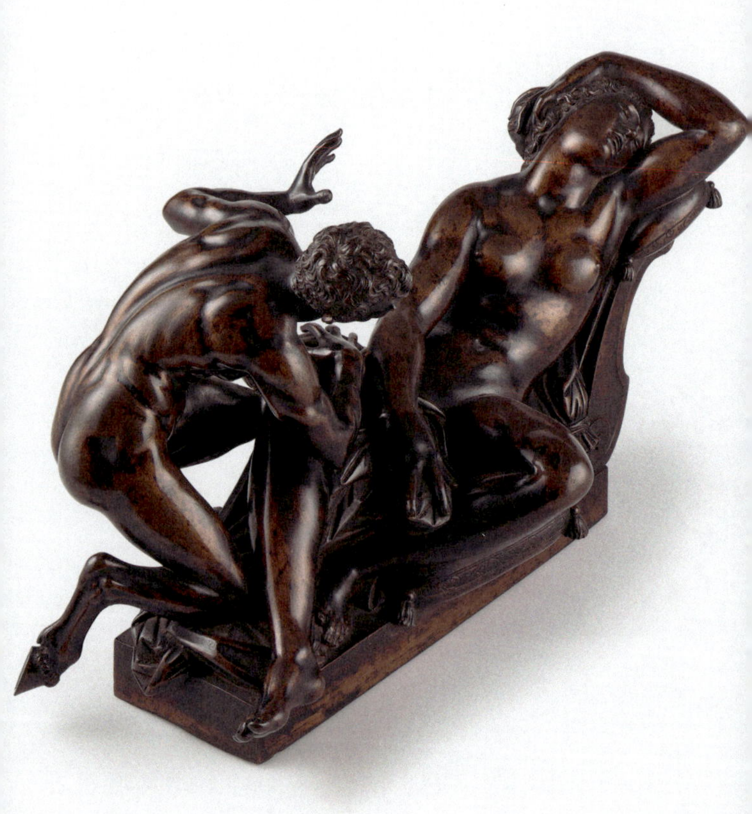

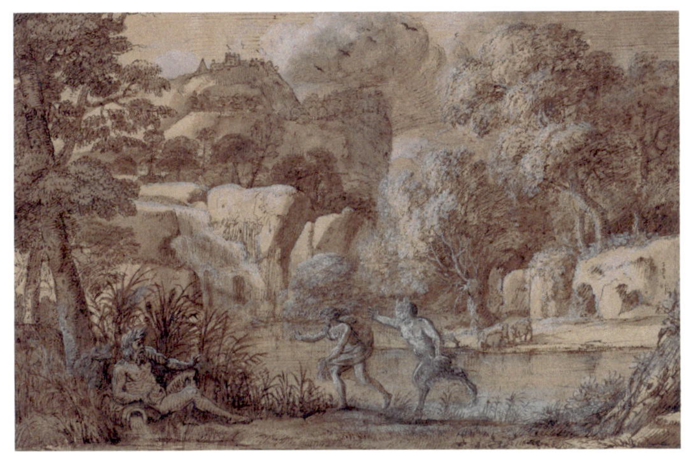

Claude Lorrain, *Landscape with Pan and Syrinx*, 1656

◂ Giambologna, *Sleeping Nymph and Satyr*, 1580-1590

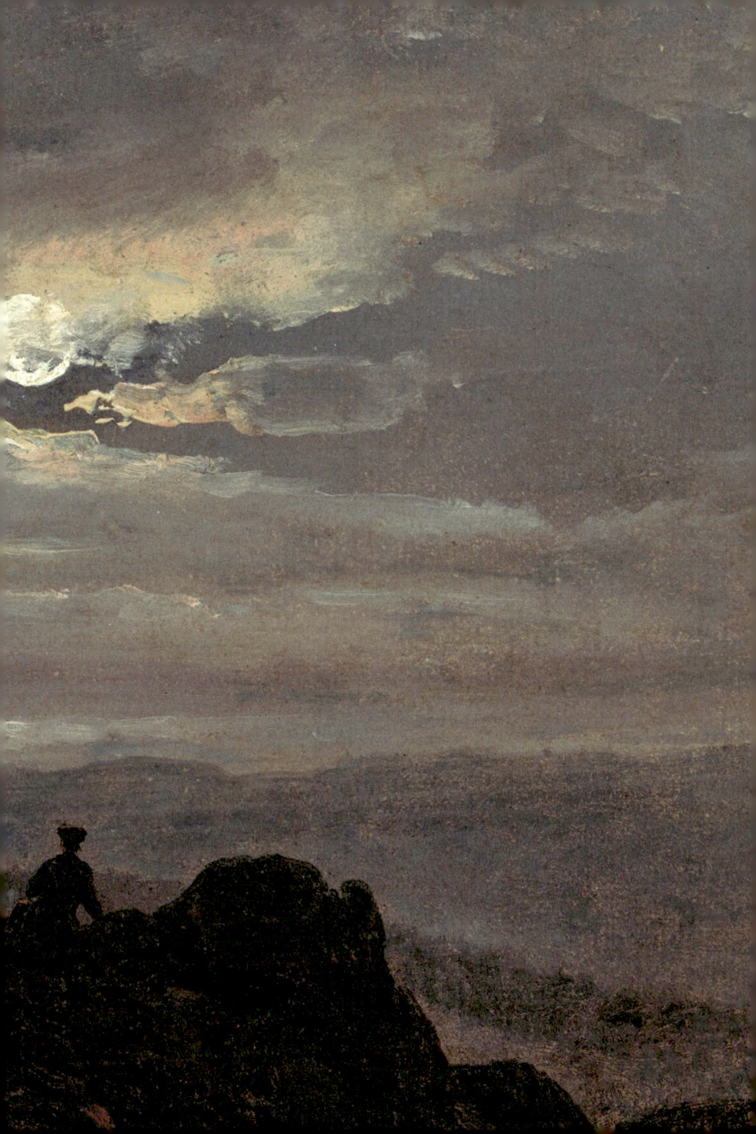

Philips Koninck, *An Extensive Landscape, with a River*, 1664

◂ Johan Christian Dahl, *Moonlit Landscape*, 1823

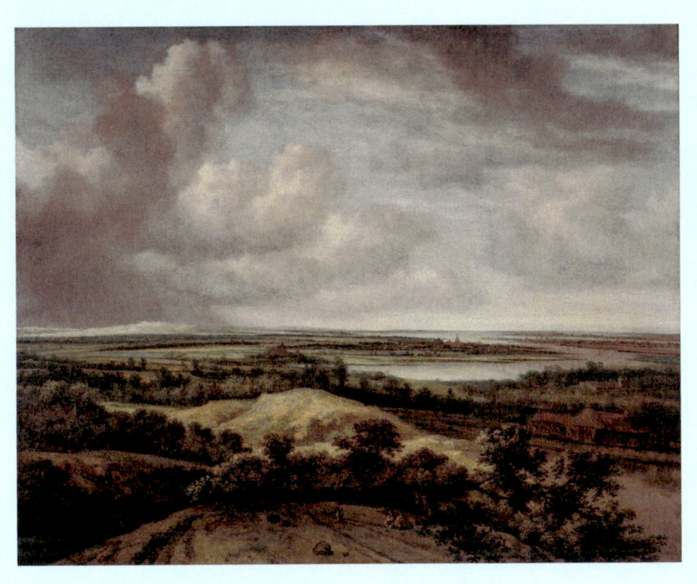

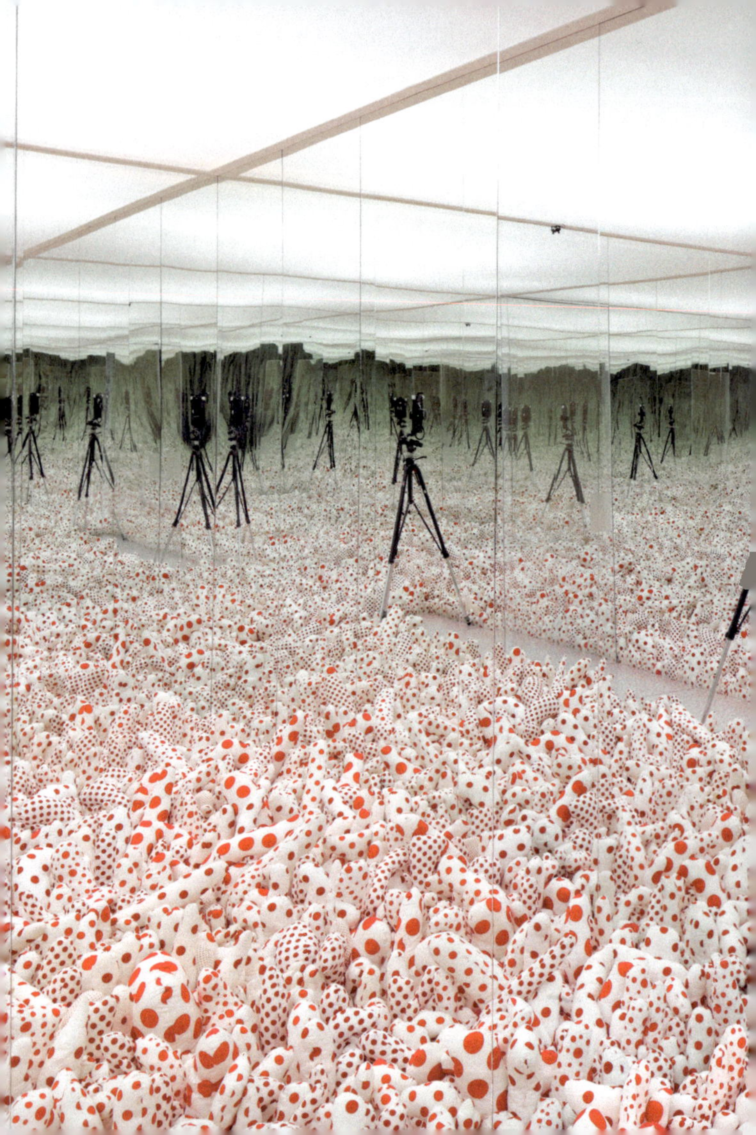

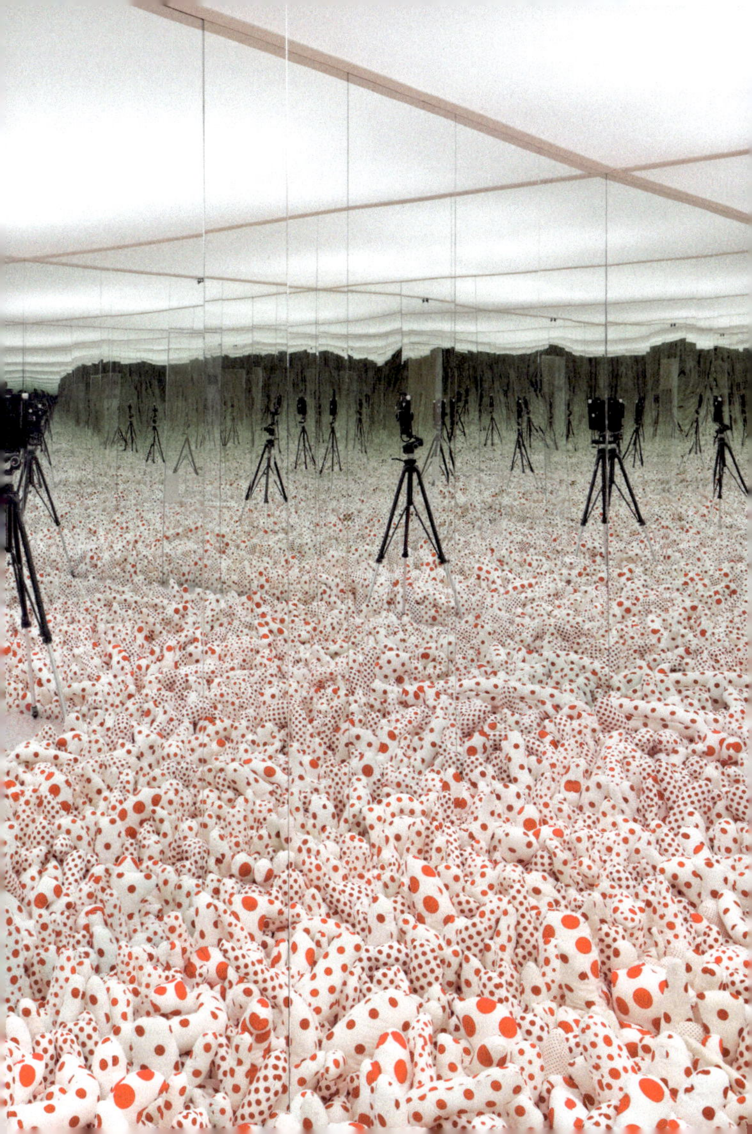

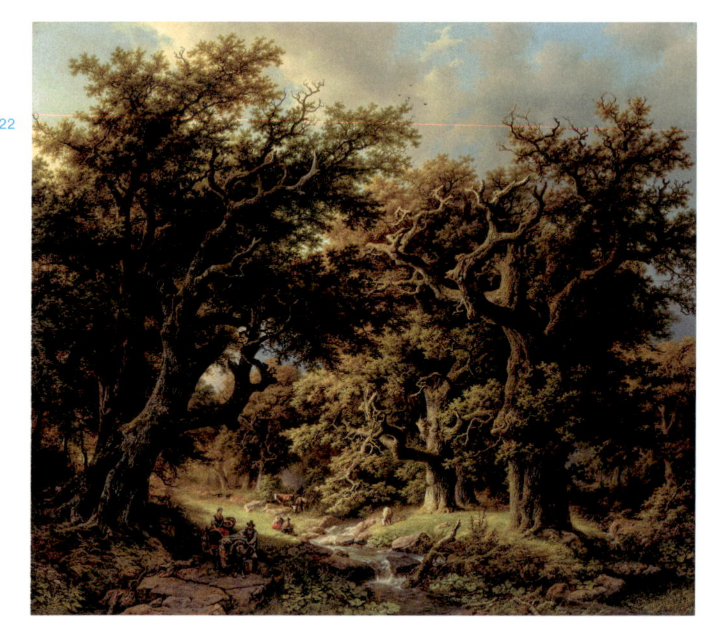

Barend Cornelis Koekkoek, *Oak Forest*, 1856

◂ Yayoi Kusama, *Infinity Mirror Room – Phalli's Field (Floor Show)*, 1965 (1998)

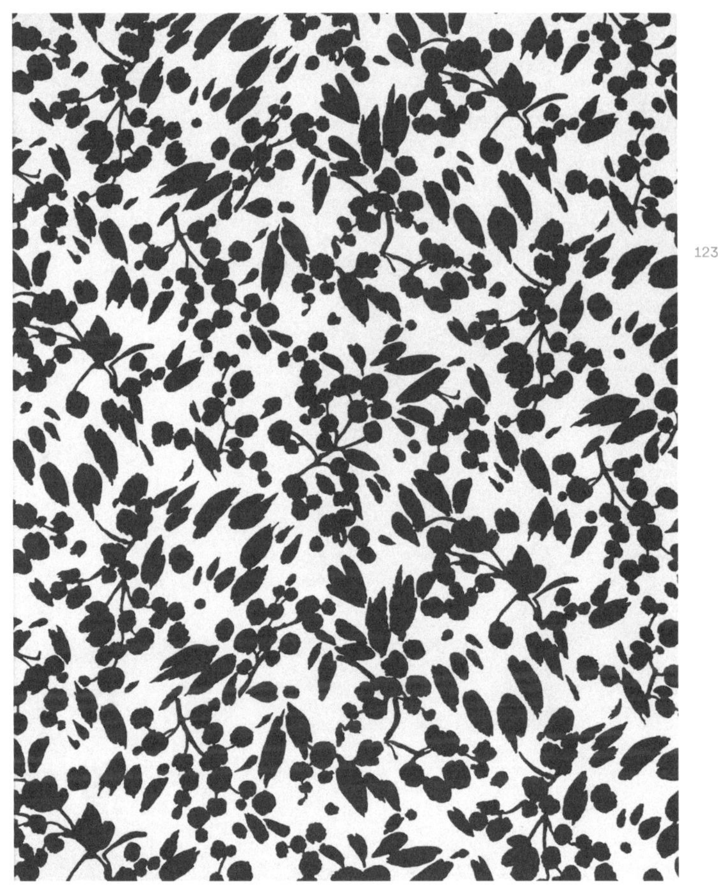

Daan van Golden, *Heerenlux III*, 1993

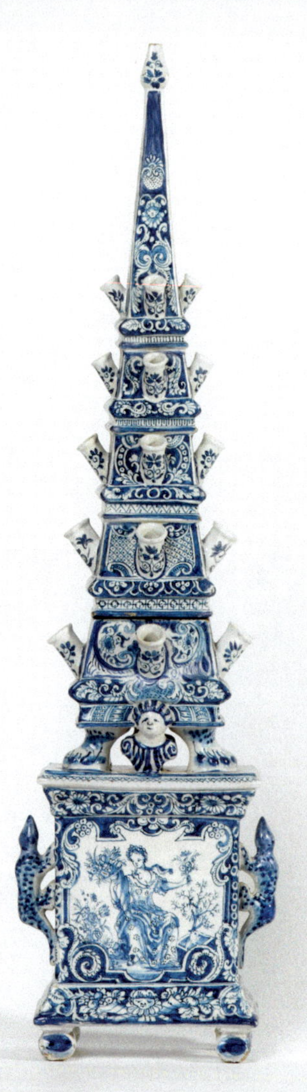

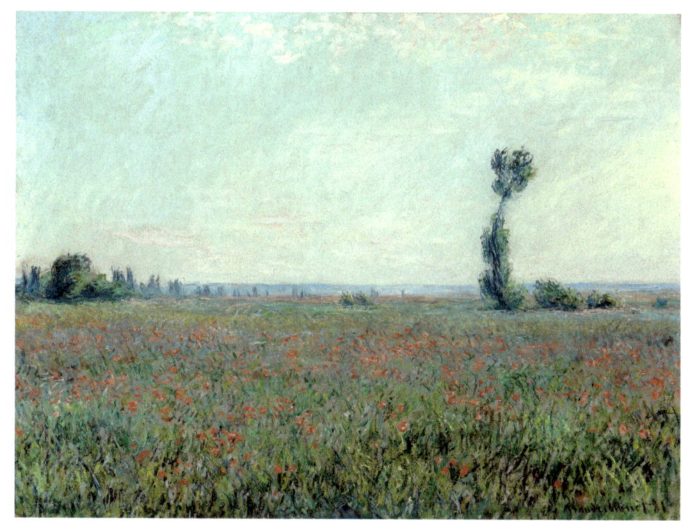

Claude Monet, *Field of Poppies*, 1881

◂ Louwys Victorsz, tulip vase, 1700-1725

This painting was given to the museum in 1903 by twenty-six friends of the arts in Rotterdam. It was the first painting by Vincent van Gogh in a public art collection.

Vincent van Gogh, *Poplars near Nuenen*, 1885

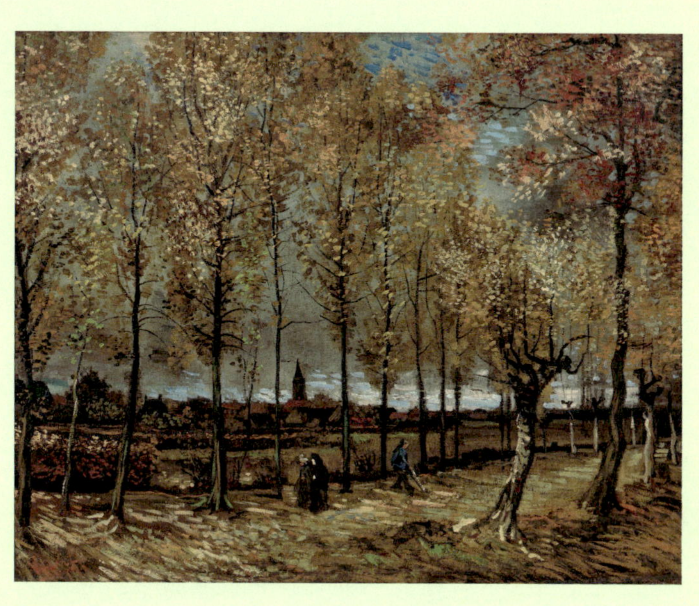

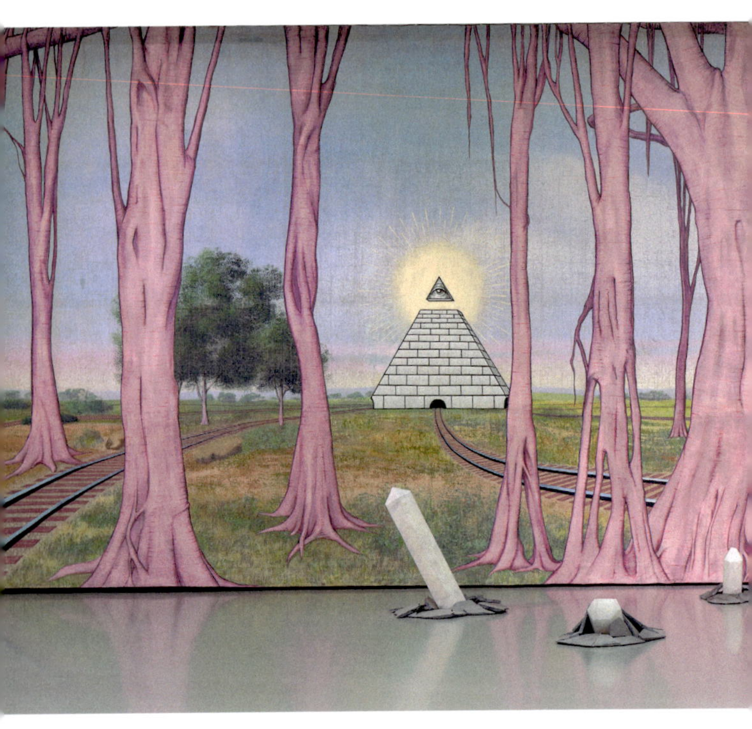

Jim Shaw, *D'red Dwarf, B'lack Hole*, 2010

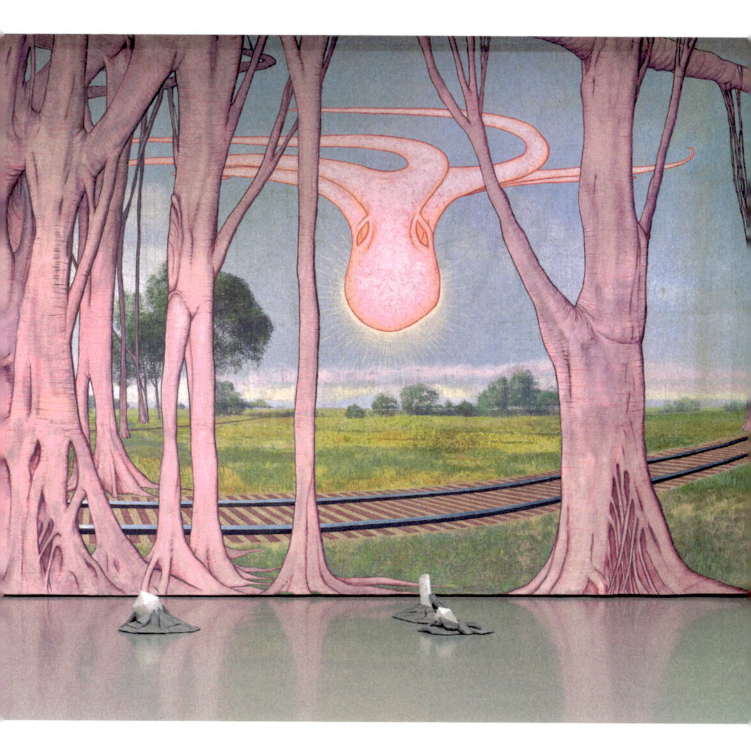

A cupboard doesn't have to be a cupboard. Break away from the rules of Modernism. This is what Ettore Sottsass and the Memphis Group stood for with their contrarian shapes in the nineteen-eighties.

Ettore Sottsass, *Carlton*, 1981

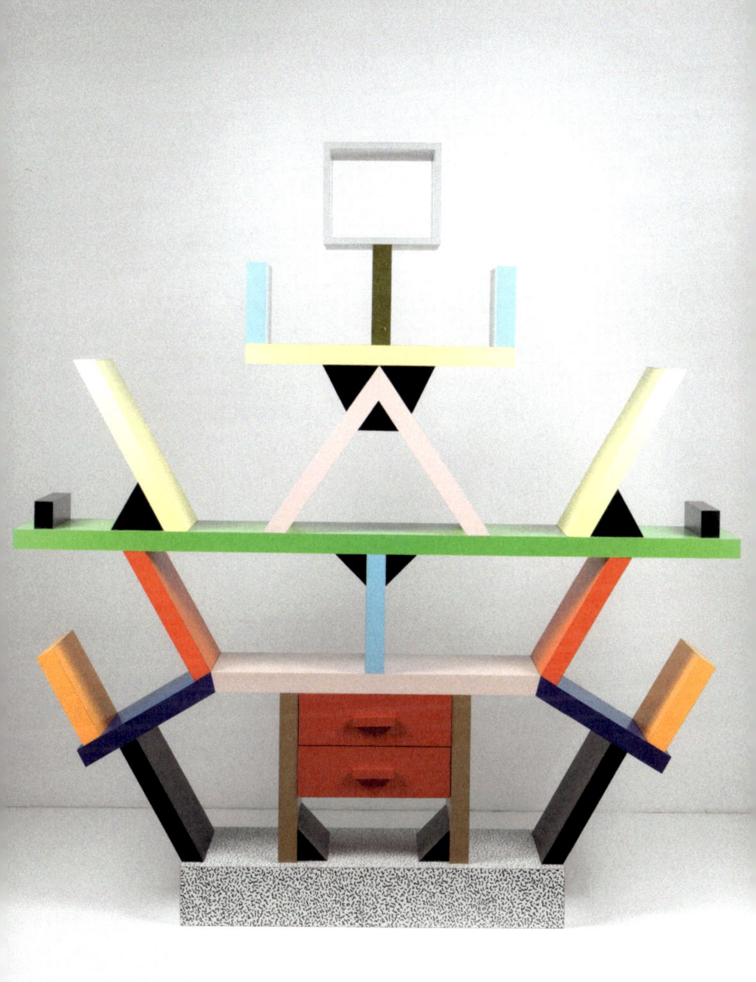

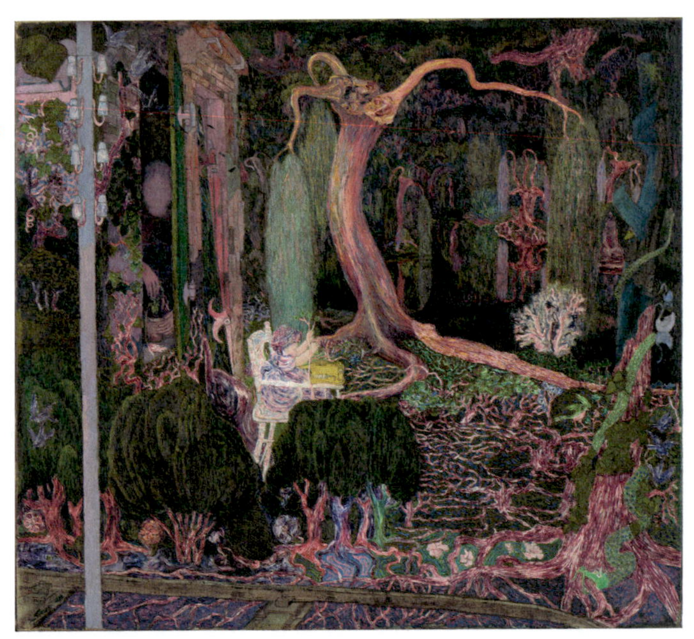

Jan Toorop, *The New Generation*, 1892

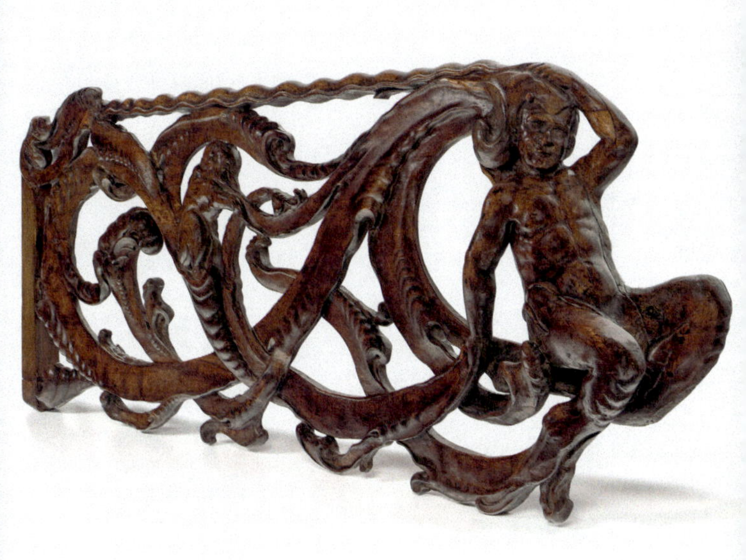

Anonymous, balustrade, c. 1650

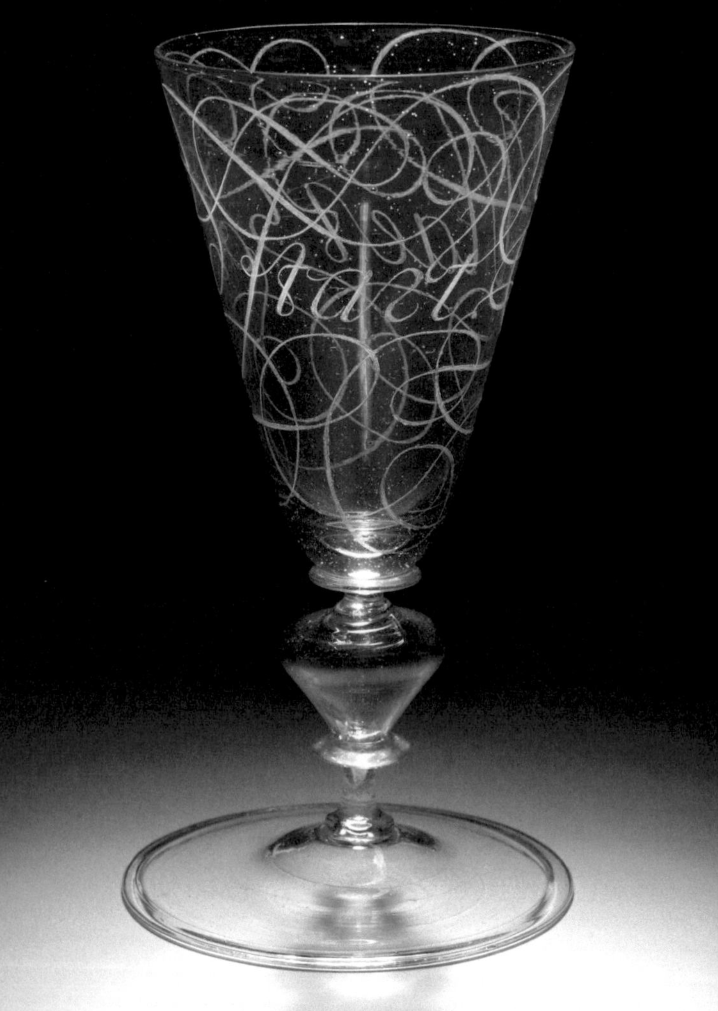

In the seventeenth century, writing in calligraphy on glass was a popular hobby of the elite. However, this is not the work of an amateur but of a particularly skilled artist.

Willem Jacobszoon van Heemskerk, goblet, 1688

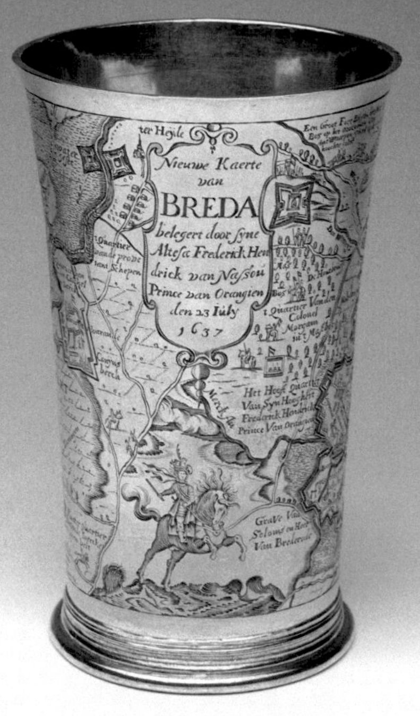

Scholte Jansen, *Memorial Beaker Commemorating the Siege of Breda in 1637*, 1648
Anonymous, coconut goblet, 1550-1600 ►

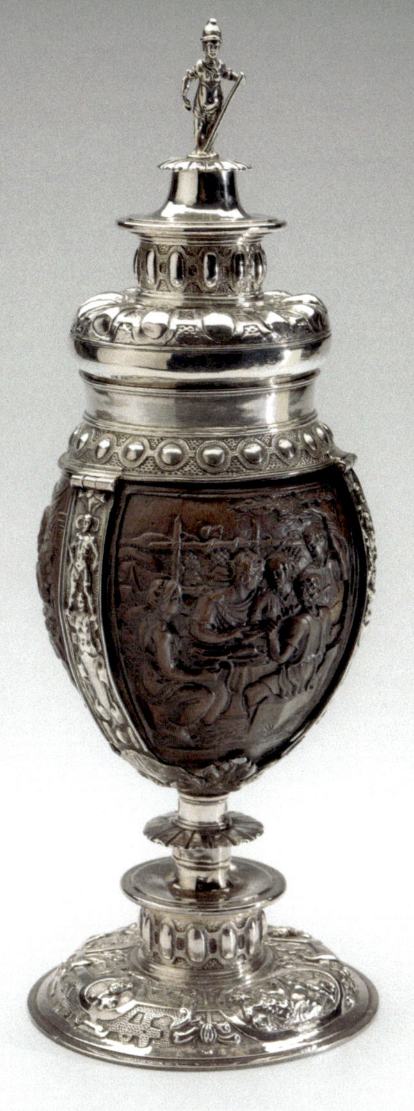

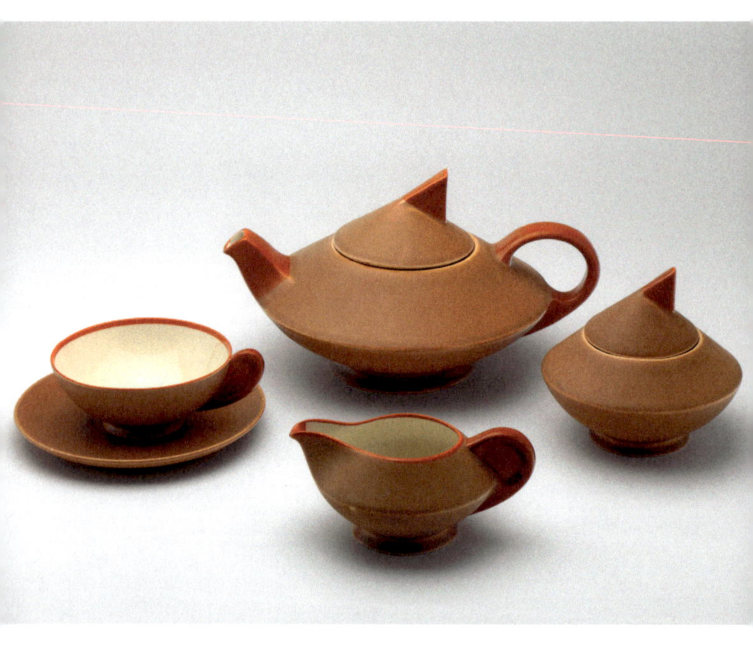

Guillaume Marie Edmond Bellefroid, *Thea* tea set, 1934

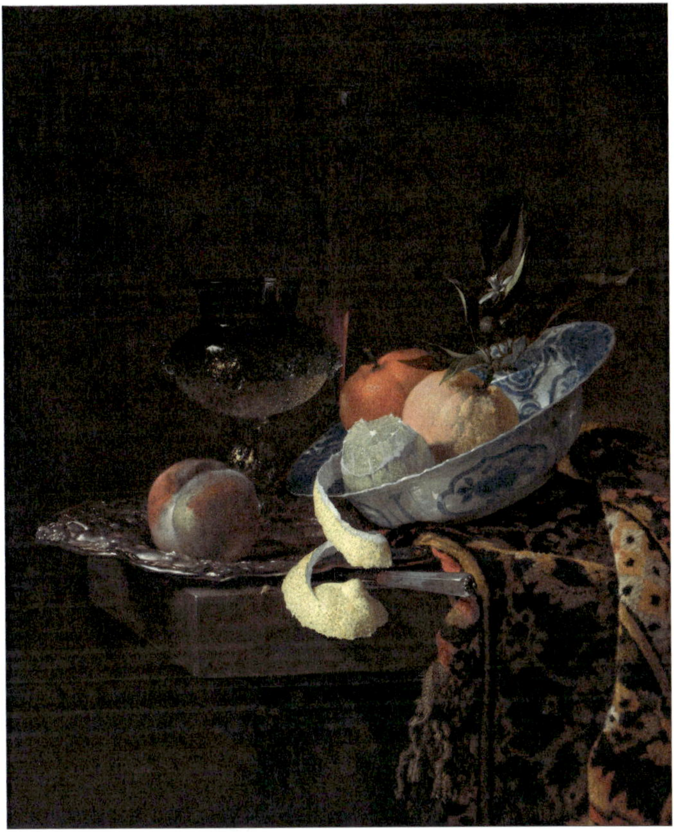

Willem Kalf, *Still Life with a Ming Bowl*, c. 1660

This fourteenth-century earthenware jug was made in Flanders and found in the submerged city of Reimerswaal, north of the Drowned Land of Reimerswaal in Zuid-Beveland.

Anonymous, *Three Kings Jug*, 1350-1400

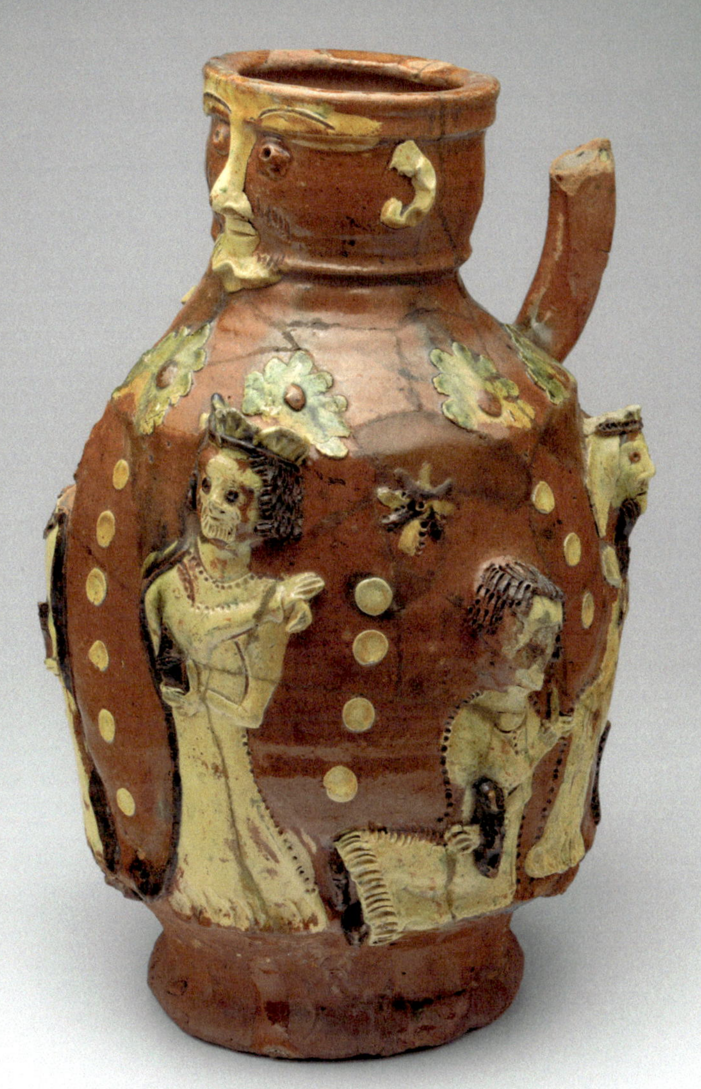

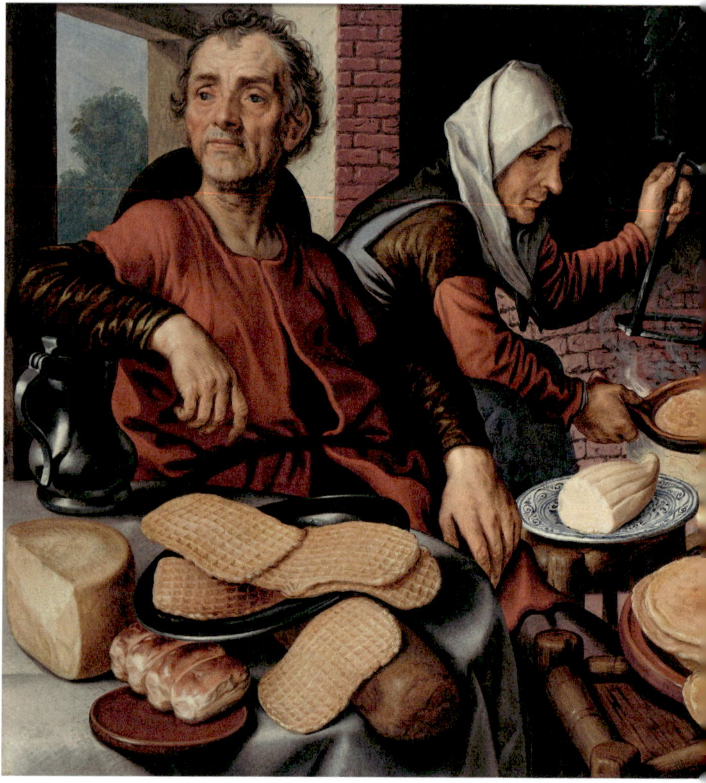

Pieter Aertsen, *The Pancake Bakery*, 1560

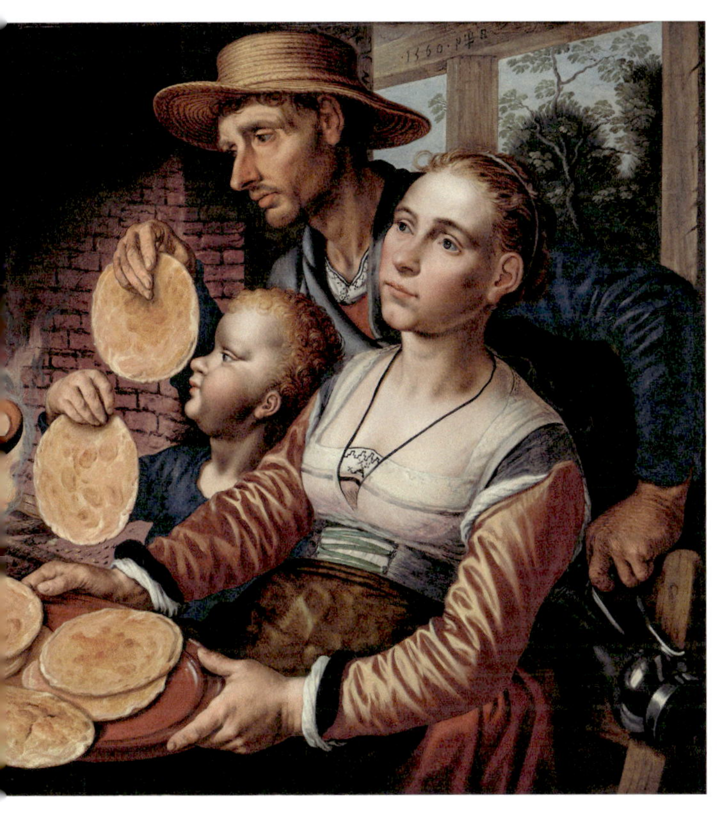

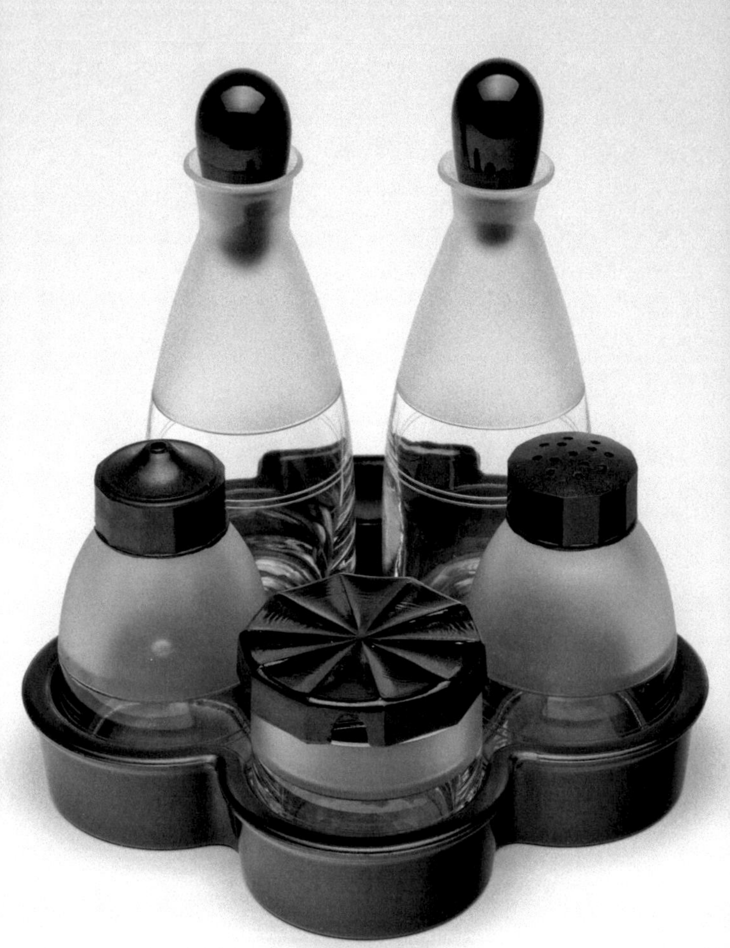

This oil and vinegar set is one of the group of affordable objects that Copier designed in the nineteen-thirties. Out of sheer necessity; sales of luxury decorated products had declined because of the recession.

Andries Copier, *Virgo*, 1937

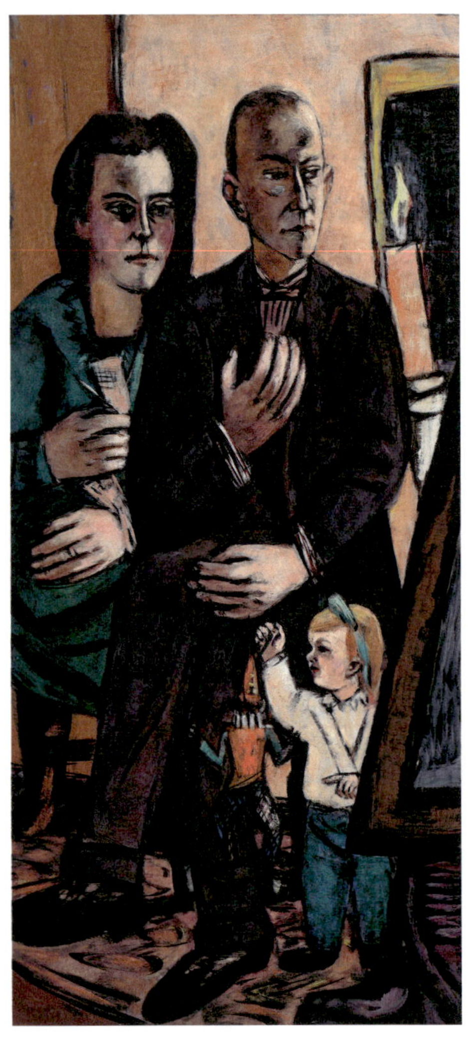

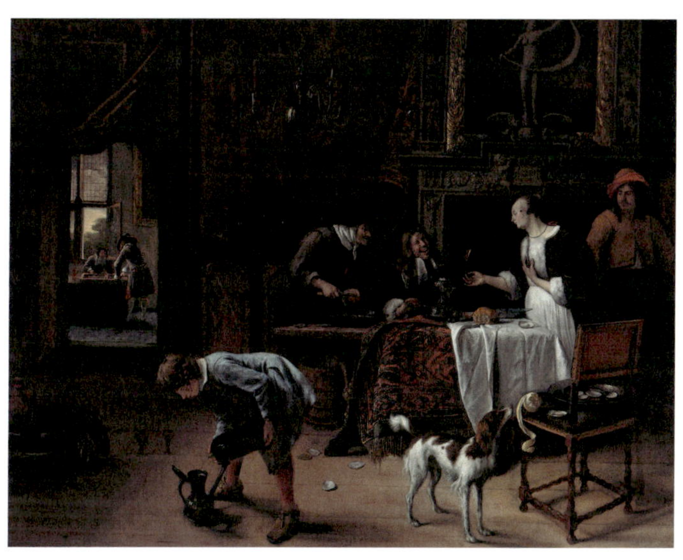

Jan Havicksz Steen, *'Easy Come, Easy Go'*, 1661

◂ Max Beckmann, *Portrait of the Lütjens Family*, 1944

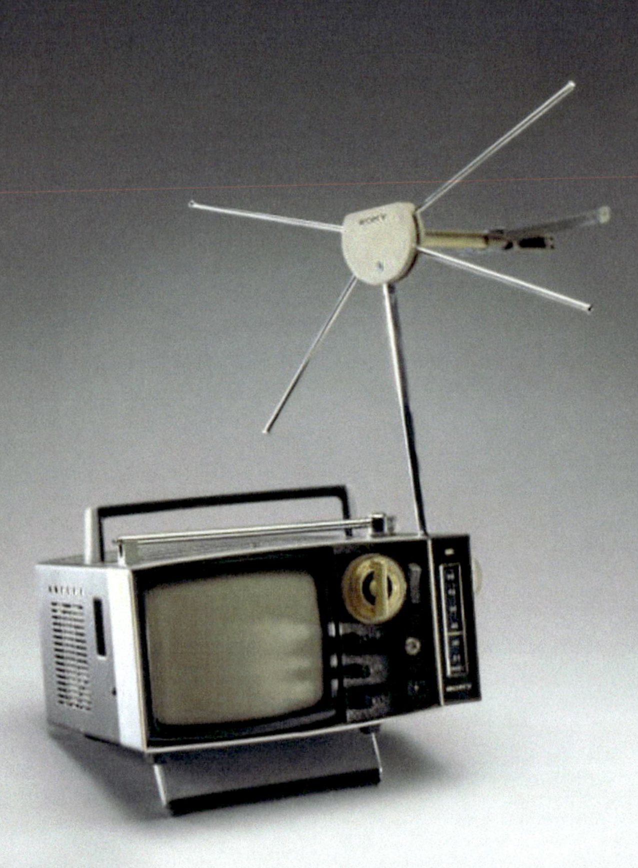

Sony Design Team, *Sony micro-tv 5-305e*, 1962
Anonymous, nautilus cup, c. 1590 ▸

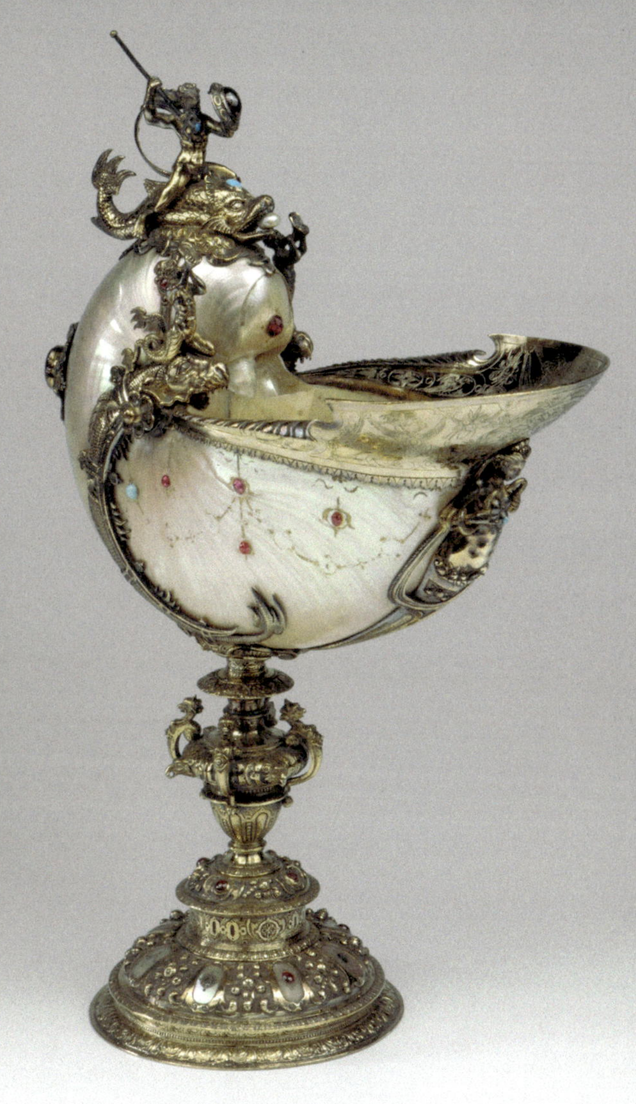

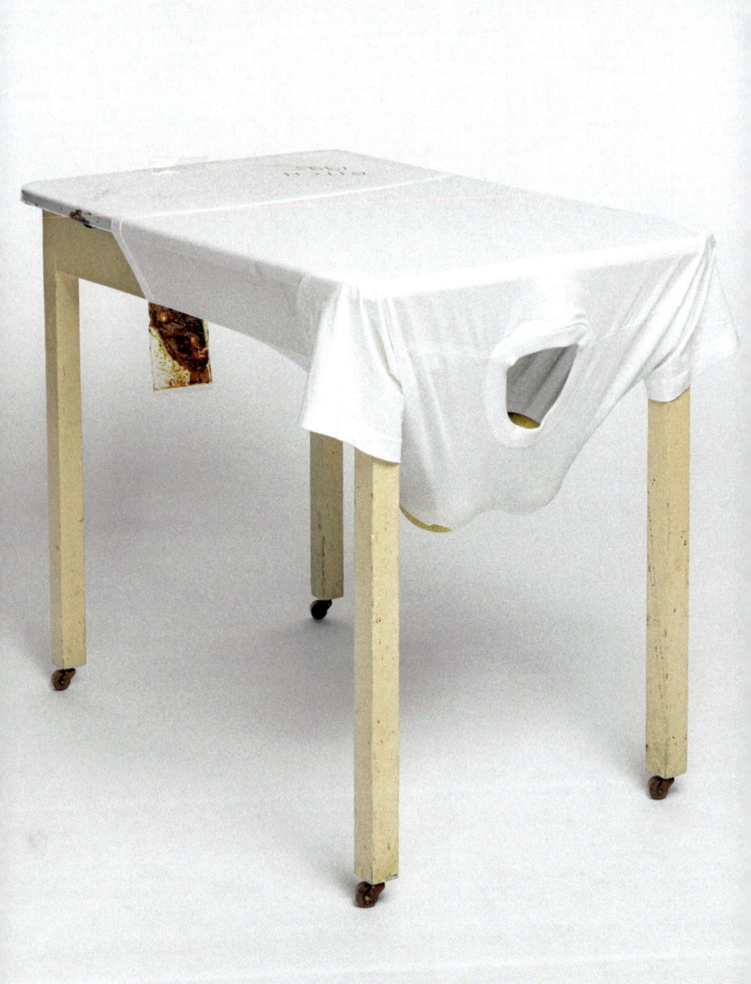

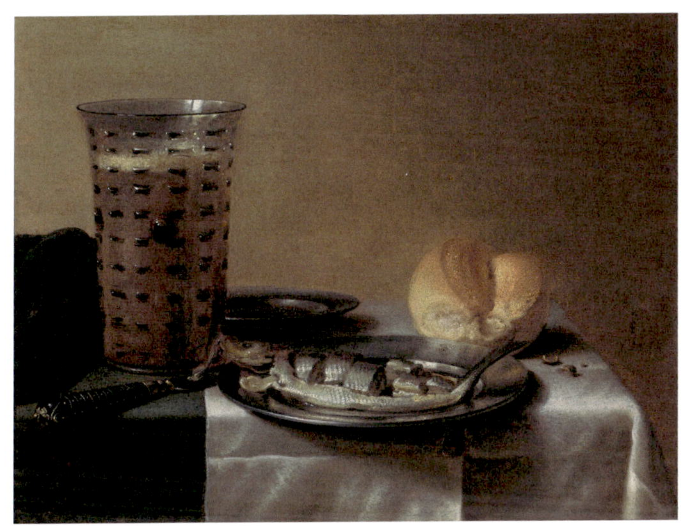

Pieter Claesz, *Breakfast Piece*, 1636

◂ Sarah Lucas, *Bitch*, 1995

Manet spent a short time in Bellevue on the River Seine to convalesce from an illness. The garden of his house was the source of inspiration for watercolours of fruit and flowers. He sent some of them to his friends as letters.

Edouard Manet, *Study Sheet with Five Plums*, 1880

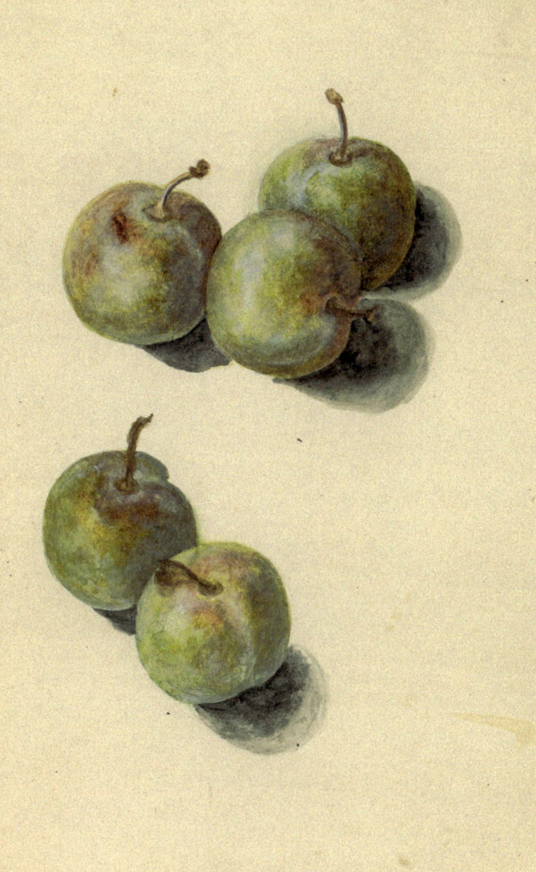

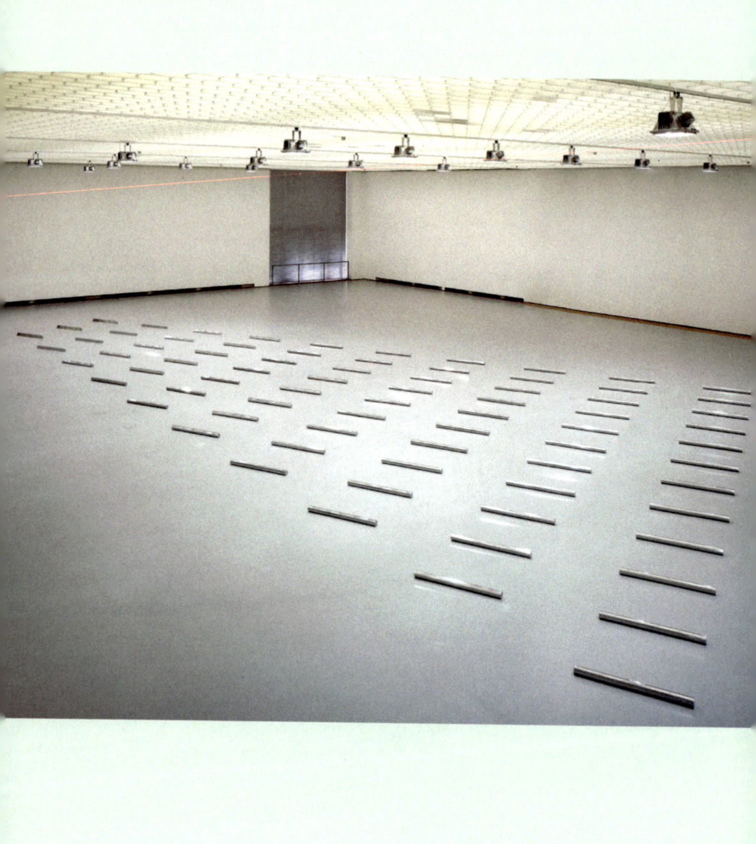

At the request of the museum's former director, Wim Beeren, Walter de Maria became the first artist to make an artwork specifically for the large exhibition space.

Walter De Maria, *A Computer Which Will Solve Every Problem in the World / 3-12 Polygon*, 1984

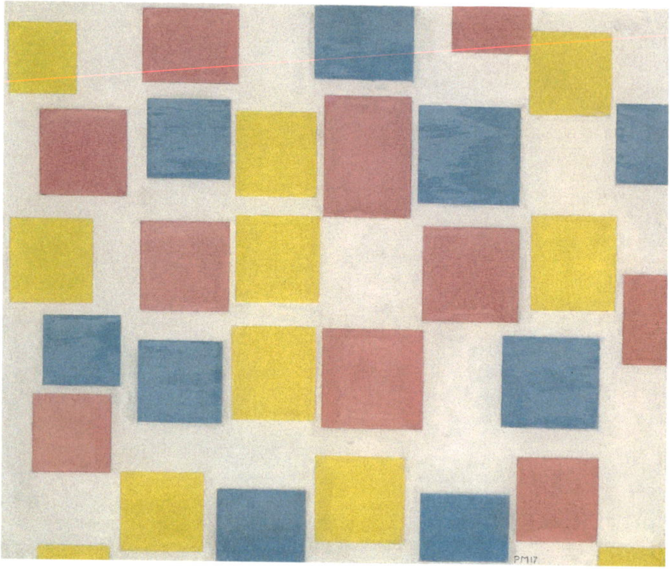

Piet Mondrian, *Composition with Colour Fields*, 1917
Gerrit Thomas Rietveld, *Zigzag Chair*, 1938 ►

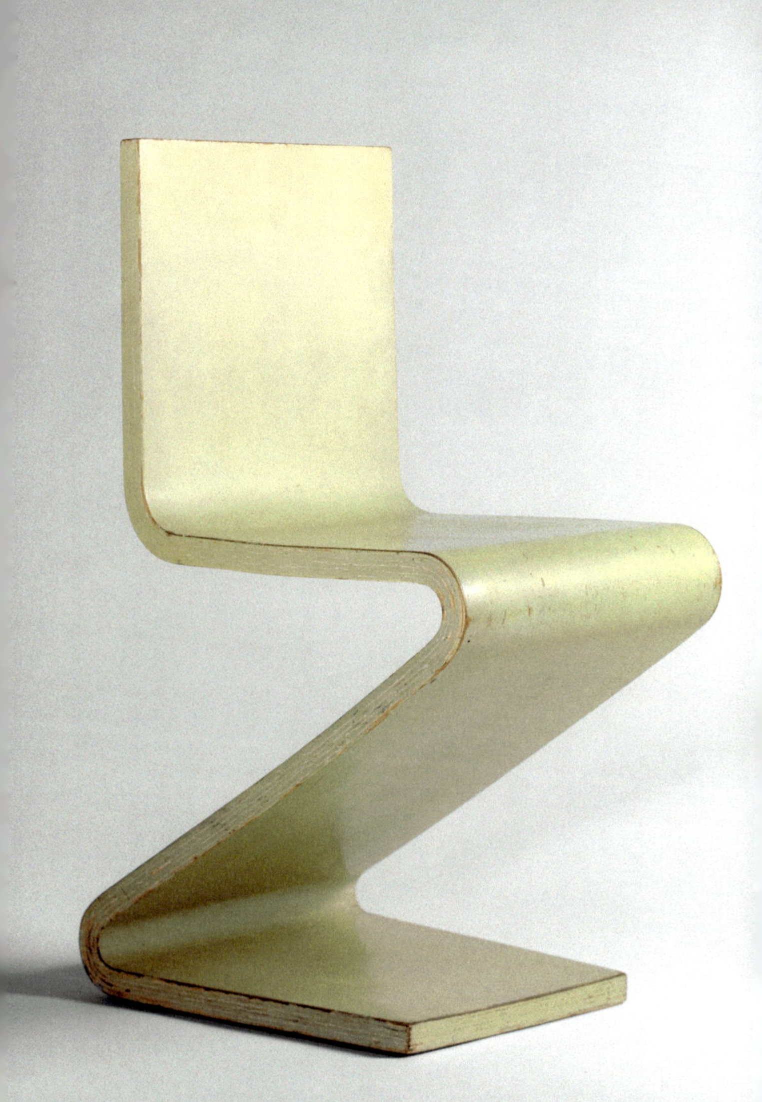

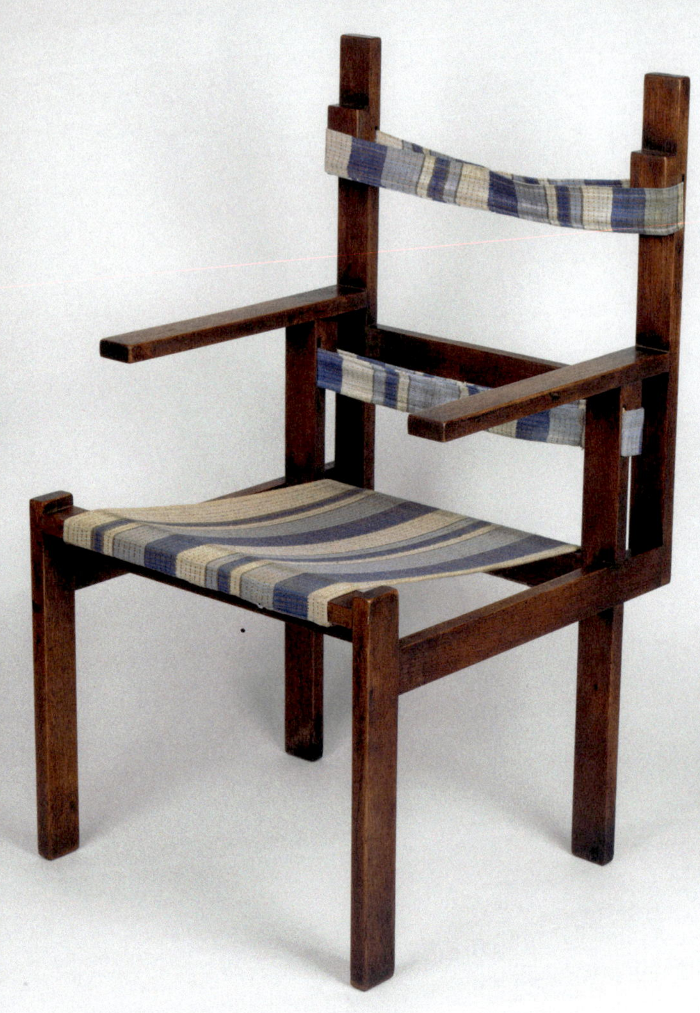

Marcel Breuer, *Slatted Chair Model ti 1a*, 1923

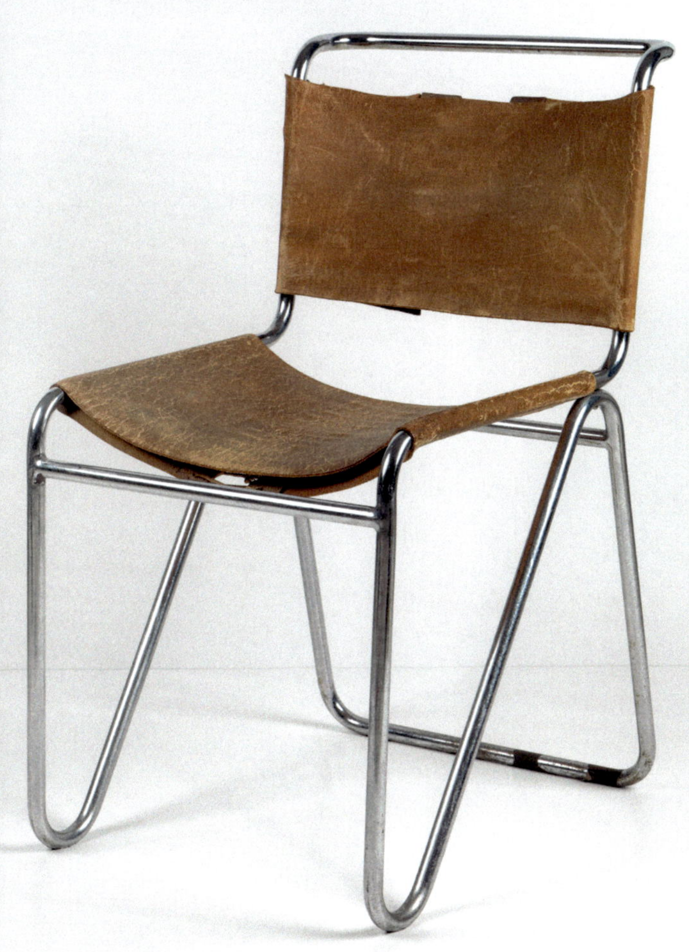

Willem Hendrik Gispen, *Diagonal Chair*, 1929-1930

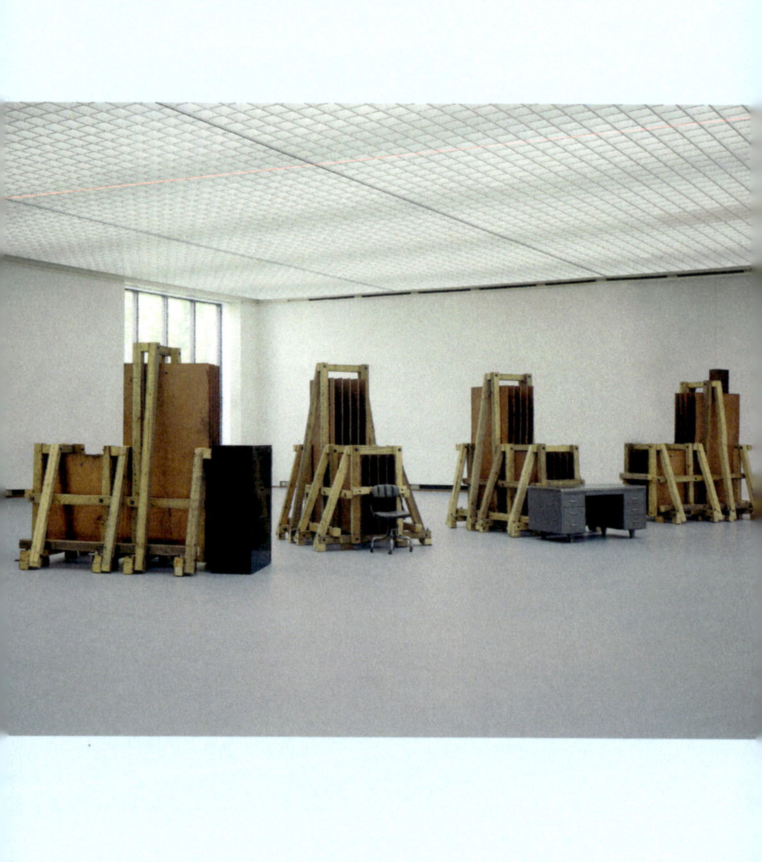

For this work Beuys removed a collection of old pieces of office furniture from René Block's gallery in Berlin and combined them with wooden racks, heavy copper plates and fragments from earlier work to create a new installation.

Joseph Beuys, *Ground*, 1980-1981

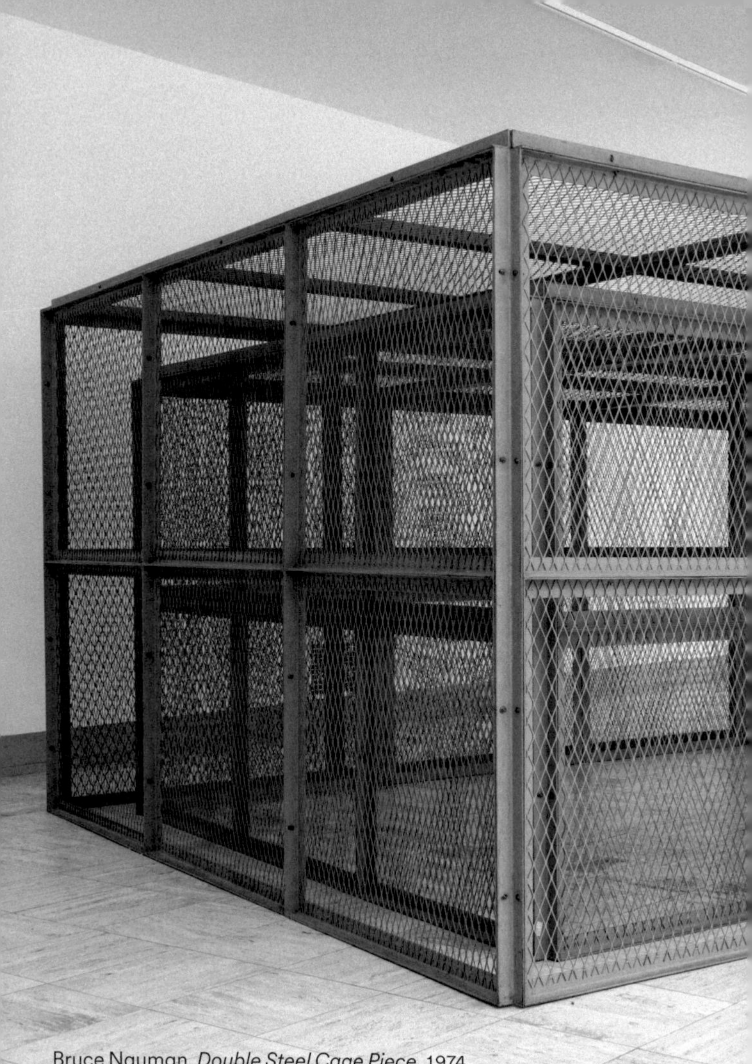

Bruce Nauman, *Double Steel Cage Piece*, 1974

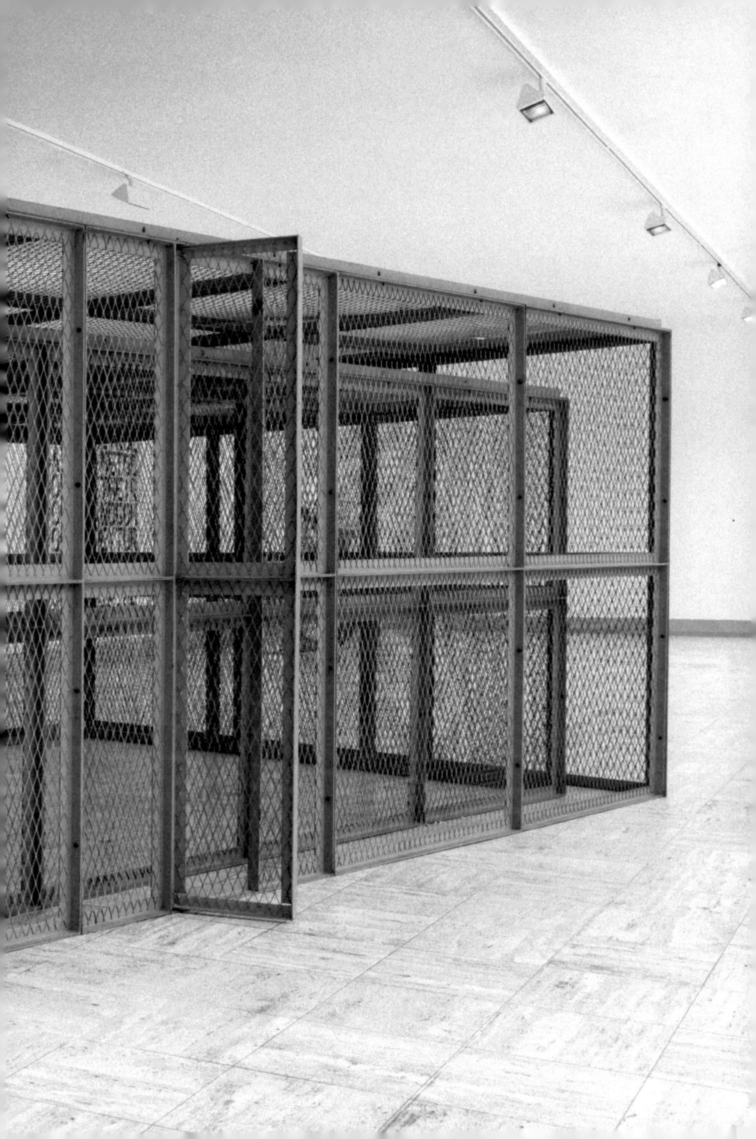

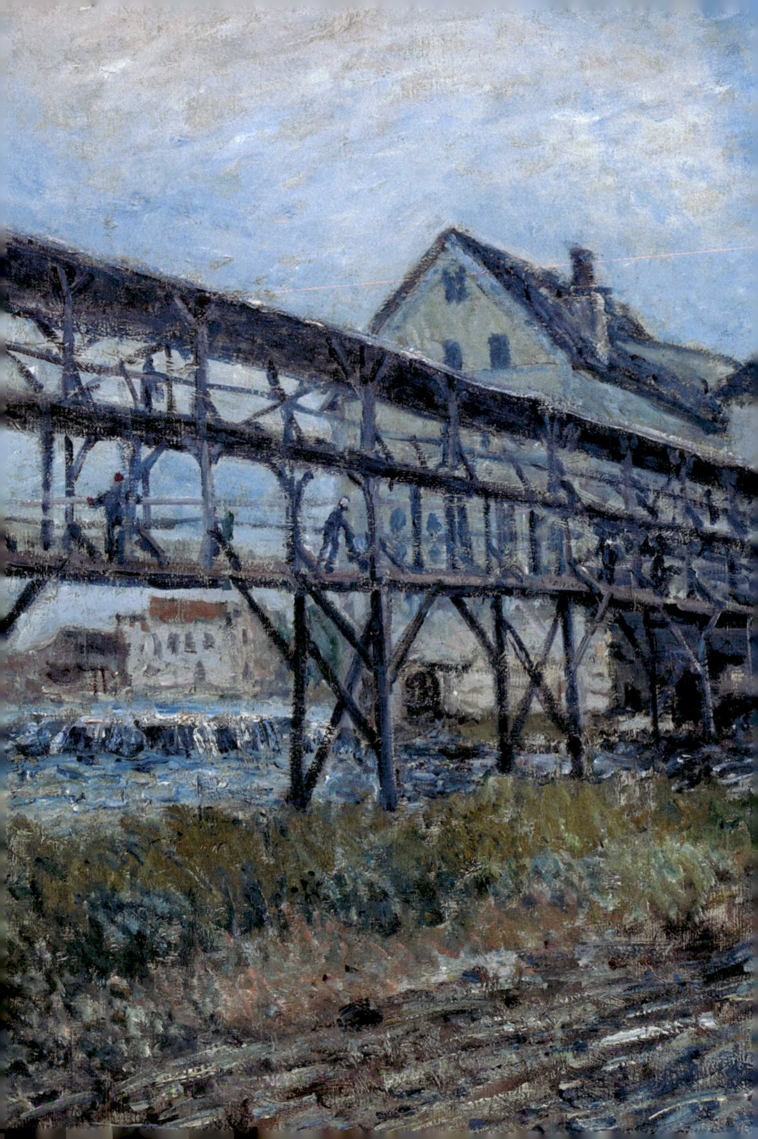

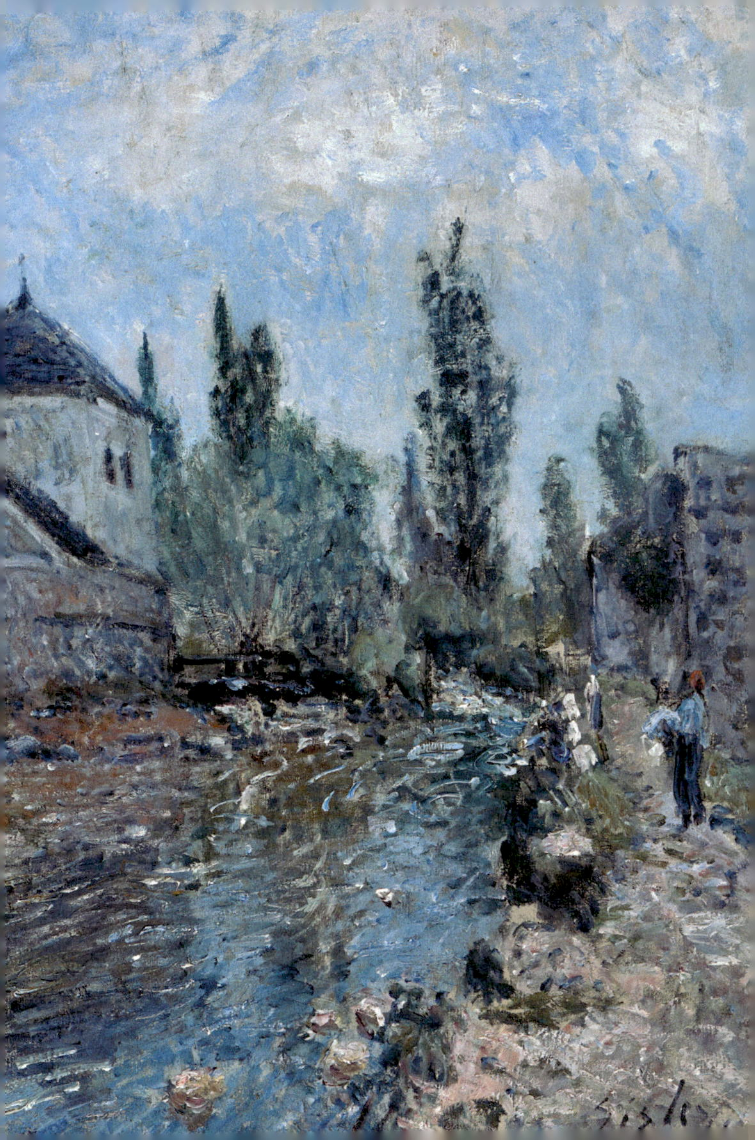

'Beyond painting and gardening, I am good for nothing.'

CLAUDE MONET

Claude Monet, *Fisherman's Cottage at Varengeville*, 1882

◂ Alfred Sisley, *Provencher's Watermill at Moret*, 1883

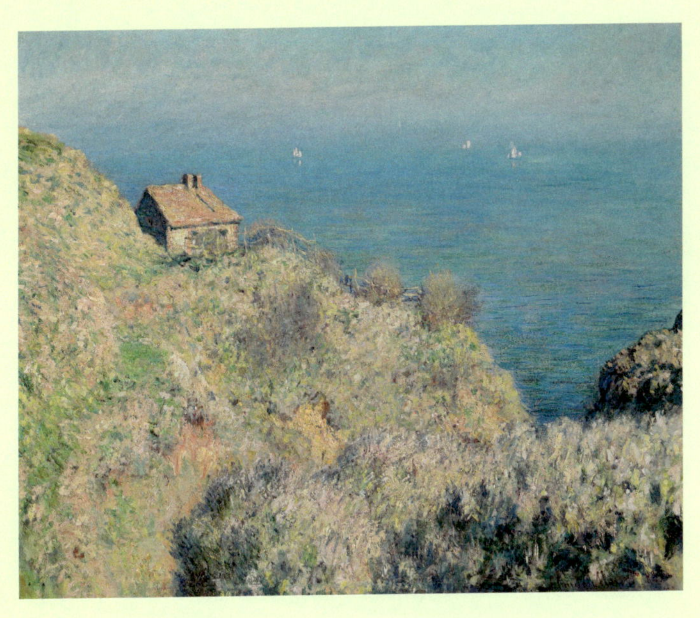

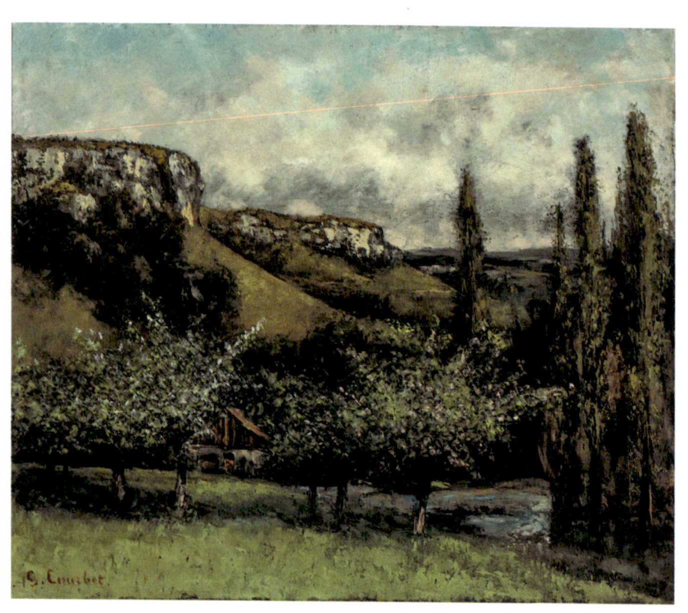

Gustave Courbet, *The Apple Orchard of Courbet's Father in Ornans*, 1873

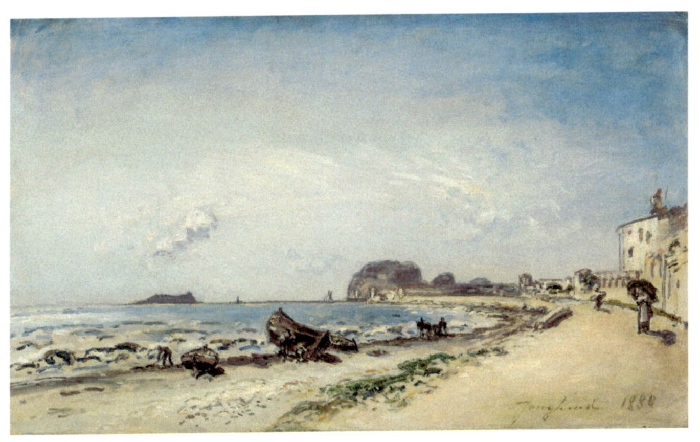

Johan Barthold Jongkind, *La Ciotat*, 1880

‘While I was taking a walk, I saw a fisherman bobbing up and down in his boat. A beautiful, hushed image. I wondered how you could interpret that same feeling in a product.’

WIEKI SOMERS

Wieki Somers, *Bathboat*, 2005

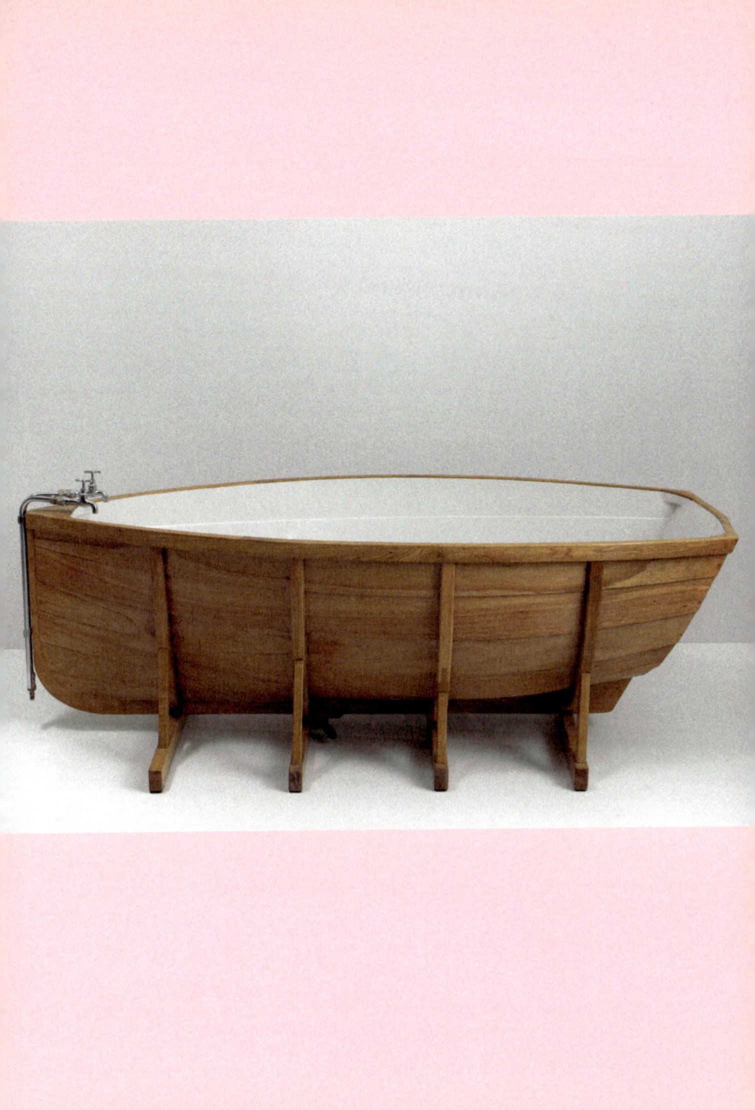

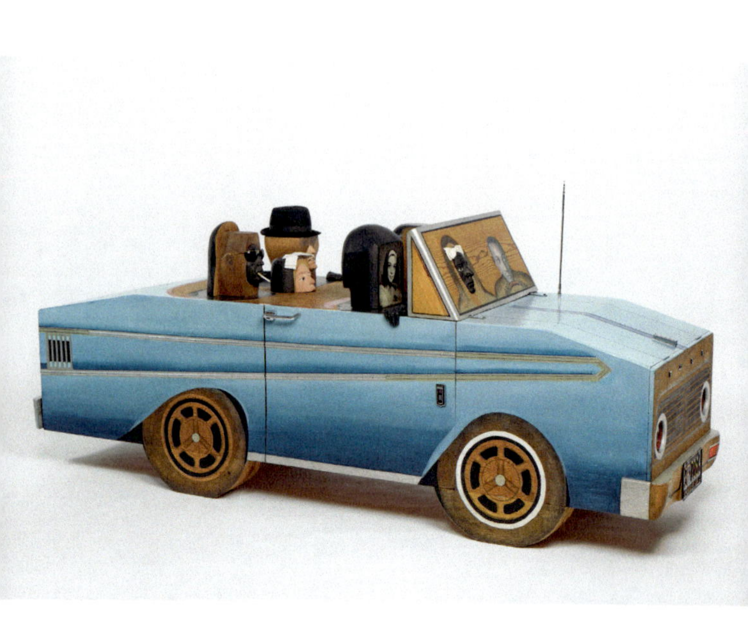

Marisol, *The Car*, 1964

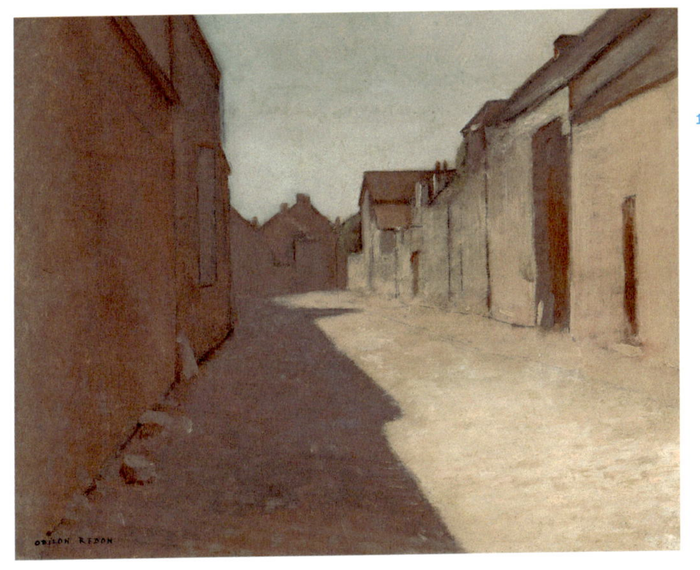

Odilon Redon, *Village Street*, c. 1875

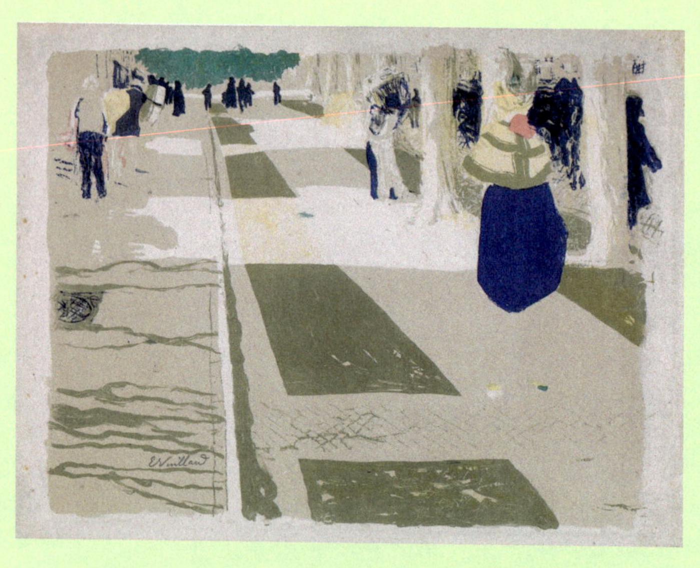
EVuillard

‘There is an effect created by a certain arrangement of colours, light, shadows etc. It’s called the music of the painting.’

ÉDOUARD VUILLARD

Édouard Vuillard, *The Avenue* from *Landscapes and Interiors*, 1899

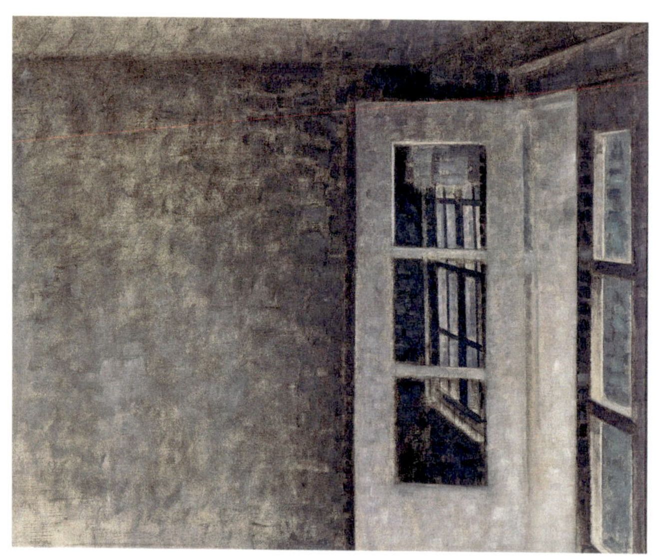

Vilhelm Hammershøi, *The Balcony Room at Spurveskjul*, 1911

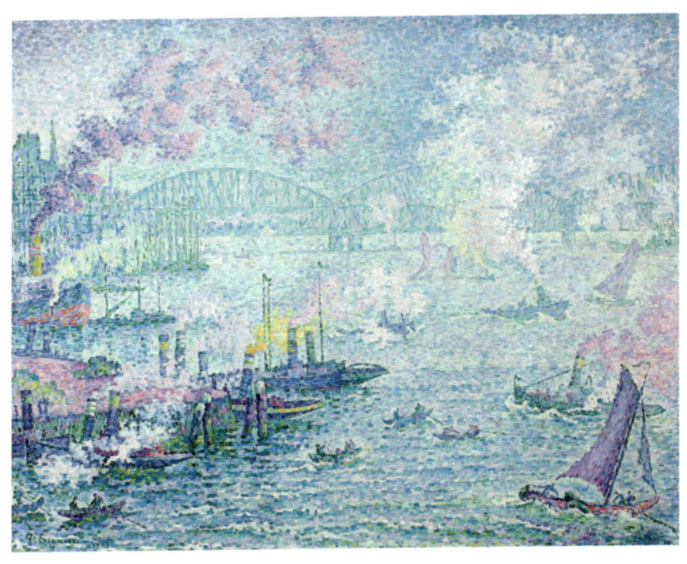

Paul Signac, *The Port of Rotterdam*, 1907

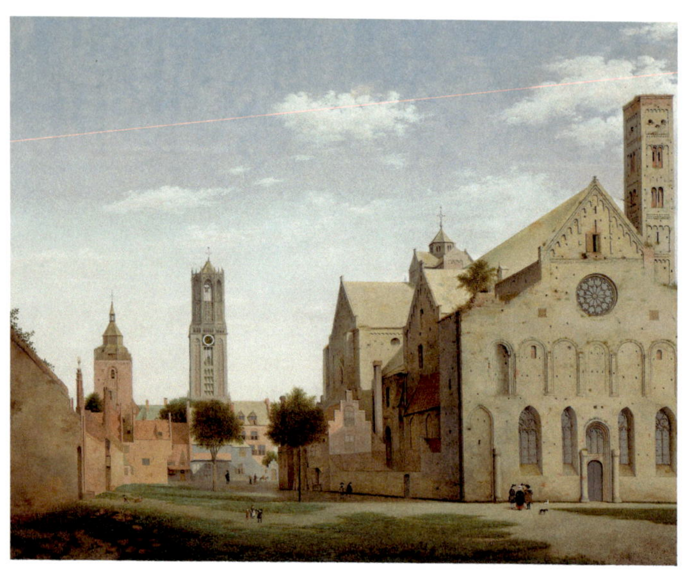

Pieter Jansz Saenredam, *View of Saint Mary's Square and Saint Mary's Church, Utrecht*, 1662

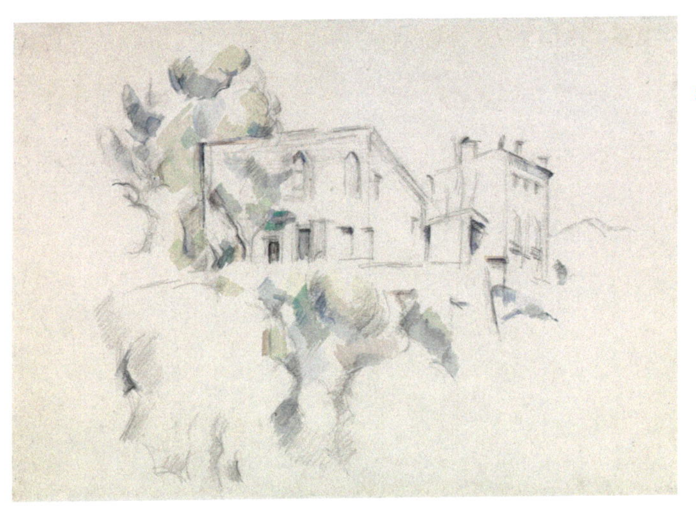

Paul Cézanne, *View of the Château Noir*, c. 1887-1890

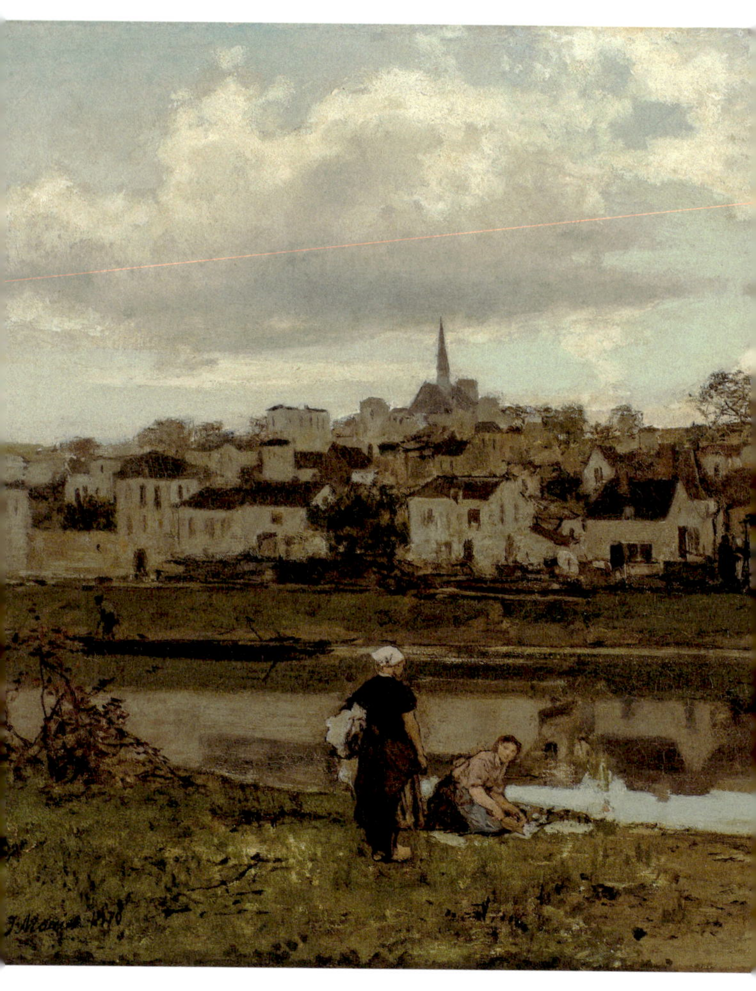

Jacob Maris, *View at Montigny-sur-Loing*, 1870

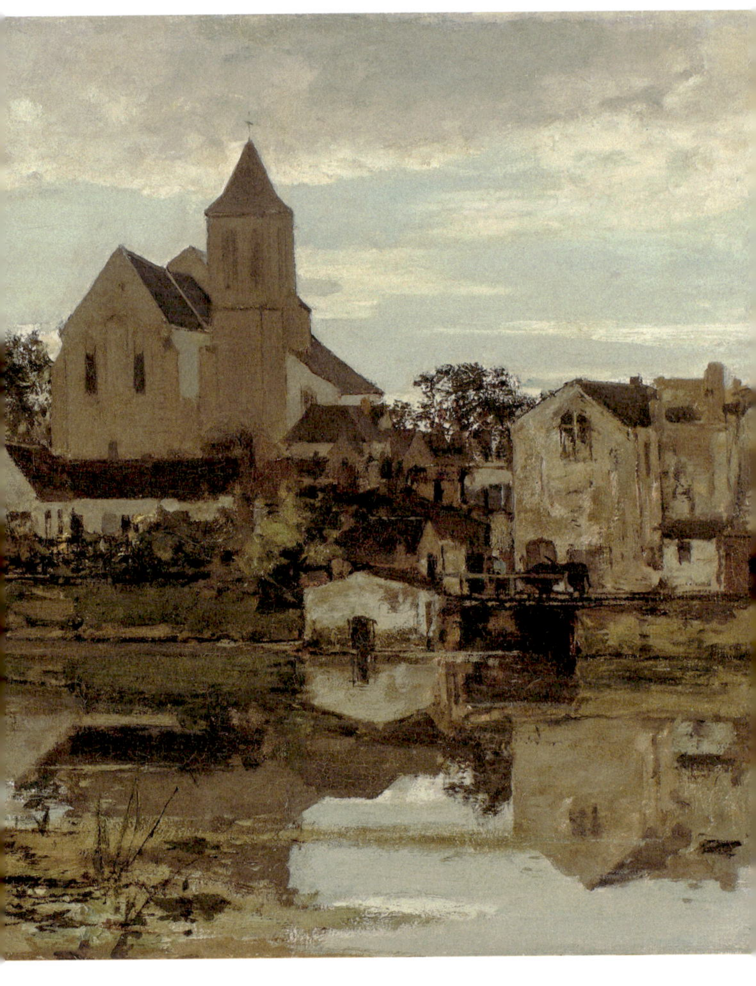

This earthenware clock is a good example of the kind of 'art for the people' that Mendes da Costa liked to make. But could everyone actually afford to buy a unique clock like this?

Joseph Mendes da Costa, clock, 1900

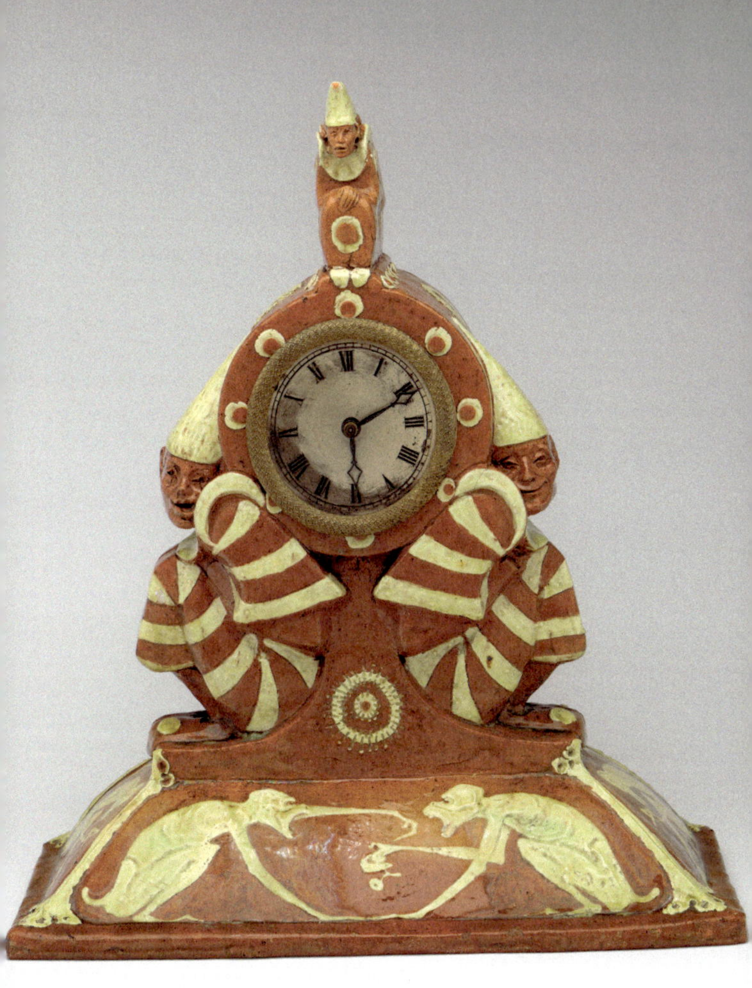

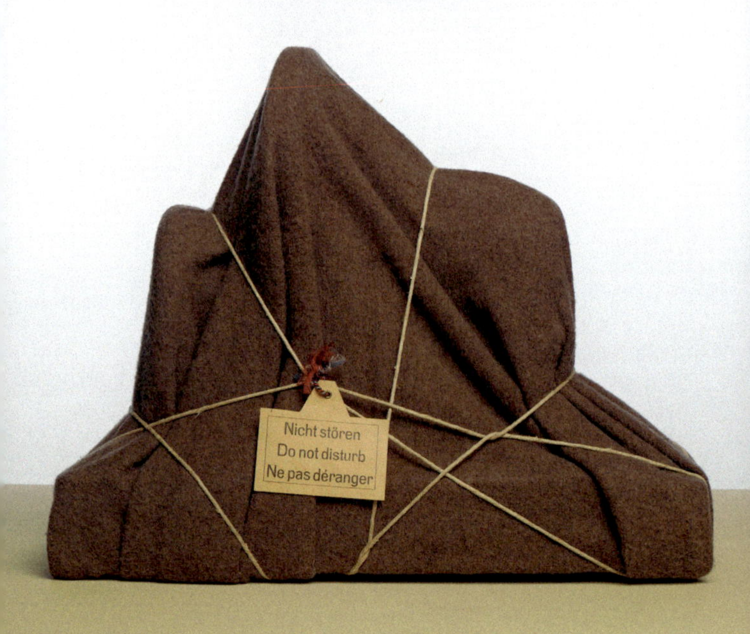
Nicht stören
Do not disturb
Ne pas déranger

‘As beautiful as the chance meeting of a sewing machine and an umbrella on a dissecting table.’ This surrealist motto inspired Man Ray to make an enigmatic wrapped object.

Man Ray, *The Enigma of Isidore Ducasse*, 1920 (1971)

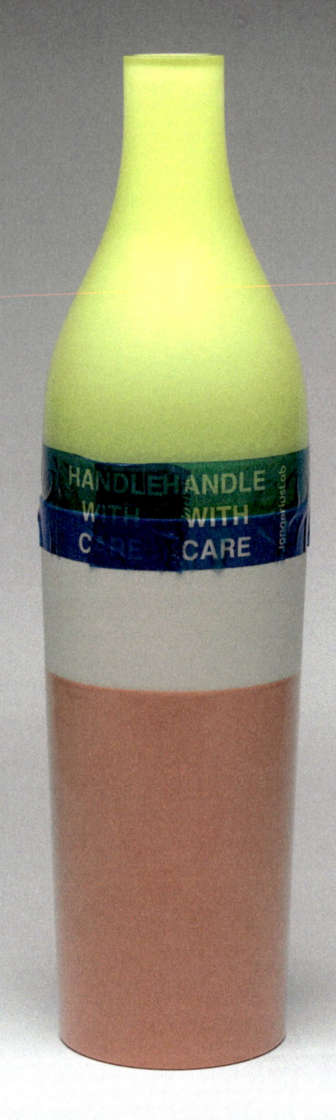
HANDLE
WITH
CARE
JongeriusLab

Glass and ceramics cannot be stuck together. This unique object can only be created by taping. The solution is imperfection.

Hella Jongerius, *Long Neck Bottle*, 2000

188

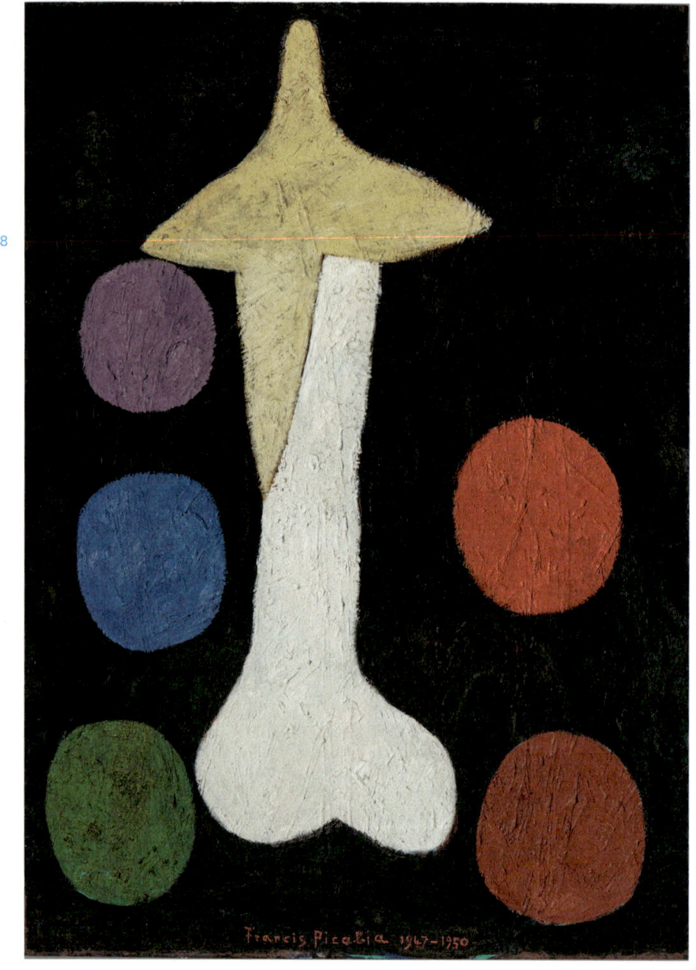

Francis Picabia, *Egoism*, 1947-1950

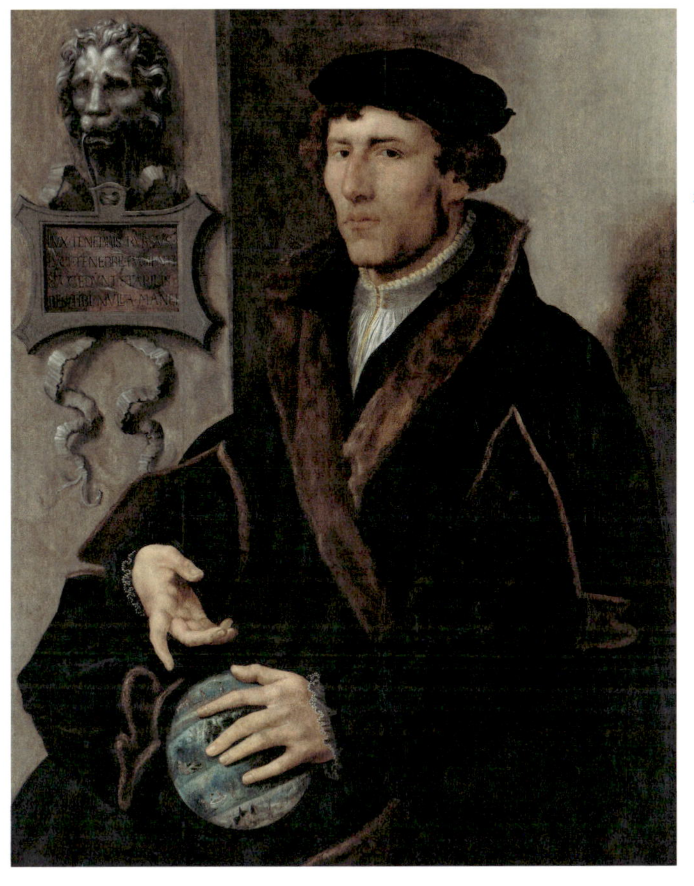

Maarten van Heemskerck, *Portrait of a Humanist*, c. 1545

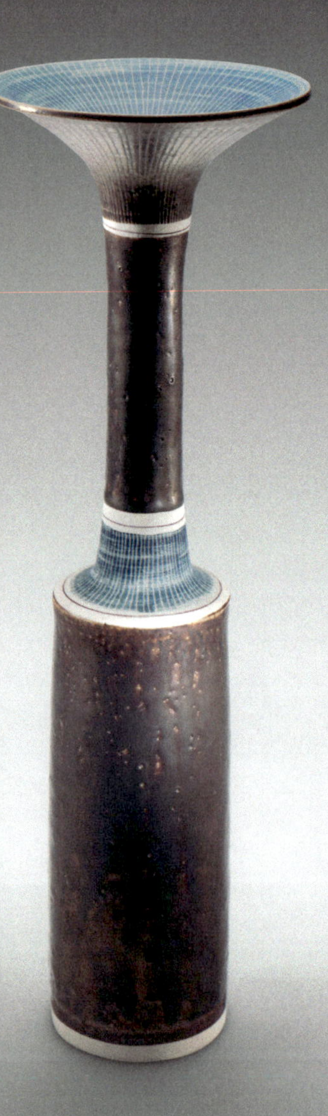

Thanks to the many years' friendship between a former curator and Lucie Rie, Museum Boijmans Van Beuningen now has a large collection of pottery by this ceramicist, who was born in Austria and fled to London during the Second World War.

Lucie Rie, *Tall Slender Bottle*, c. 1960

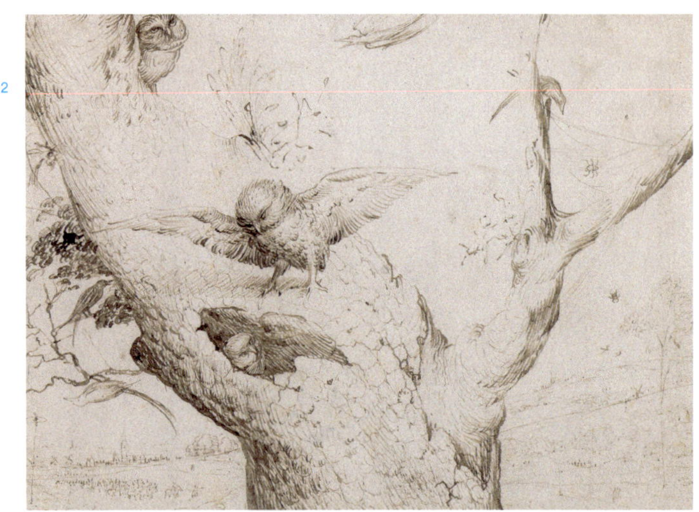

Jheronimus Bosch, *The Owls' Nest*, c. 1505-1515
J. Jurriaan Kok, Sam Schellink, N.V. Haagsche Plateelfabriek Rozenburg, vase, 1904 ▸

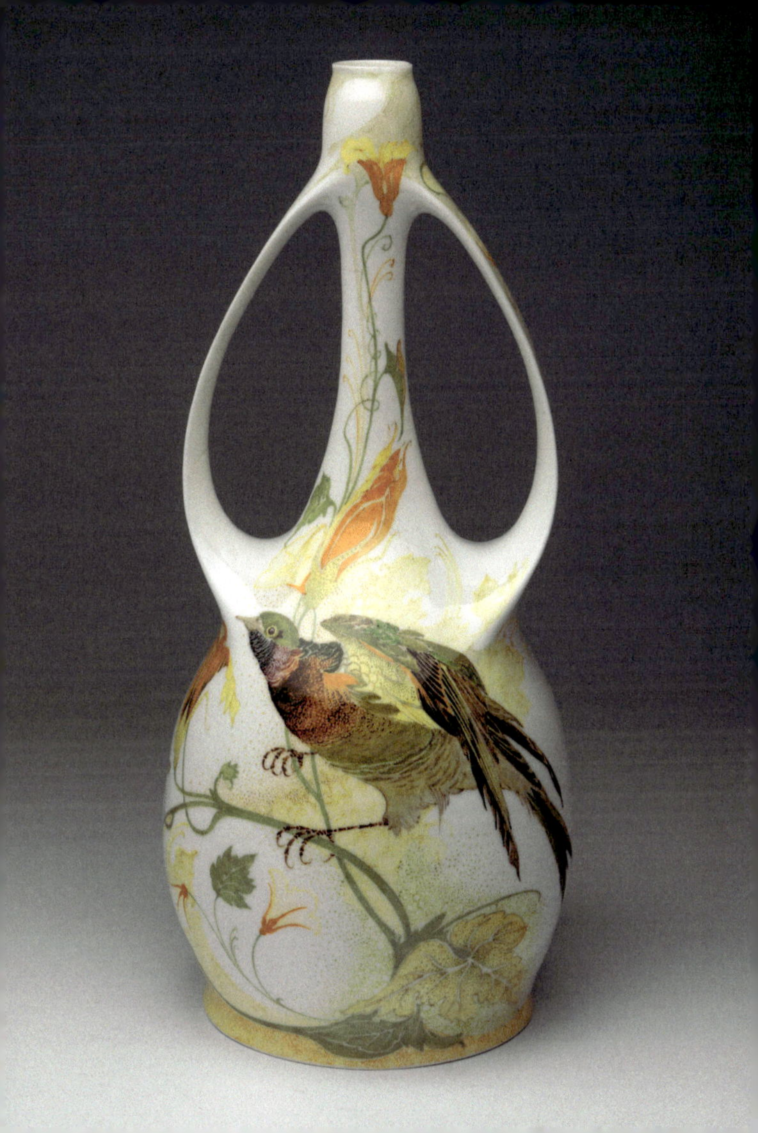

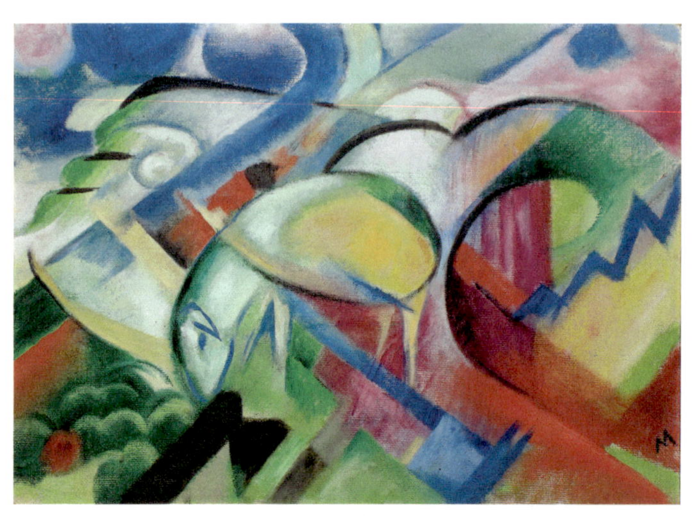

Franz Marc, *The Sheep*, 1913-1914

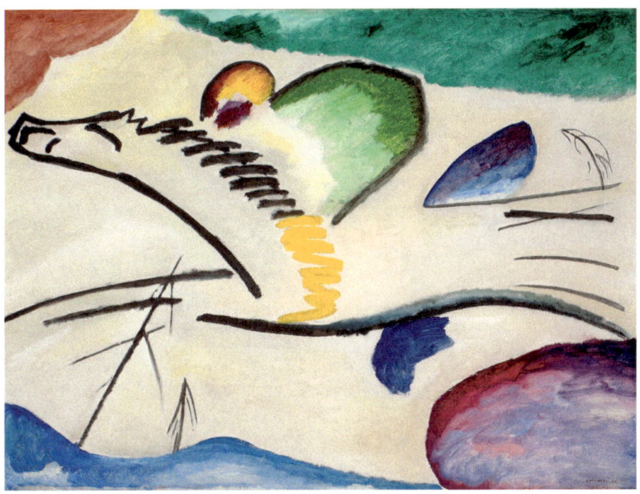

Wassily Kandinsky, *Lyrical*, 1911

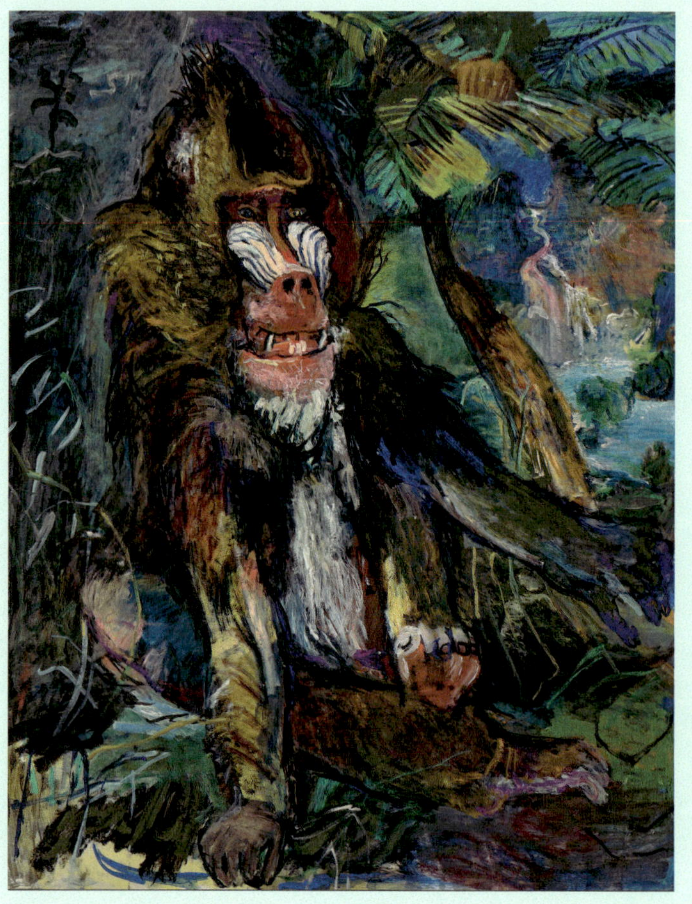

The Austrian expressionist Oskar Kokoschka got permission to paint in London Zoo after closing time. He painted this impressive portrait of a mandrill there.

Oskar Kokoschka, *The Mandrill*, 1926

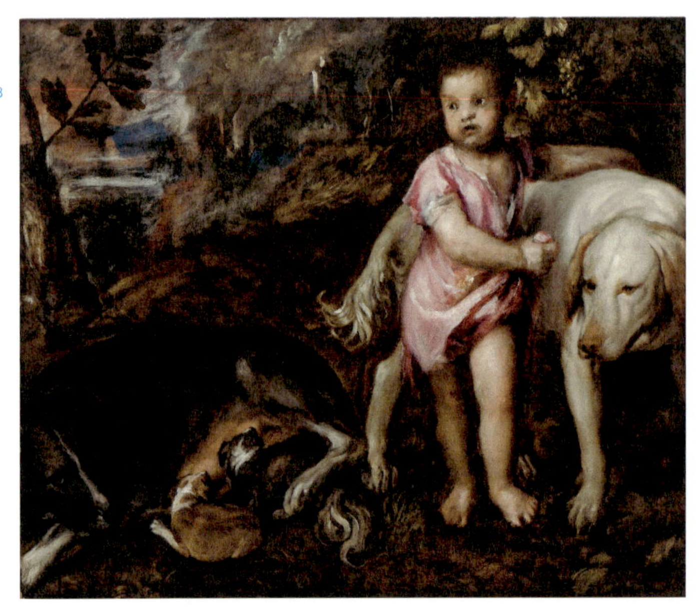

Titian, *Boy with Dogs in a Landscape*, 1565-1576

Anonymous, aquamanile, 1200-1300 ▸

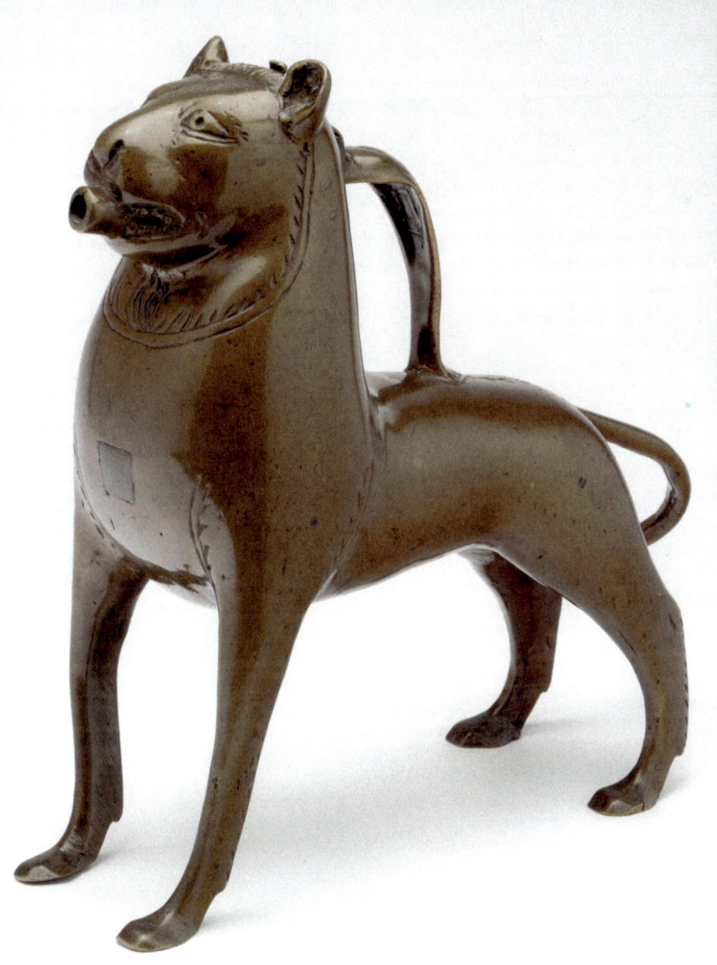

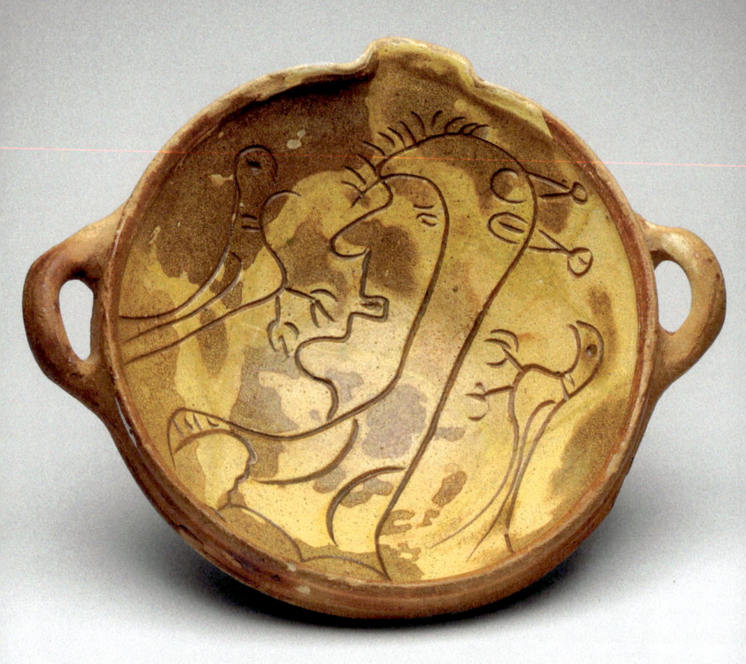

Anonymous, batter tub, 1475-1525
Fra Bartolommeo, *Studies for Bystanders in the 'Madonna della Misericordia'*, c. 1515 ▸

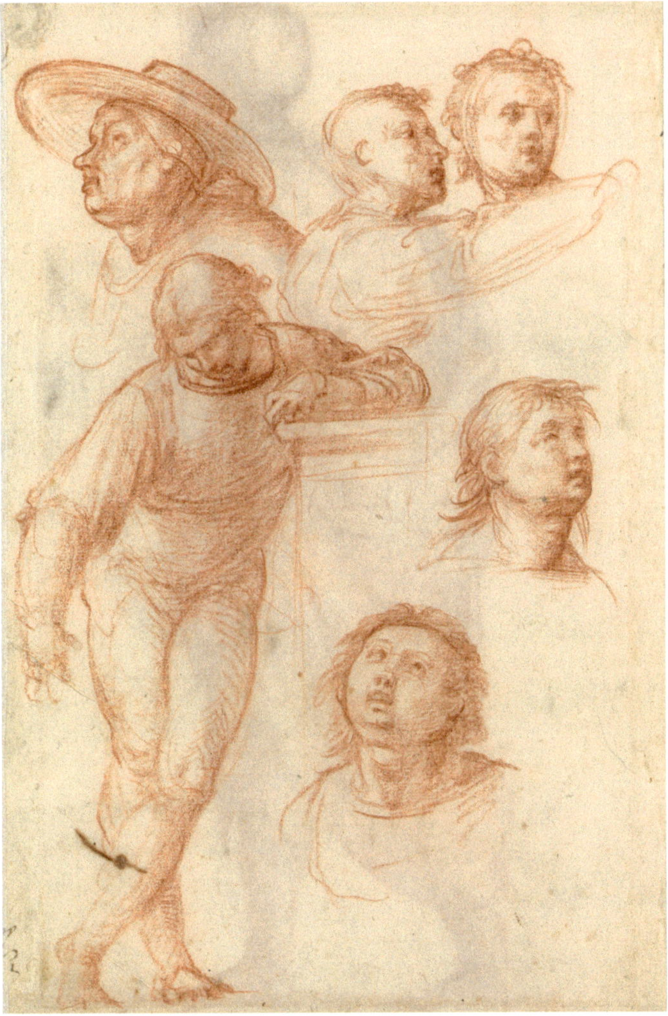

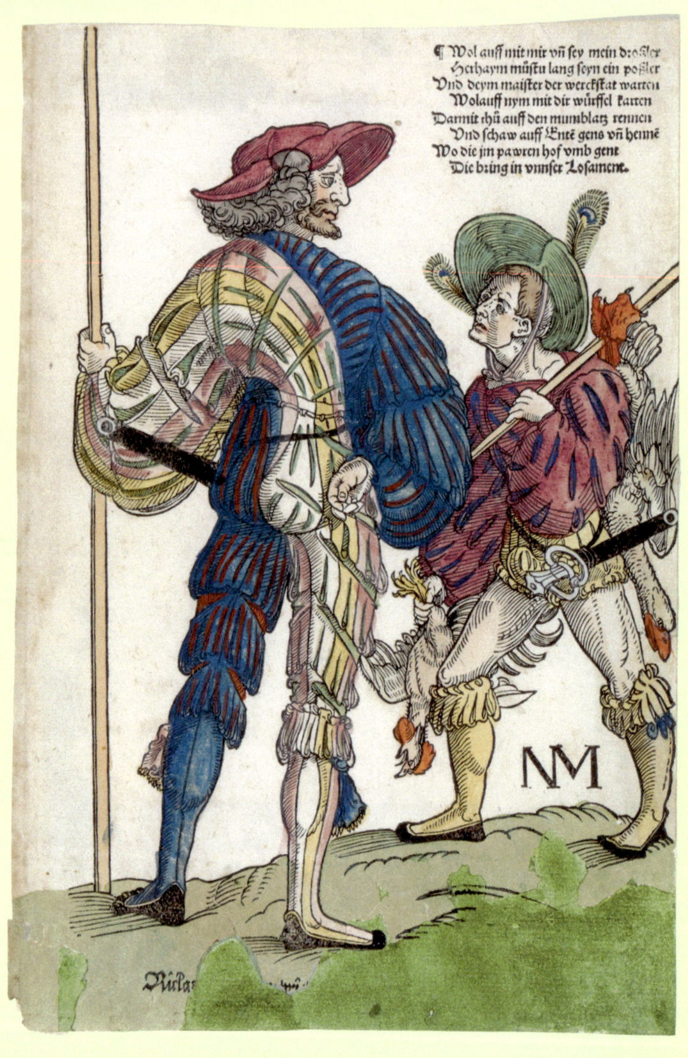
¶ Wol auff mit mir vñ sey mein droßler
Herhaym müstu lang seyn ein poßler
Vnd deym maister der werckstat warten
Wolauff nym mit dir würffel karten
Darmit thů auff den mumblatz rennen
Vnd schaw auff Entē gens vñ hennē
Wo die jm pawren hof vmb gent
Die bring in vnnser Losament.
NM

Hand-coloured prints are rarely represented in museums. It used to be said that 'colouring is spoiling', but now we appreciate such colourful prints all the more.

Erhard Schön, *Lansquenet with Helper*, c. 1530

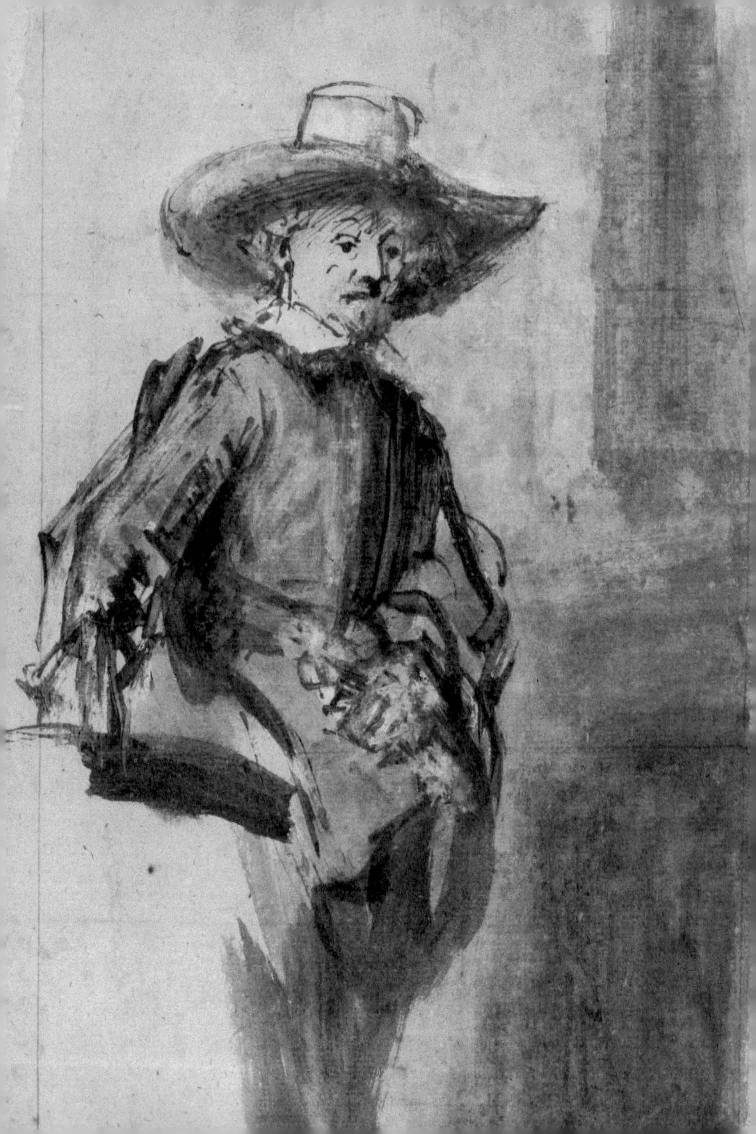

This is one of the three surviving preliminary studies for Rembrandt's painting of The Syndics in the Rijksmuseum. The sitter is the Amsterdam wool merchant Volckert Jansz.

Rembrandt van Rijn, *Study for one of the Syndics, Volkert Jansz*, c. 1662

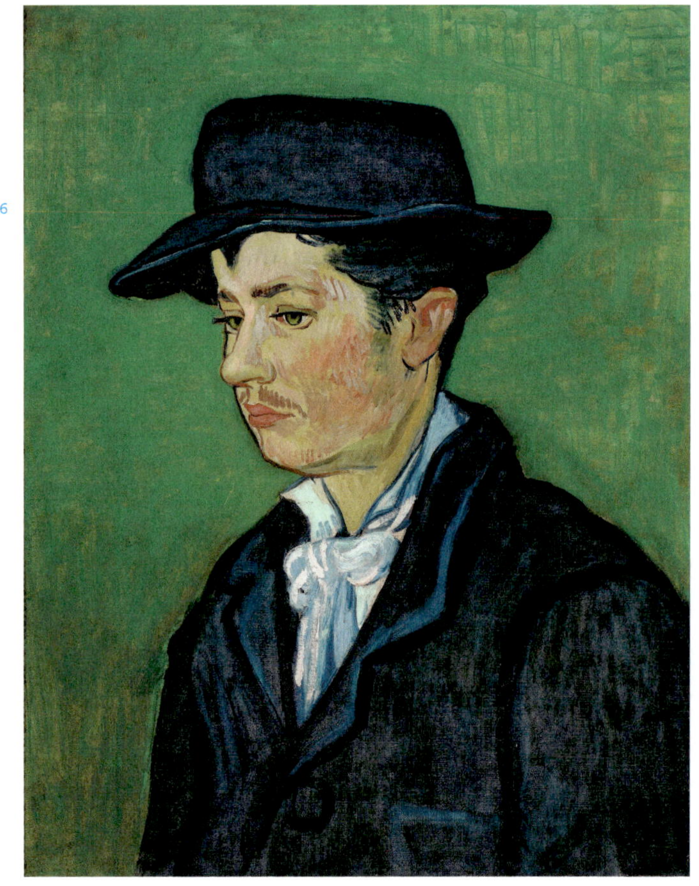

Vincent van Gogh, *Portrait of Armand Roulin*, 1888

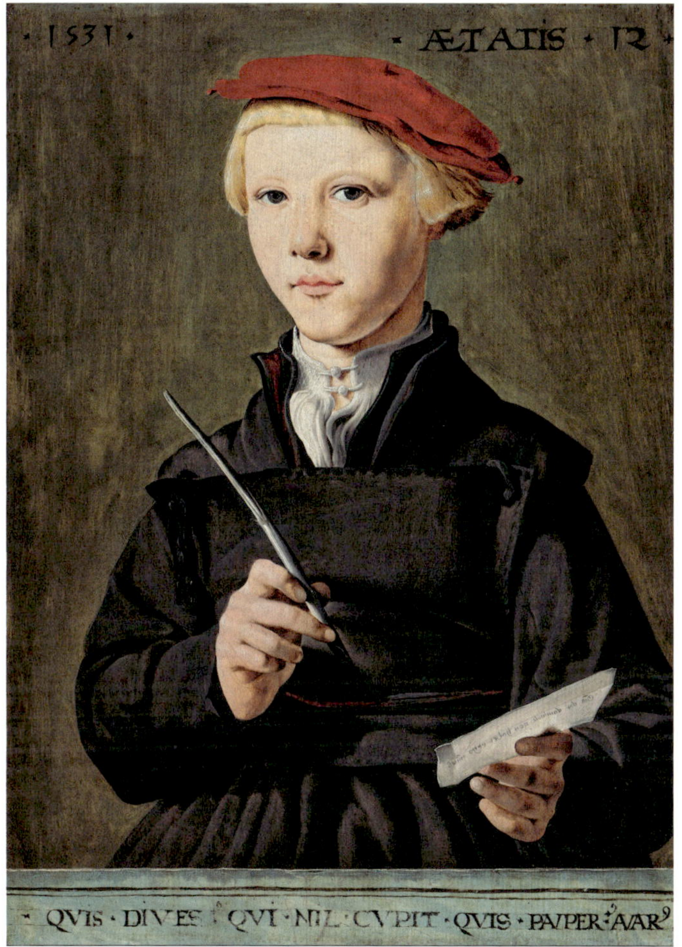

Maarten van Heemskerck, *Portrait of a Young Student*, 1531

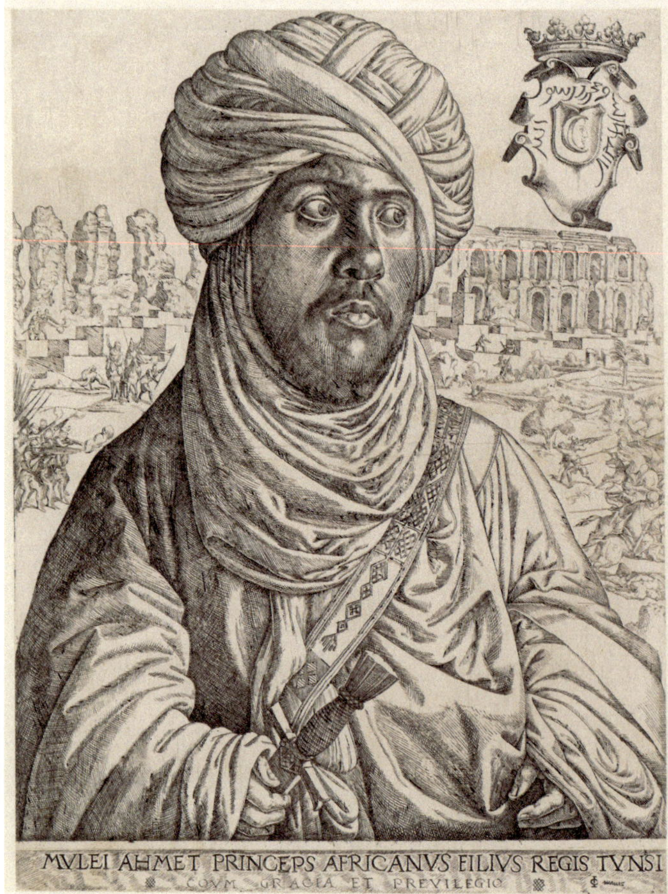

Jan Cornelisz Vermeyen, *Portrait of Muley Ahmed*, c. 1535-1536

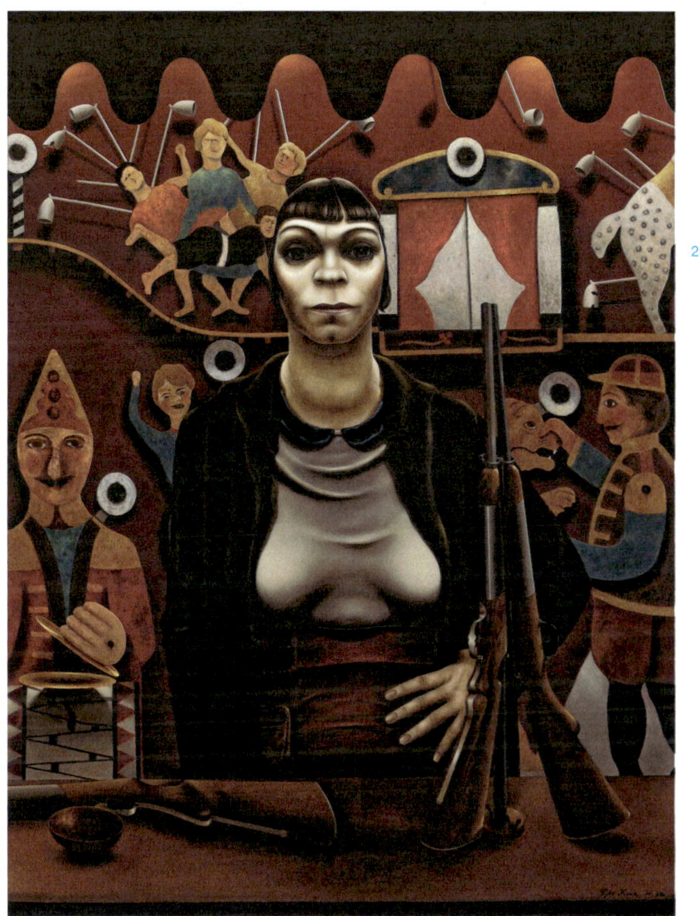

Pyke Koch, *The Shooting Gallery*, 1931

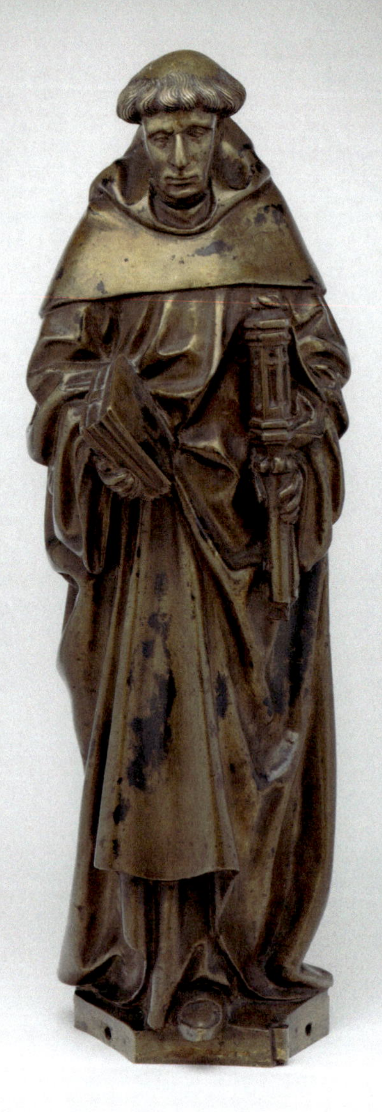

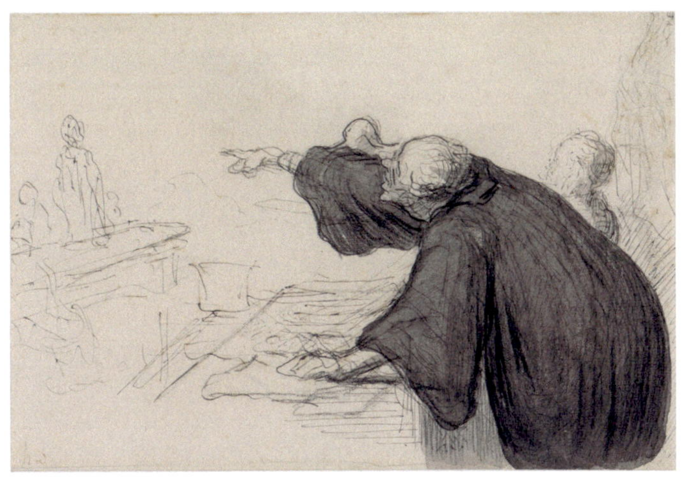

Honoré Daumier, *Pleading Lawyer ('L'argument décisif')*, c. 1860-1870

◂ Arnold van Maeler, *Saint Leonard*, c. 1480

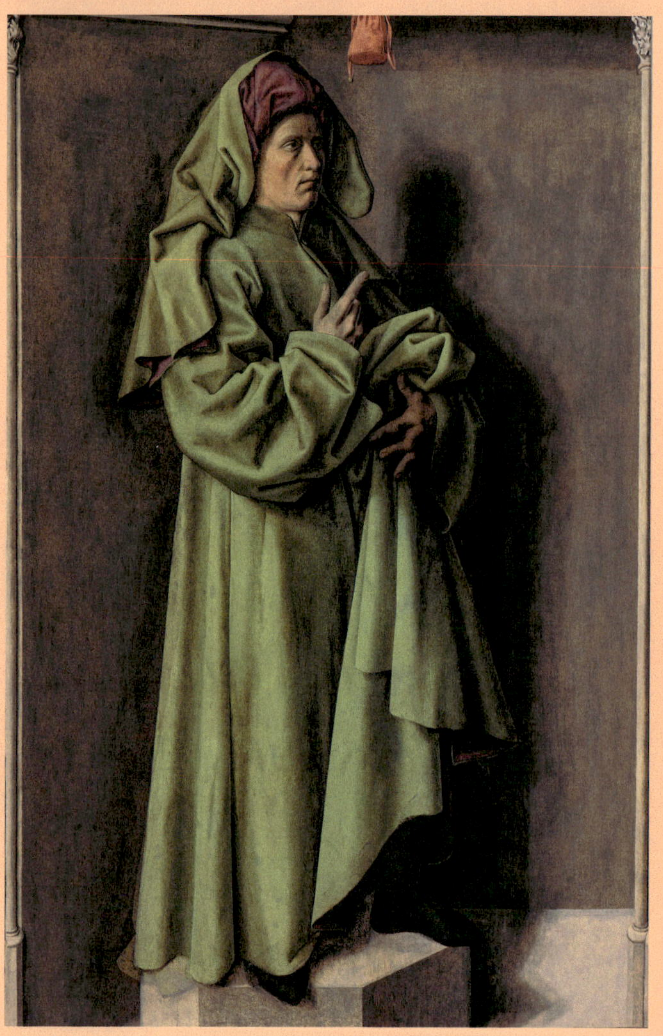

Some paintings go through a lot. This panel started as the left shutter of a triptych. After the altarpiece was disassembled, probably in the nineteenth century, this side shutter was sawn in two: a book still life at the top was separated from the prophet below it.

Barthélémy d'Eyck, *Isaiah*, 1442-1445

There is a small plank made of a different wood in the oak panel. Because it is at precisely the place where Christ is painted, it has been suggested that it is a relic.

Anonymous, *The Norfolk Triptych* (detail), 1415-1420

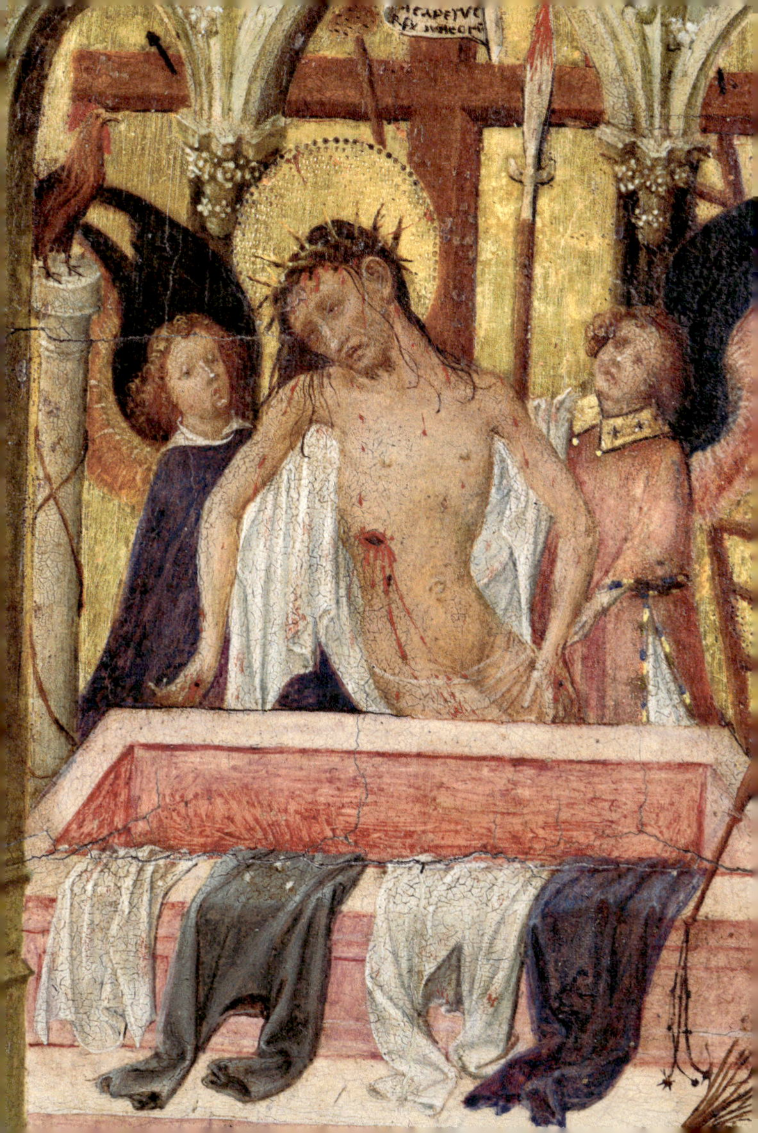

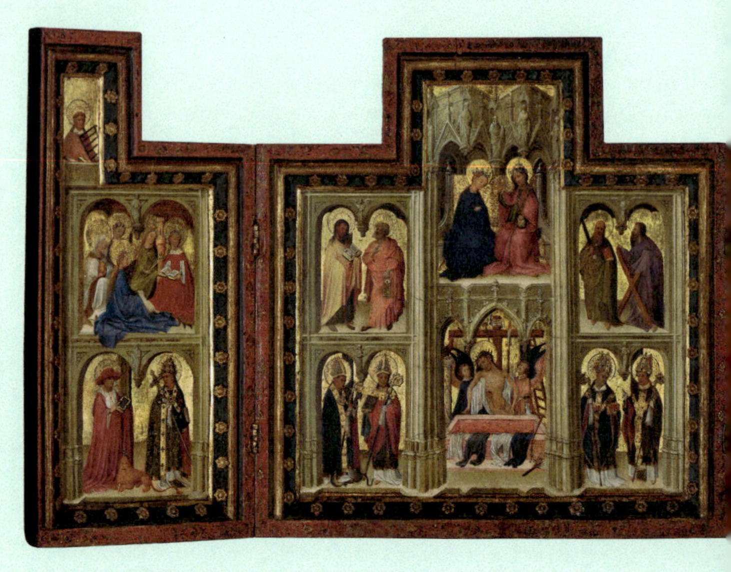

Anonymous, *The Norfolk Triptych*, 1415-1420

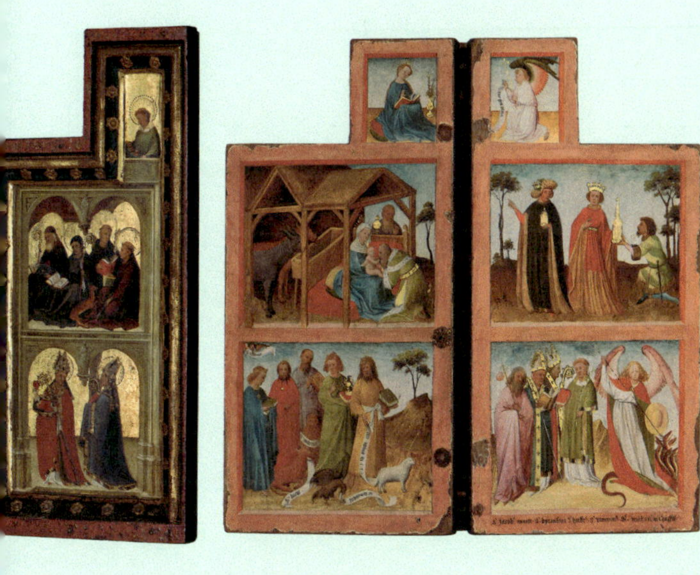

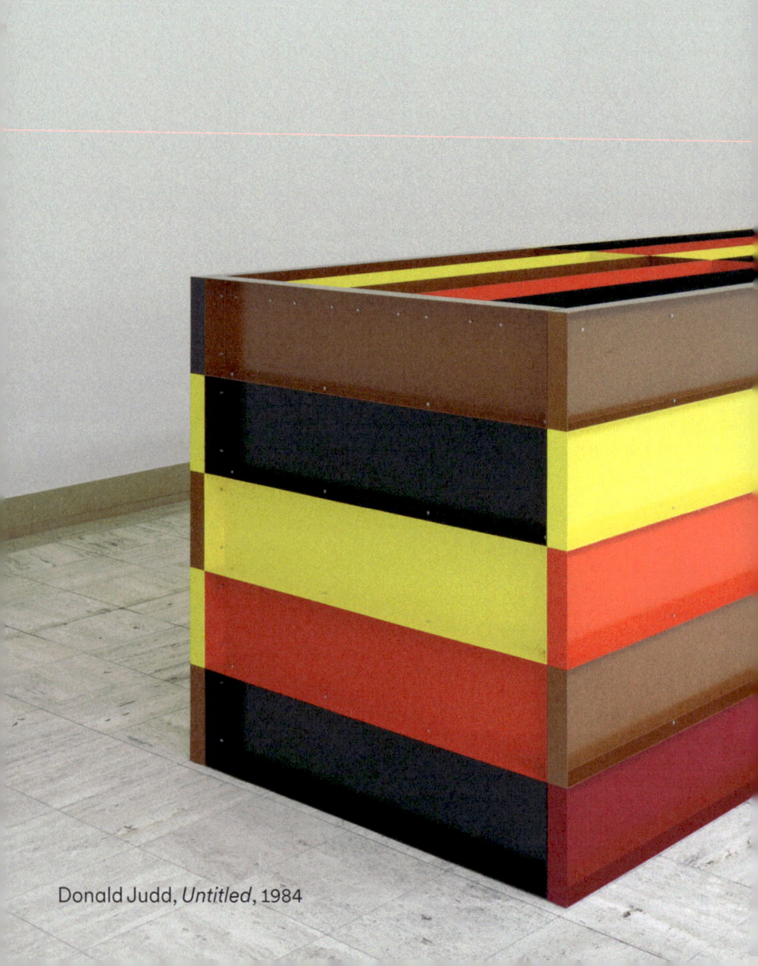

Donald Judd, *Untitled*, 1984

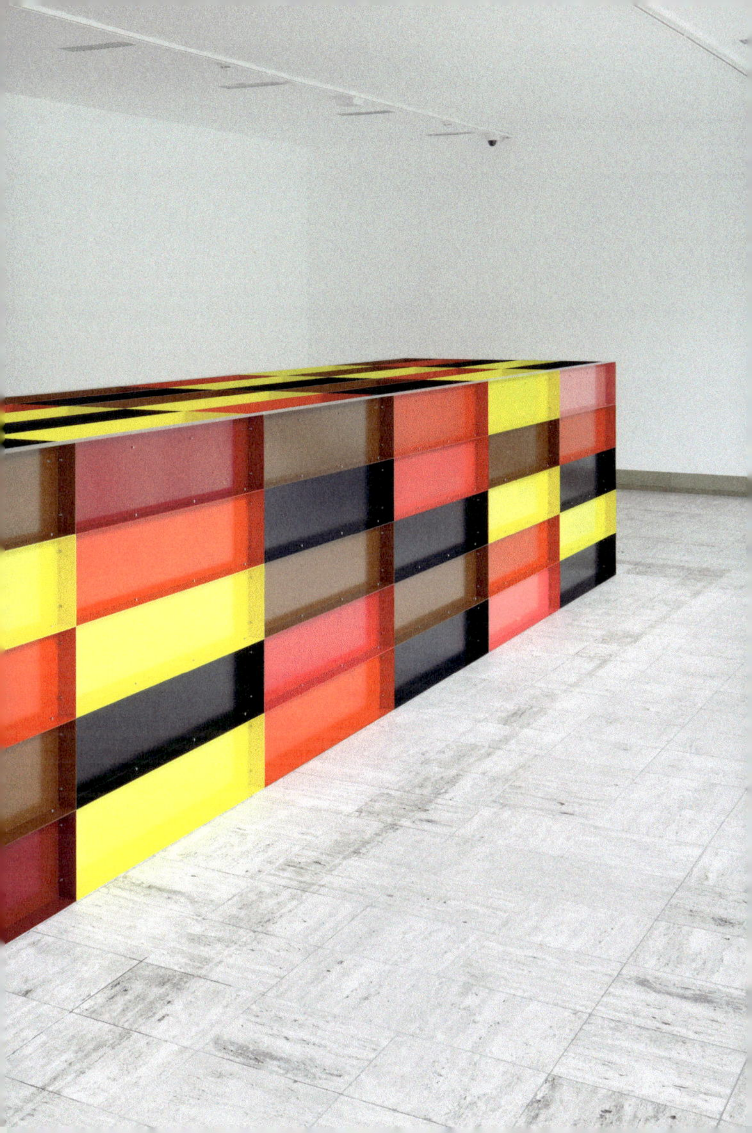

Bruegel's way of suggesting that the building of the tower had been going on for a long time is masterly: weeds grow in the joints and the bricks are weathered at the base, however they are still bright red at the top.

Pieter Bruegel (I), *The Tower of Babel*, c. 1568

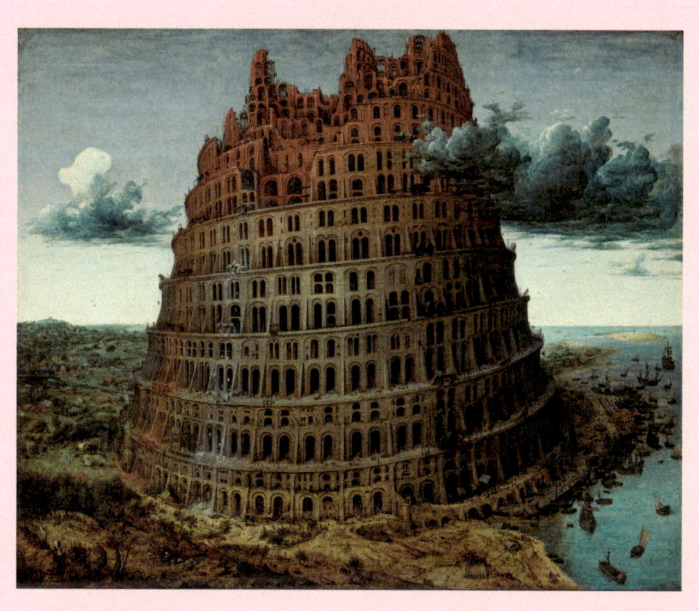

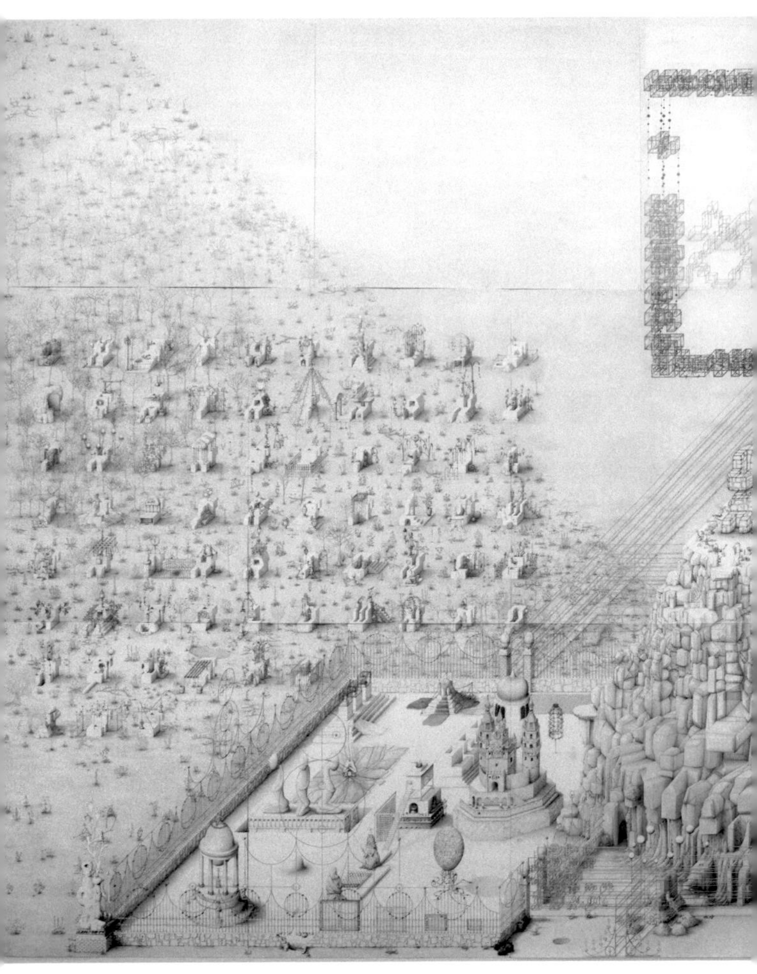

Paul Noble, *Ye Olde Ruin*, 2003-2004

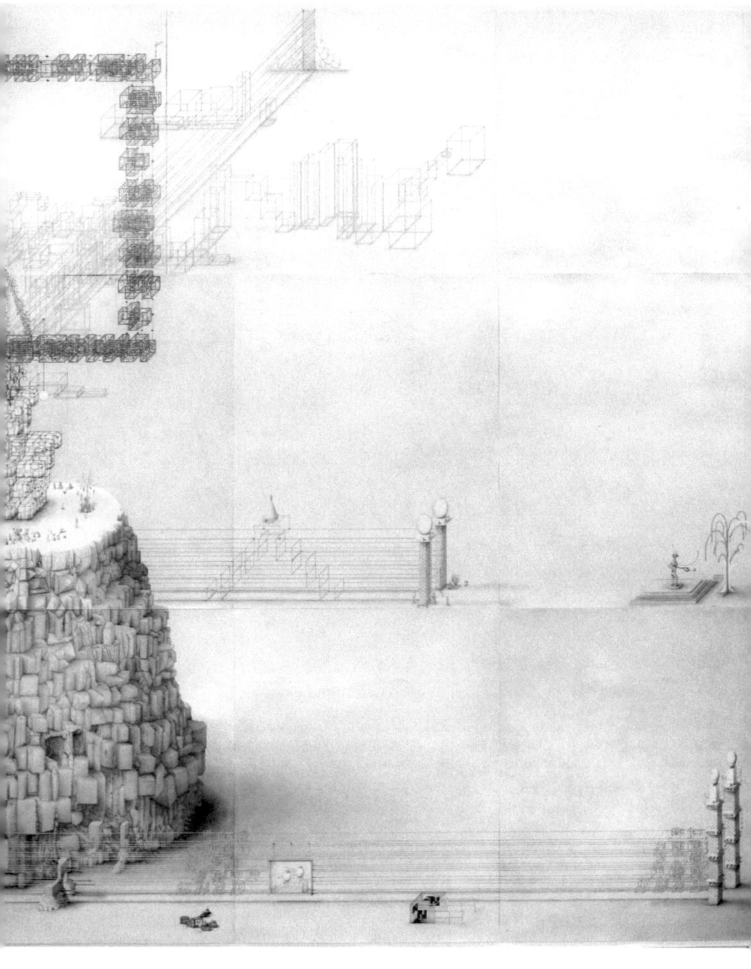

Gio Ponti, Piero Fornasetti, *Bureau Architettura*, 1960-1965

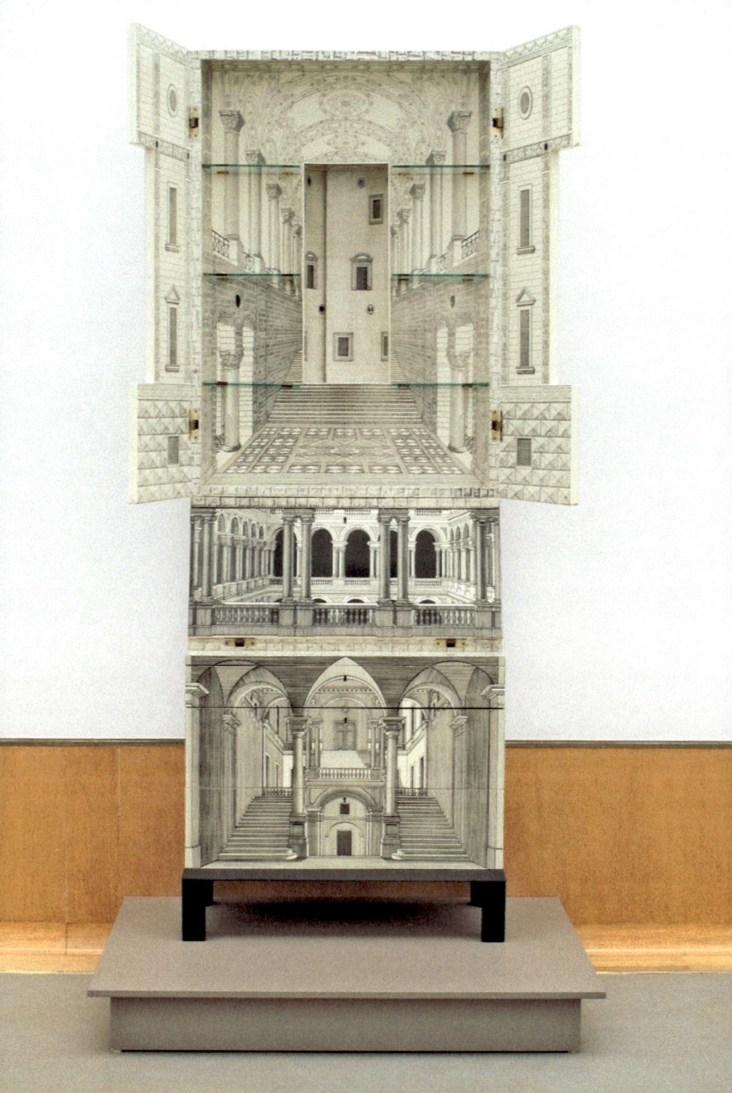

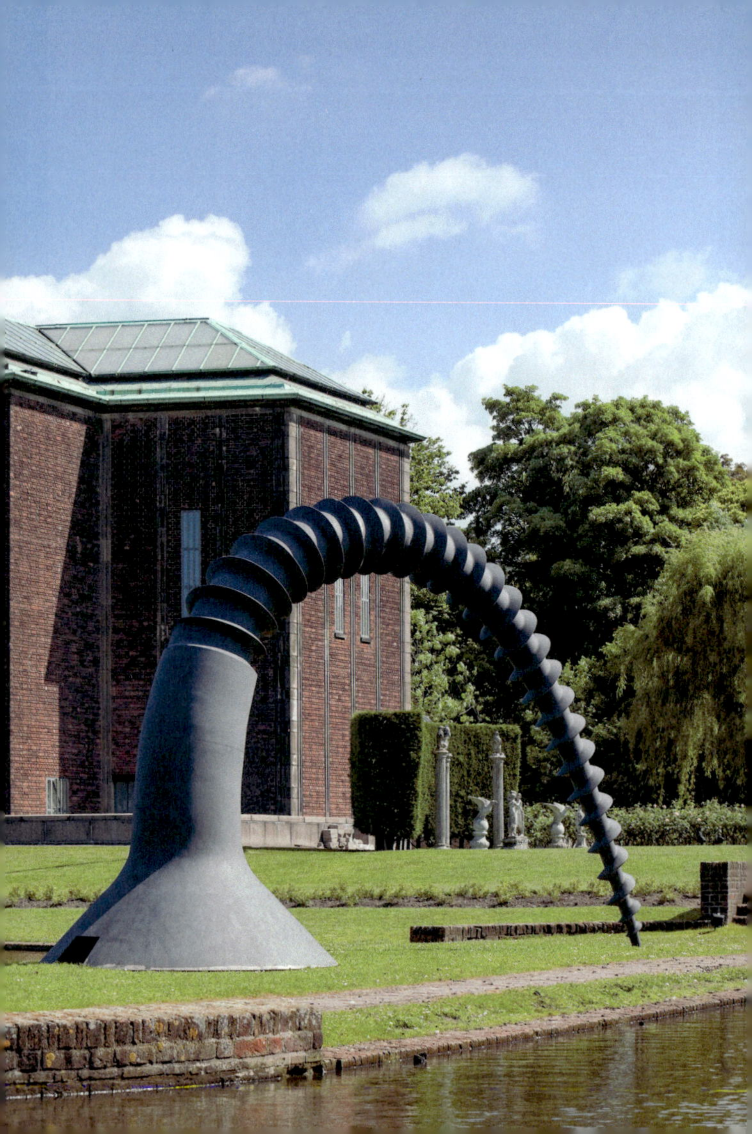

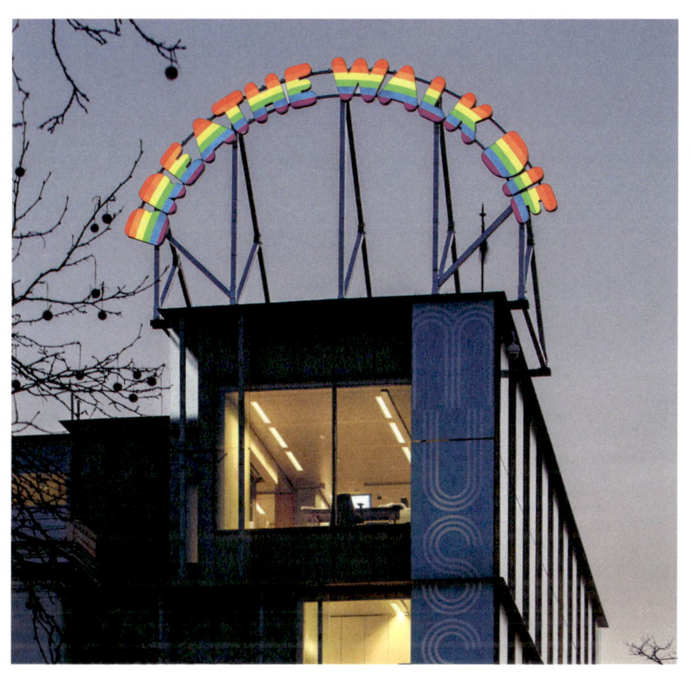

Ugo Rondinone, *Breathe, Walk, Die*, 2014

◂ Claes Oldenburg, Coosje van Bruggen, *Screwarch*, 1982

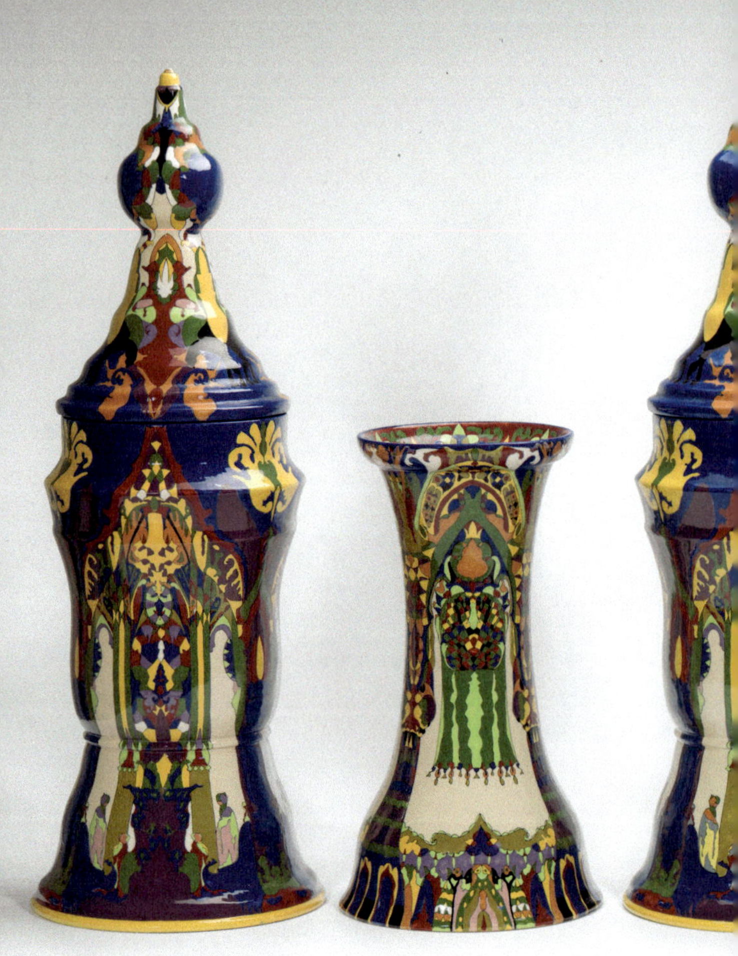

Theo Colenbrander, *Cathedral*, 1922

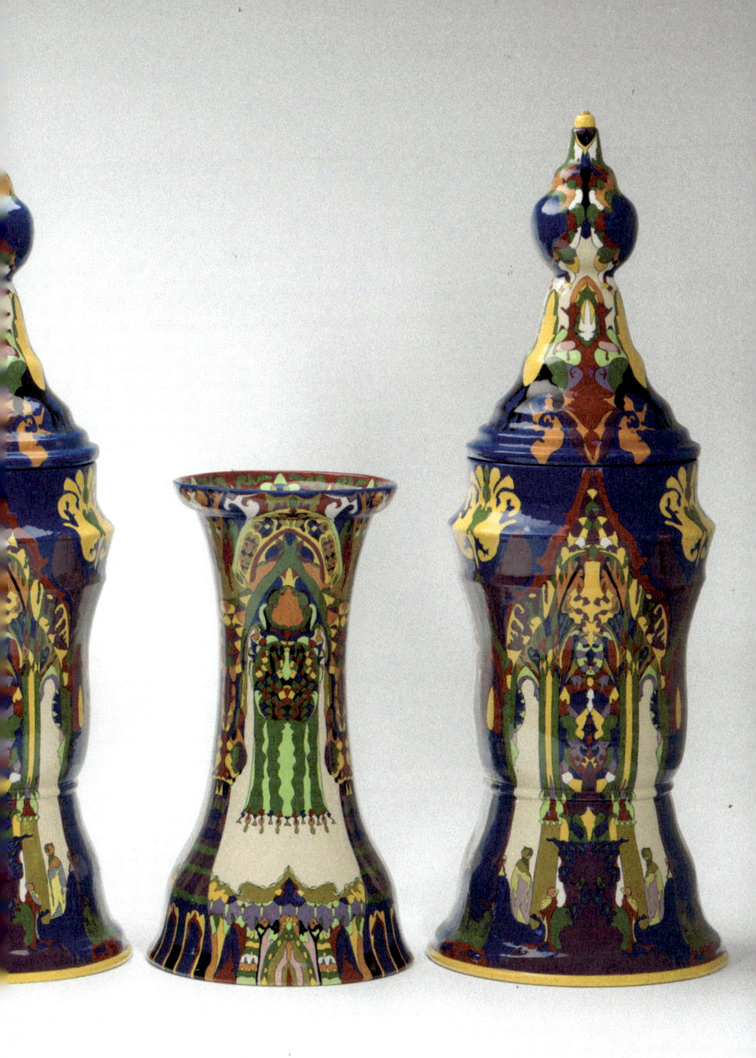

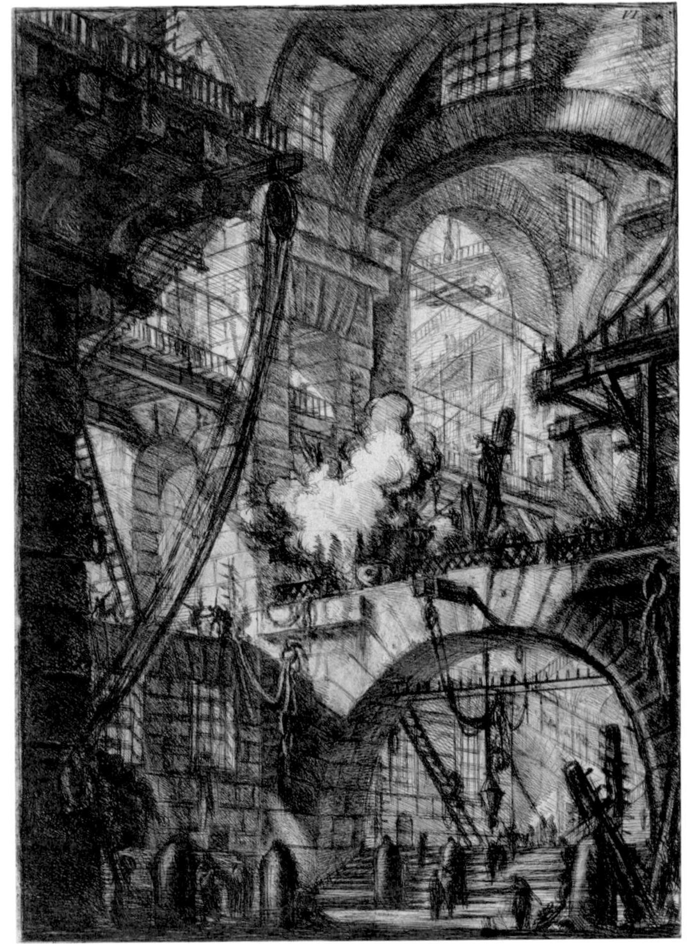

Giovanni Battista Piranesi, *The Smoking Fire*, 1761

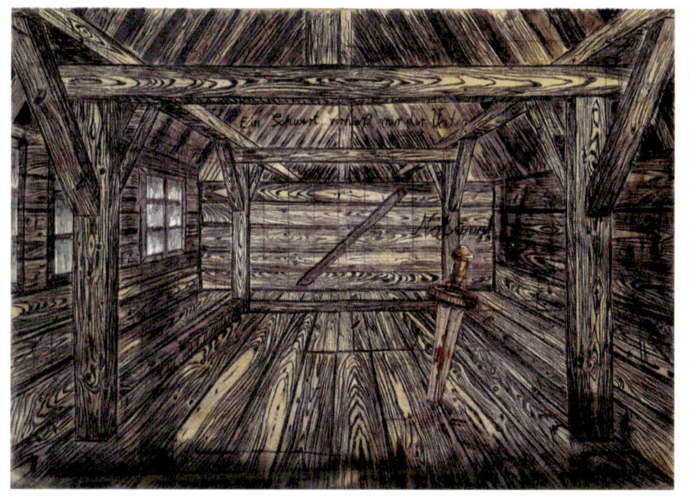

Anselm Kiefer, *Notung*, 1973

In 1521 the German artist Albrecht Dürer visited Antwerp. The town clerk gave him this little panel by Joachim Patinir. Dürer knew the landscape painter well and even attended his wedding later that year.

Joachim Patinir, *Landscape with the Destruction of Sodom and Gomorrah*, c. 1520

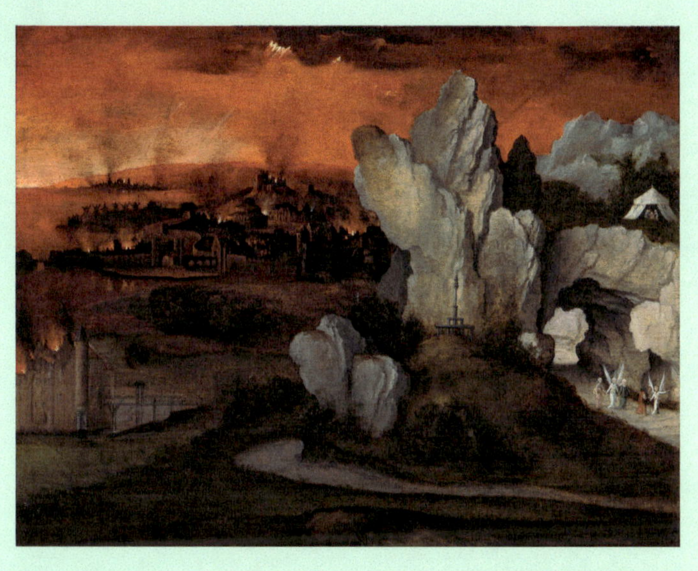

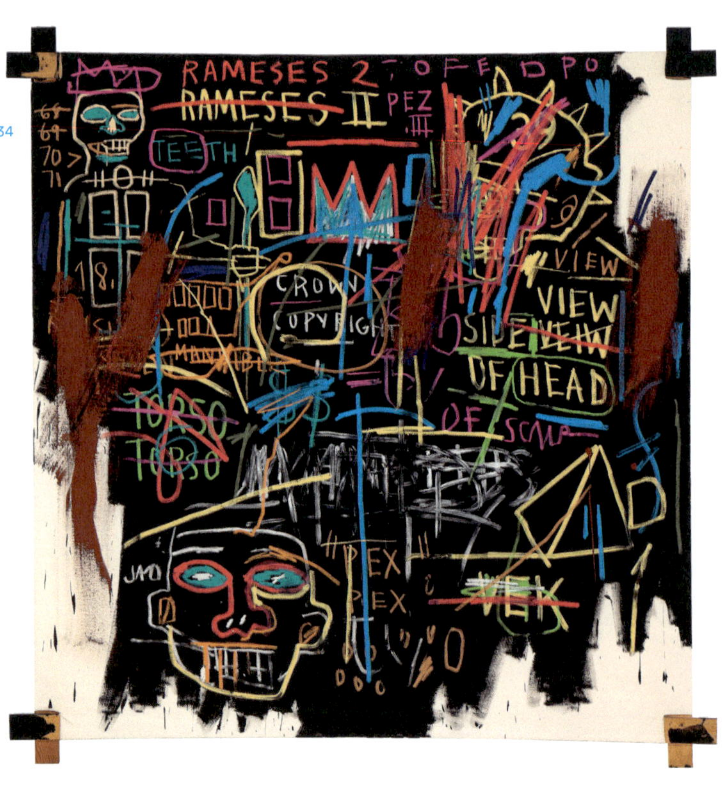

Jean-Michel Basquiat, *Kings of Egypt II*, 1982
Christopher Wool, *Untitled*, 1988 ▸

HEL
TER
HEL
TER

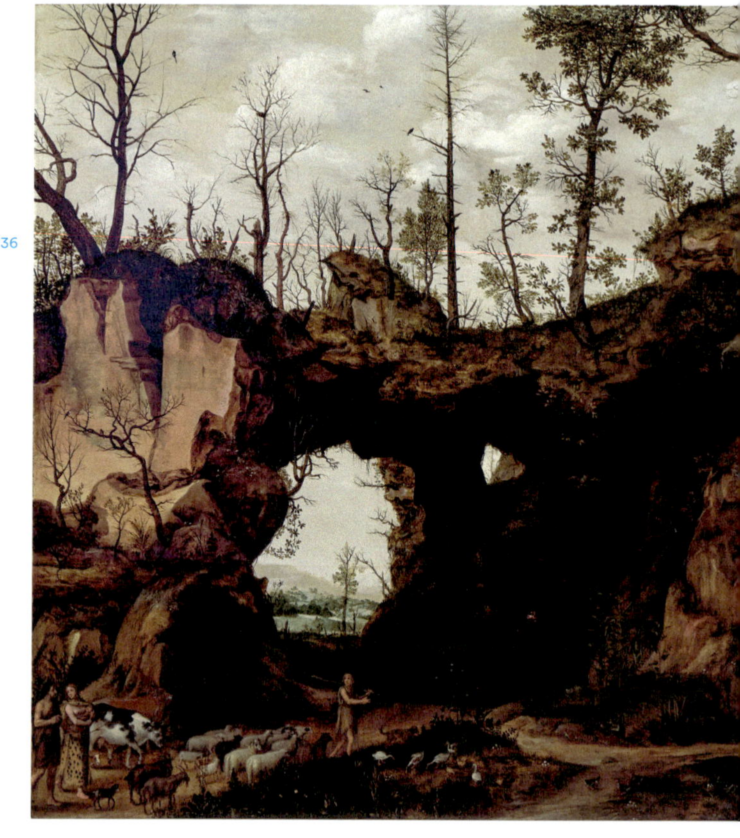

Cornelis van Dalem, *Landscape with the Dawn of Civilisation*, 1560-1570

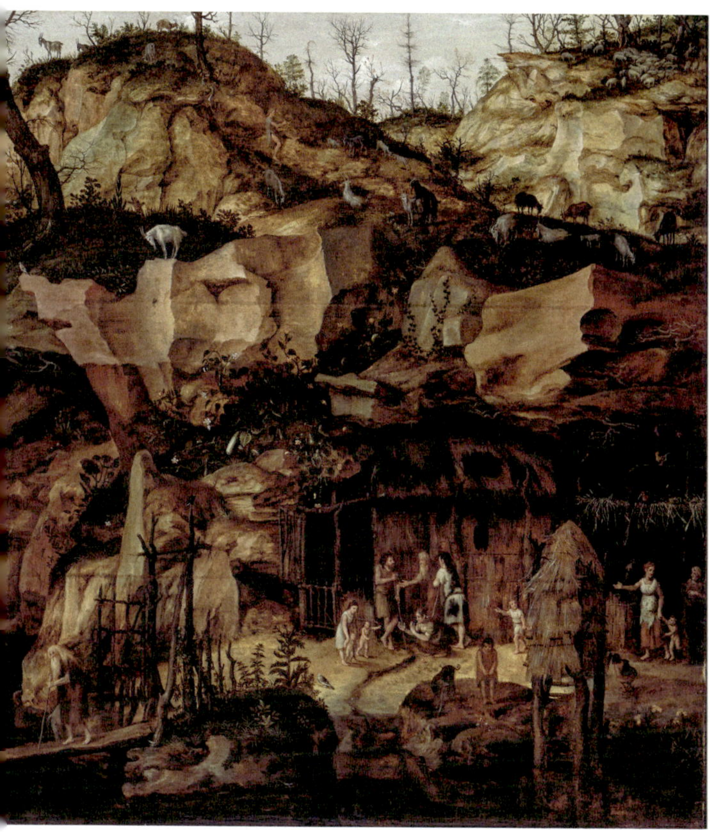

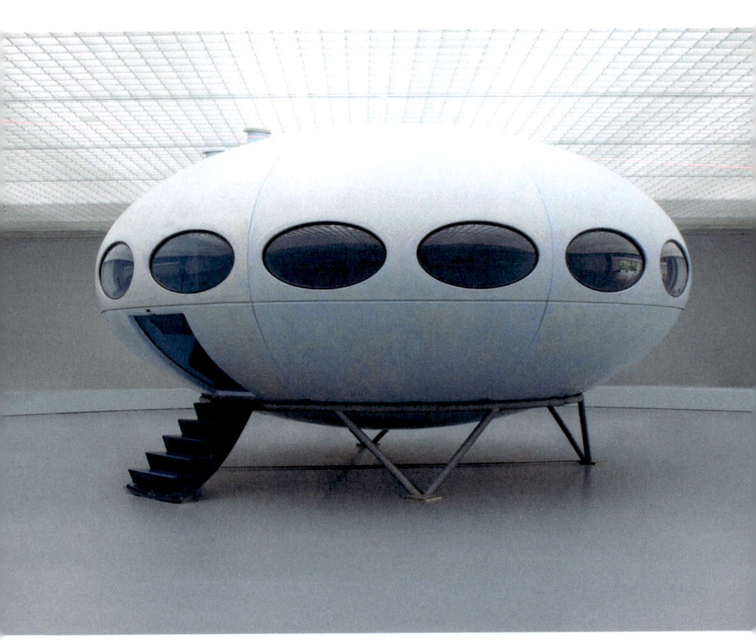

Matti Suuronen, *Futuro*, 1968

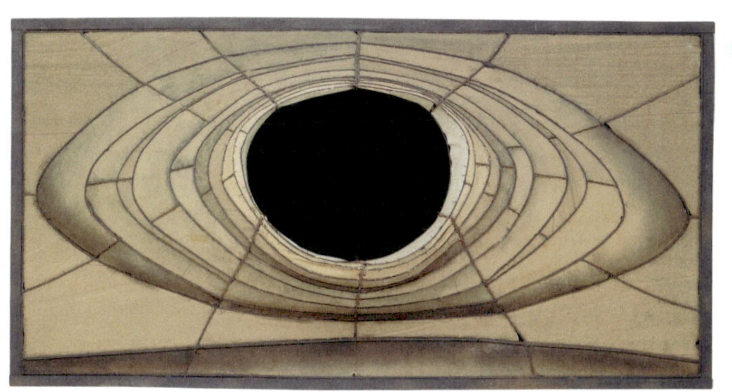

Lee Bontecou, *Untitled*, 1960

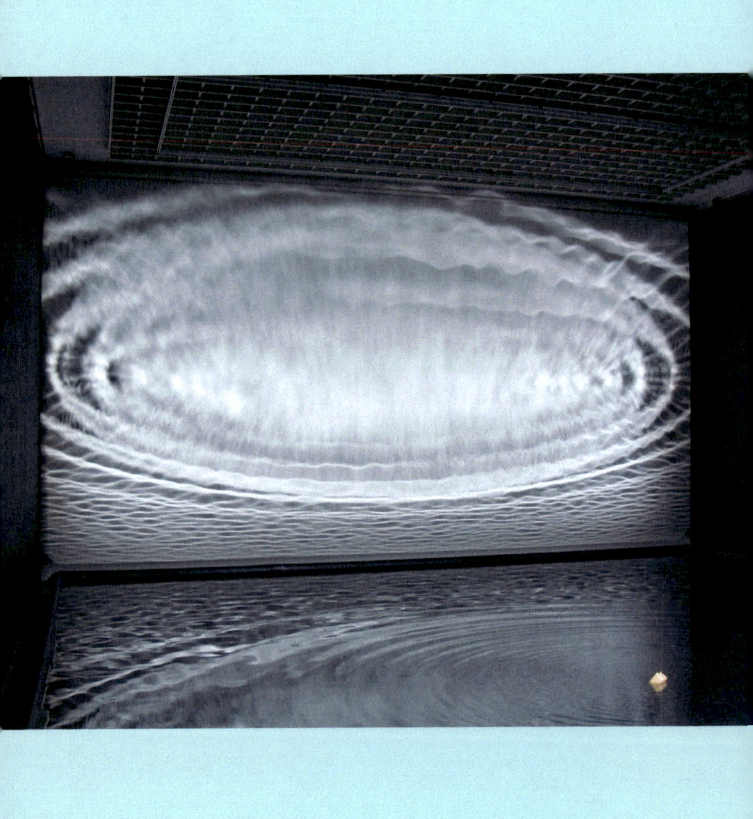

20,562 litres of water, eight hundred duckboard elements and three six-kilowatt lamps respond to visitors' footsteps and create a magical spectacle in the museum's large exhibition space.

Olafur Eliasson, *Notion motion*, 2005

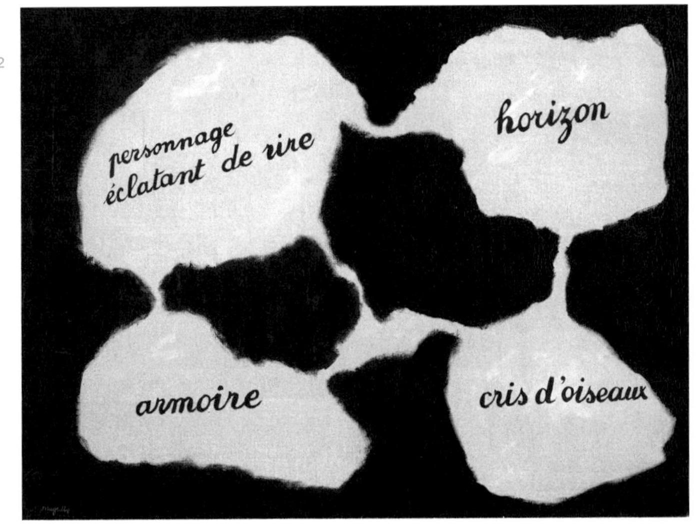

René Magritte, *The Living Mirror*, 1928

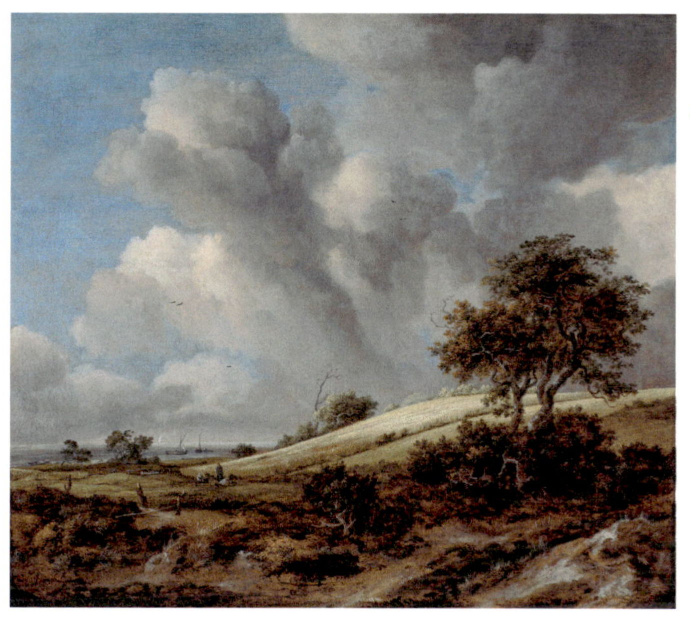

Jacob Isaacksz van Ruisdael, *A Cornfield, in the Background the Zuiderzee*, c. 1660

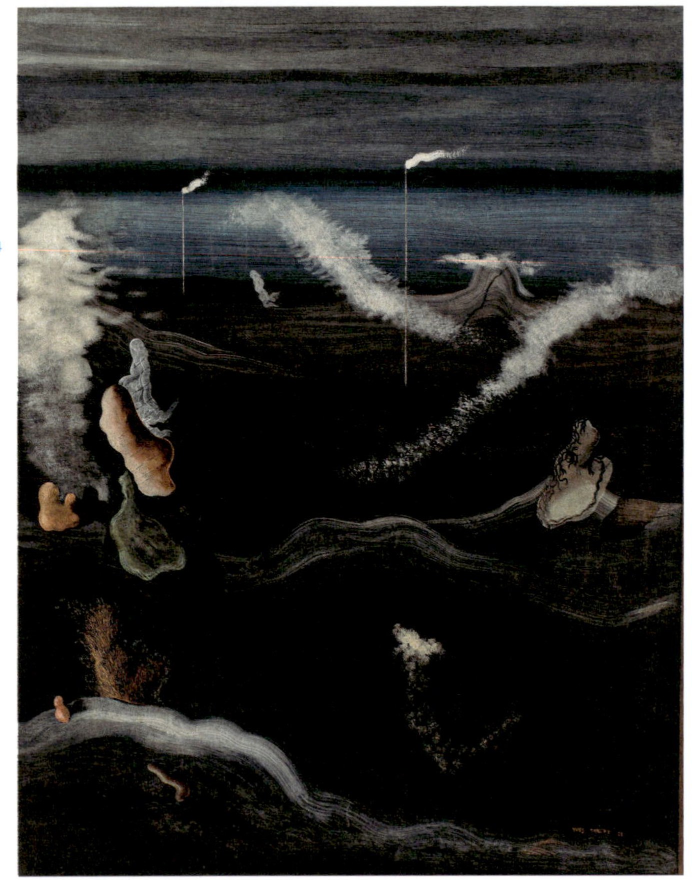

Yves Tanguy, *Landscape with Pink Clouds*, 1928

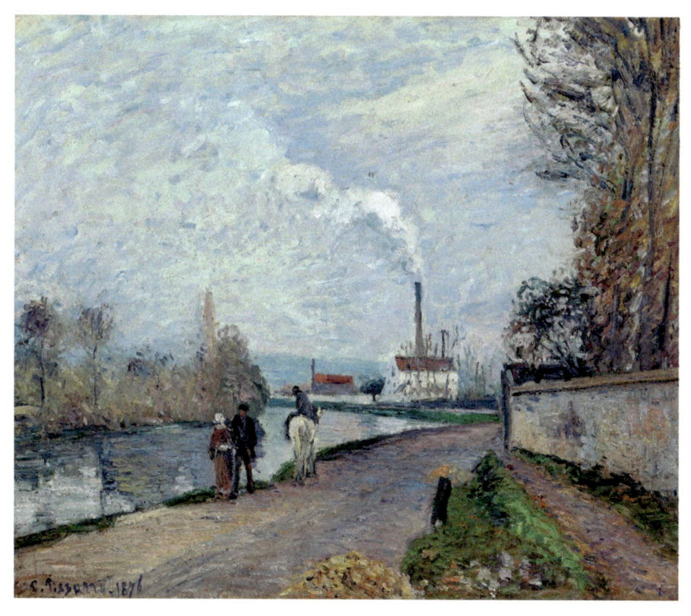

Camille Pissarro, *The Oise near Pontoise in Grey Weather*, 1876

‘I think my mind becomes clearer when I’m in nature. Unfortunately, I always find it an extremely painful process to become aware of my sensory sensations. I simply can’t manage to express the intensity that batters my senses.’

PAUL CÉZANNE

Paul Cézanne, *Landscape near Aix with the Tour de César*, 1895

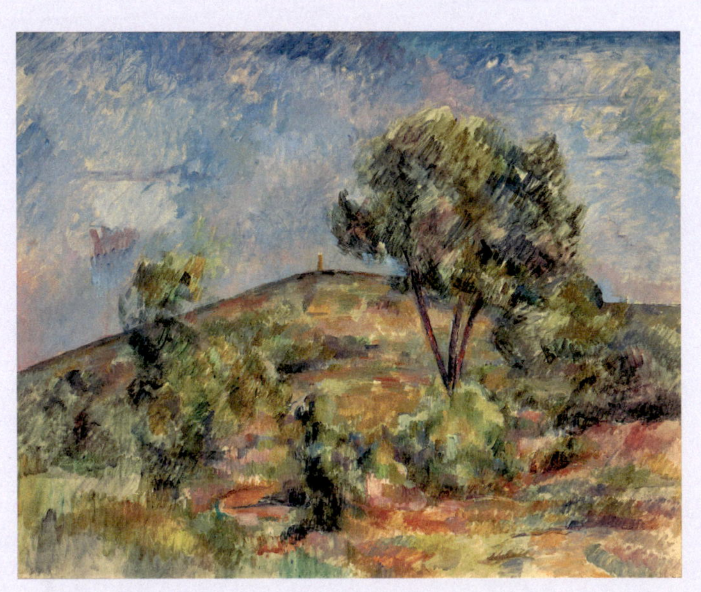

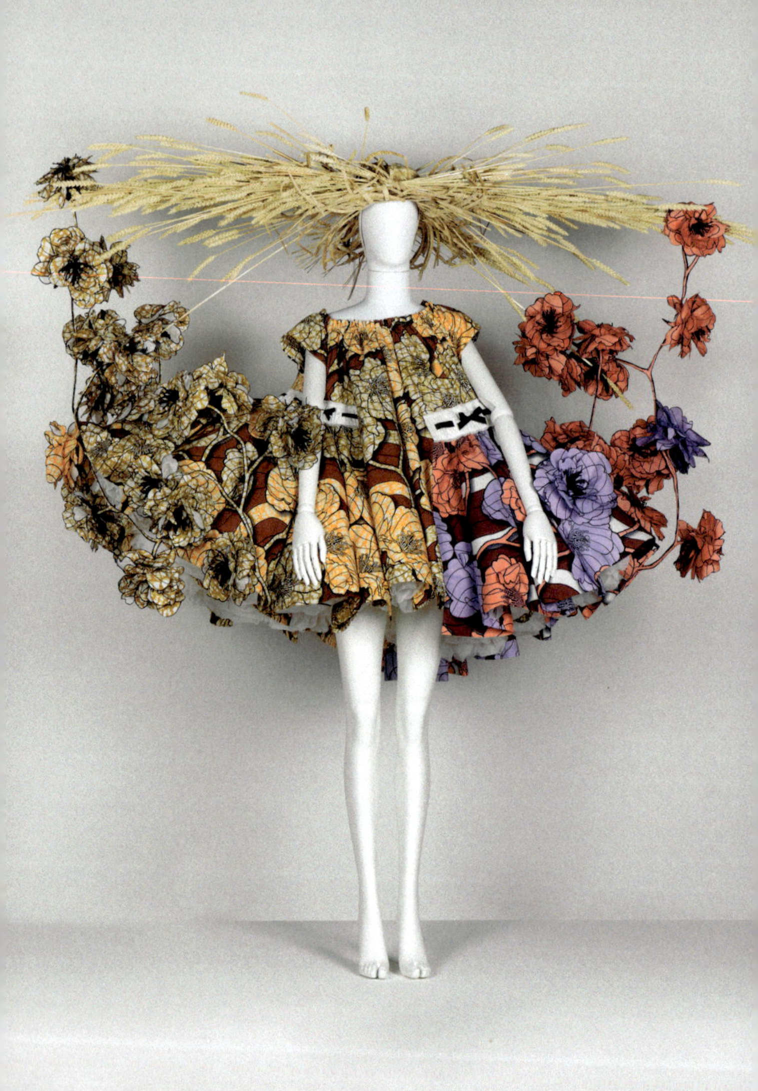

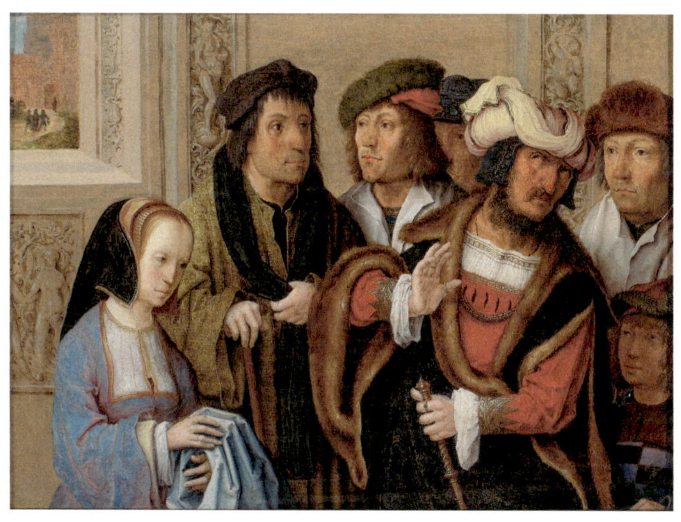

Lucas van Leyden, *Potiphar's Wife Displays Joseph's Garment*, c. 1512
◂ Viktor&Rolf, *Look 18, Van Gogh Girls, Haute Couture Collection*, spring/summer 2015

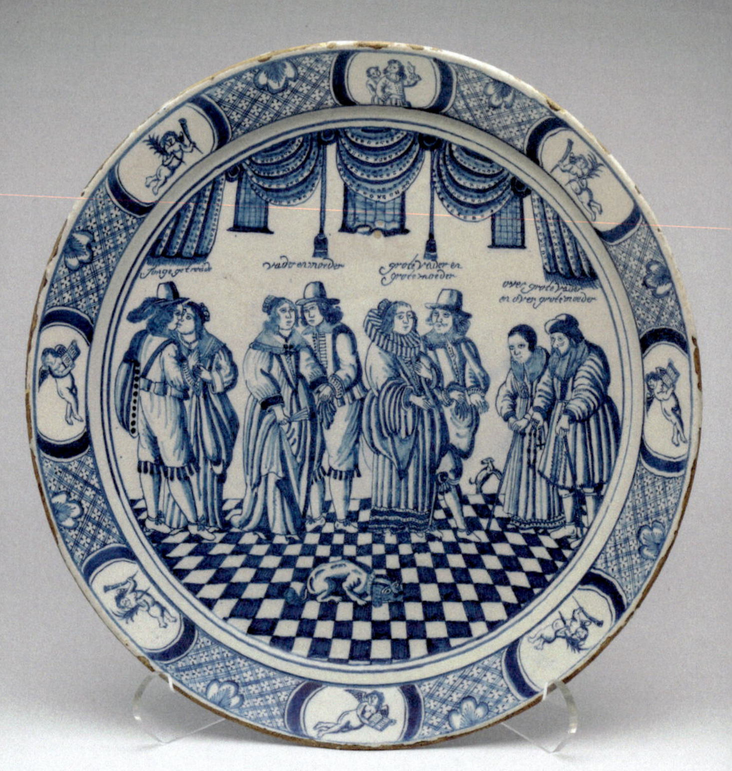
vader en moeder
grote Vader en
grote moeder

This monumental dish was made as a wedding gift. We can only wonder whether the young couple enjoyed its less than cheerful depiction of married life.

Anonymous, dish, 1729

Caritas (Charity) has two children beside her, a heart in her hand and a pelican on her head. The seven works of charity are depicted in all kinds of little scenes around her.

Pieter Bruegel (I), *One of the Seven Virtues: Caritas (Charity)*, 1559

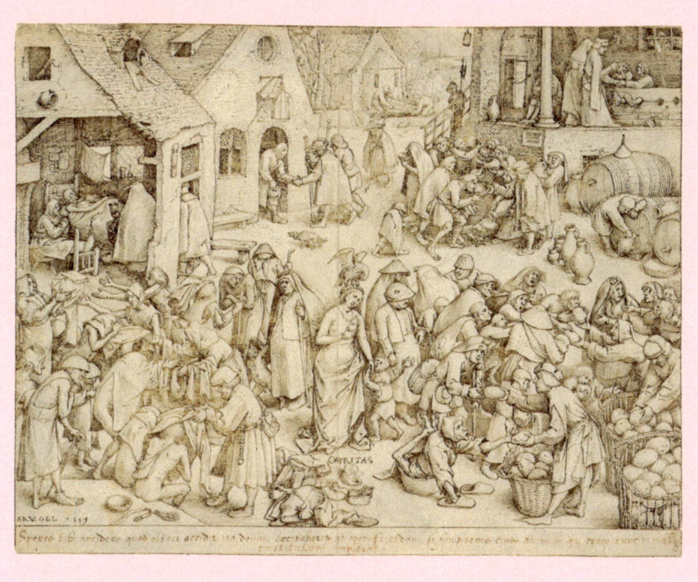
CARITAS
BRVEGEL 1559

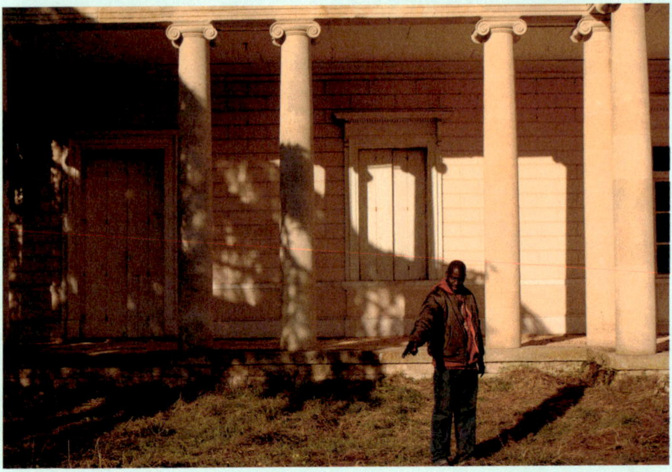

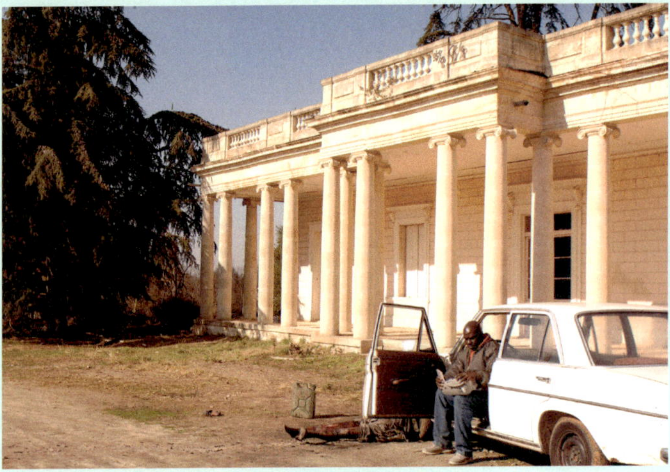

White House has a time span from sunrise to sunset. Two actors repeat a gruesome murder scene seventy-three times in thirteen hours. Claerbout stages the barely ten-minute-long event against the passing of real time.

David Claerbout, *White House*, 2006, video, 13 hrs. 27 min. 53 sec.

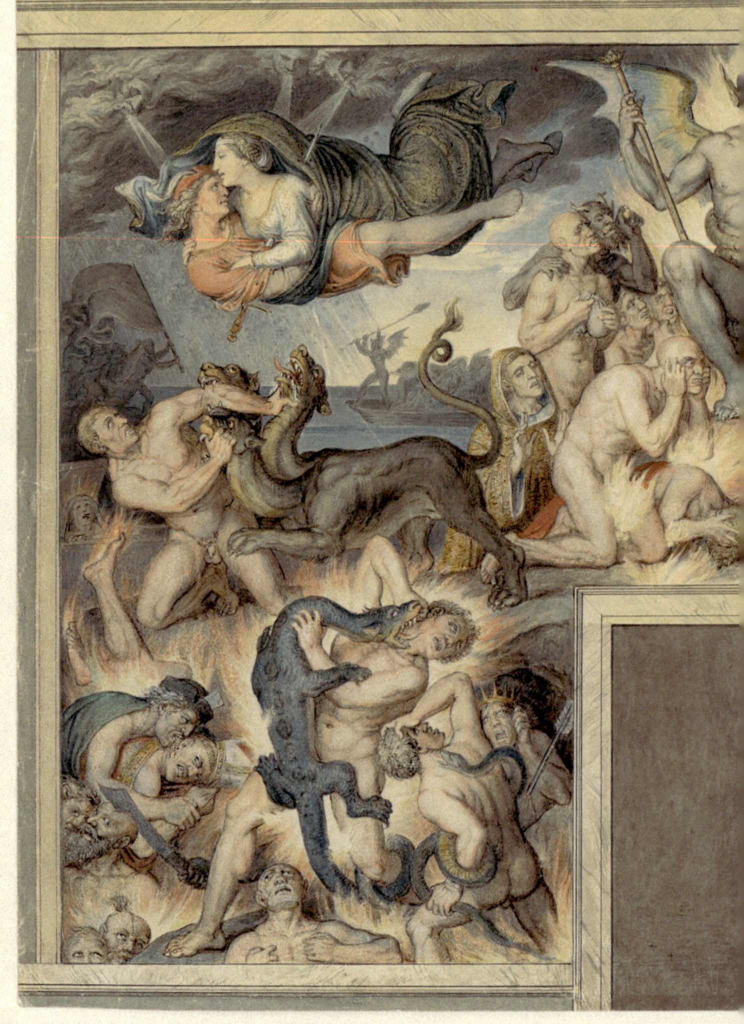

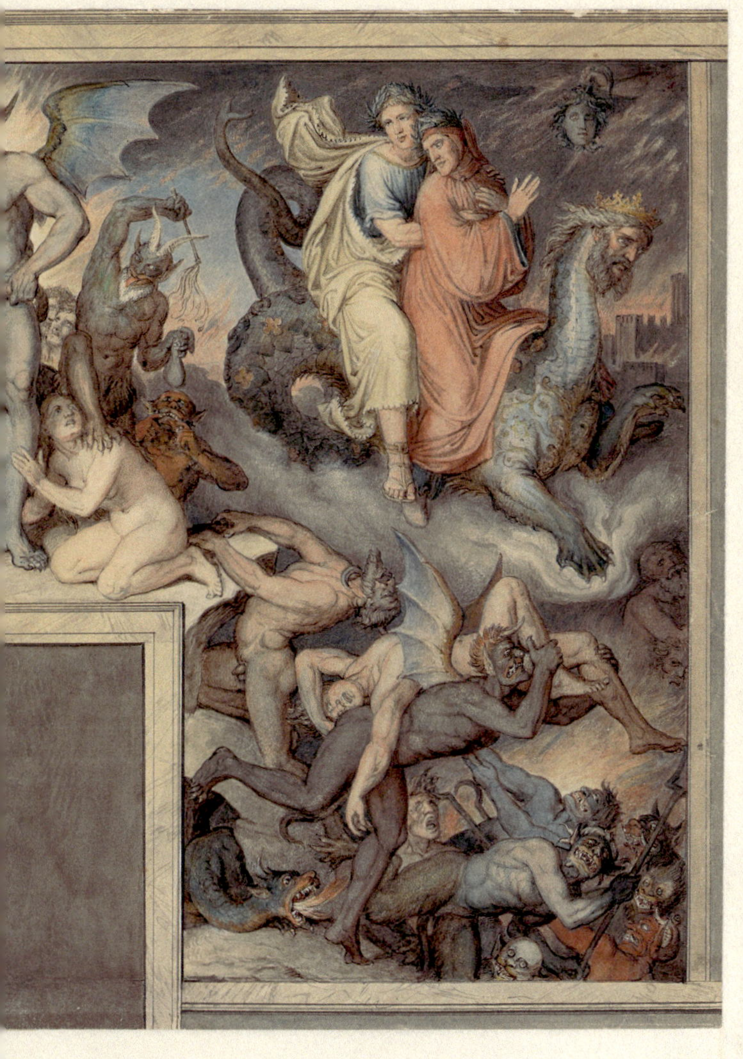

D.G. van Beuningen regarded this painting as the undisputed crown in his collection. After lengthy negotiations it came to Rotterdam from London on 8 May 1940, just two days before the Second World War broke out in the Netherlands.

Jan van Eyck, *The Three Marys at the Tomb*, 1425-1435

◂ Joseph Anton Koch, *Dante's Inferno*, 1825

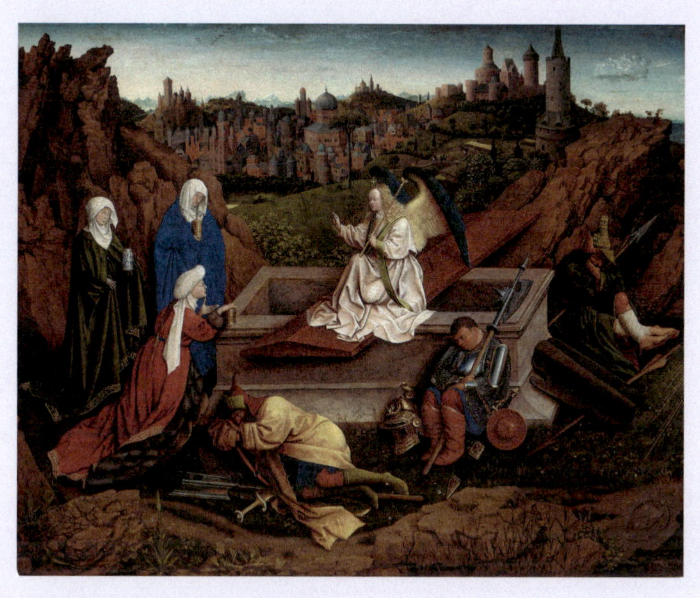

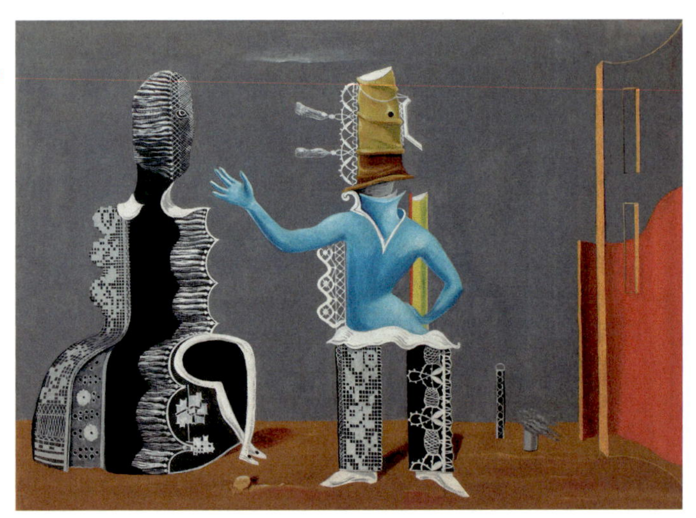

Max Ernst, *The Couple*, 1923

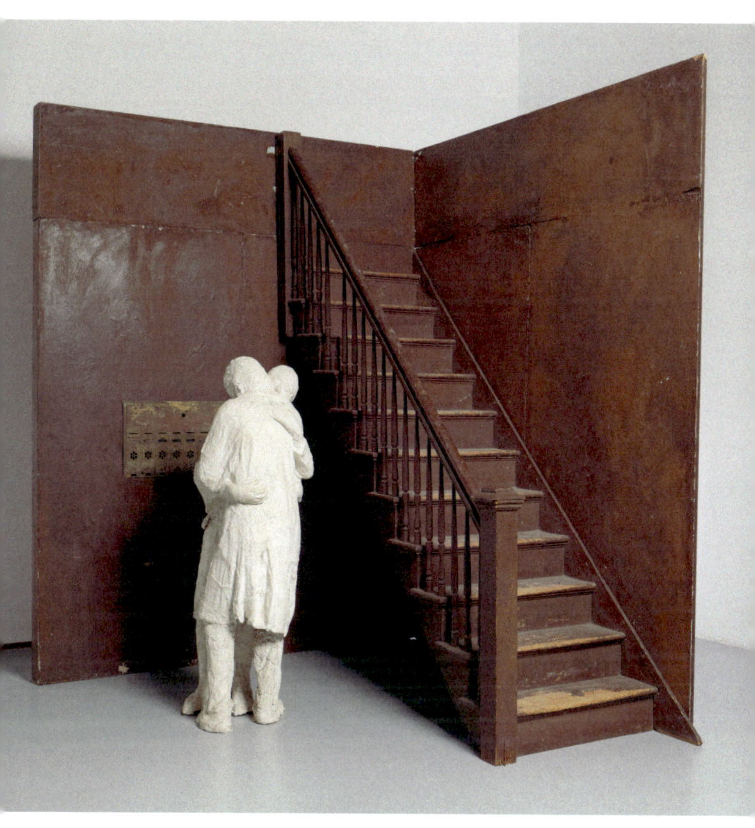

George Segal, *Couple at the Stairs*, 1964

In 1954 Bacon stayed in the Imperial Hotel in Henley-on-Thames. Anonymous businessmen drinking in the hotel bar inspired him to make a series of seven claustrophobic, deep blue paintings; this is number one.

Francis Bacon, *Man in Blue I*, 1954

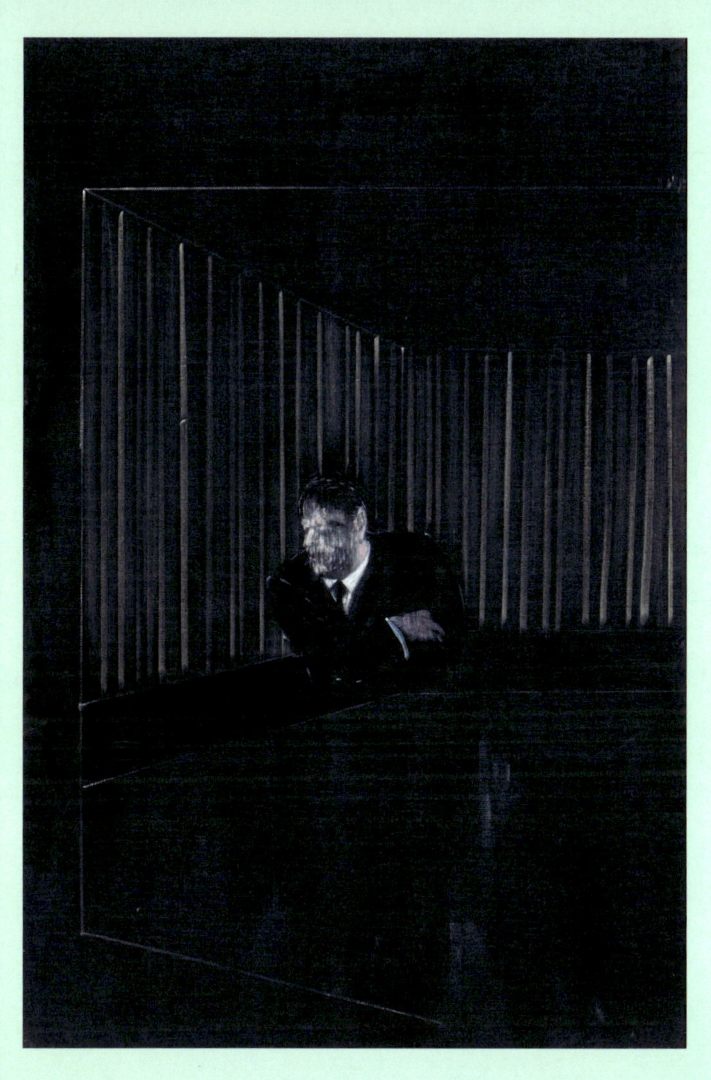

Bas Jan Ader, *I'm Too Sad To Tell You*, 1970

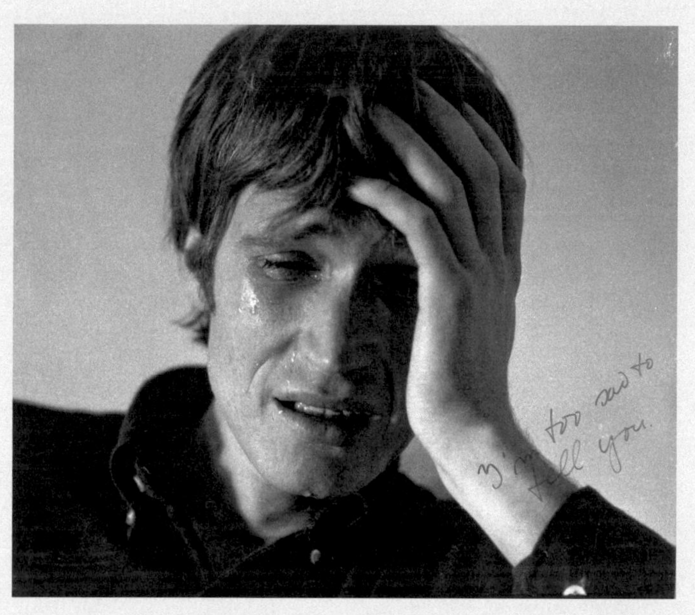
I'm too sad to
tell you.

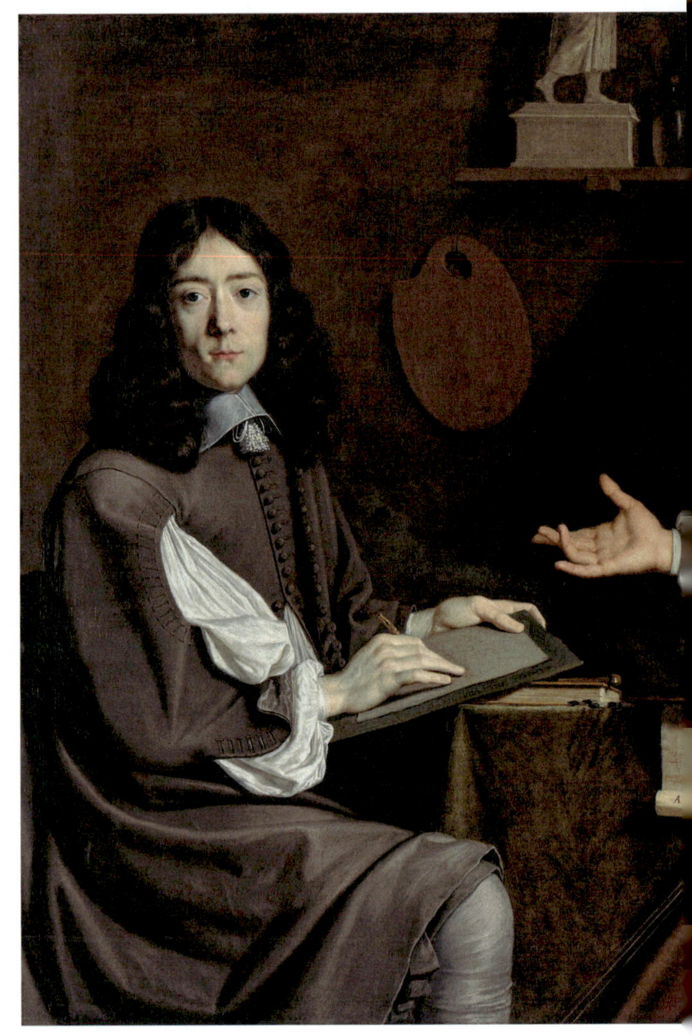

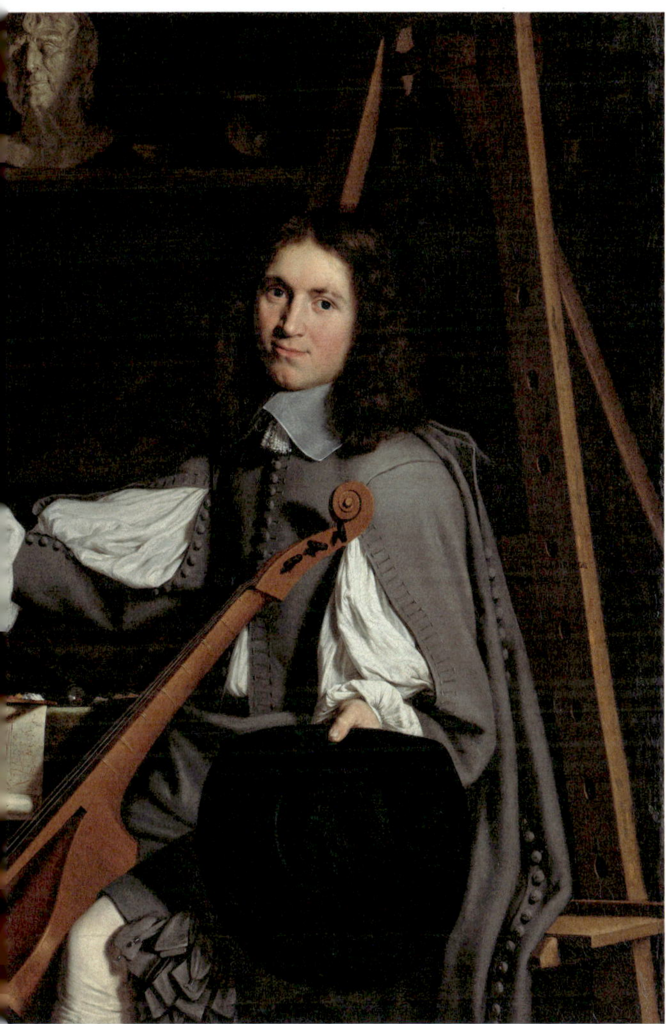

Hubert Robert, *The Artist in His Studio*, 1763-1765

◂ Jean-Baptiste de Champaigne, Nicolas de Plattemontagne, *Double Portrait of the Two Artists*, 1654

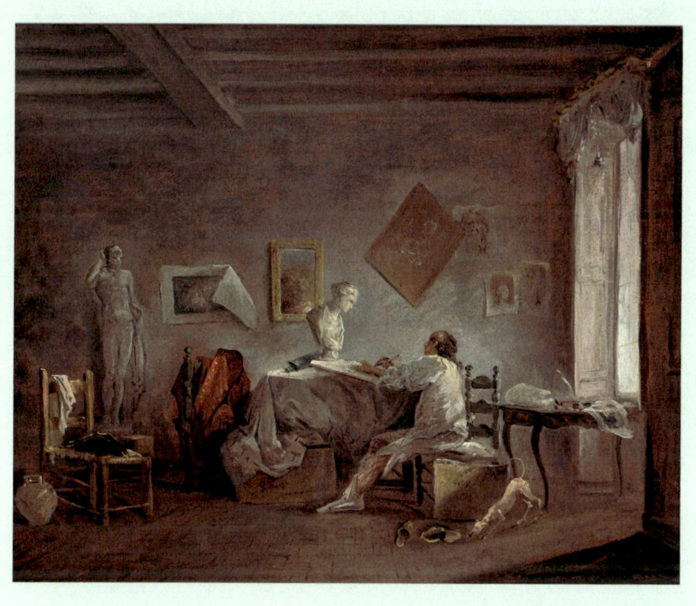

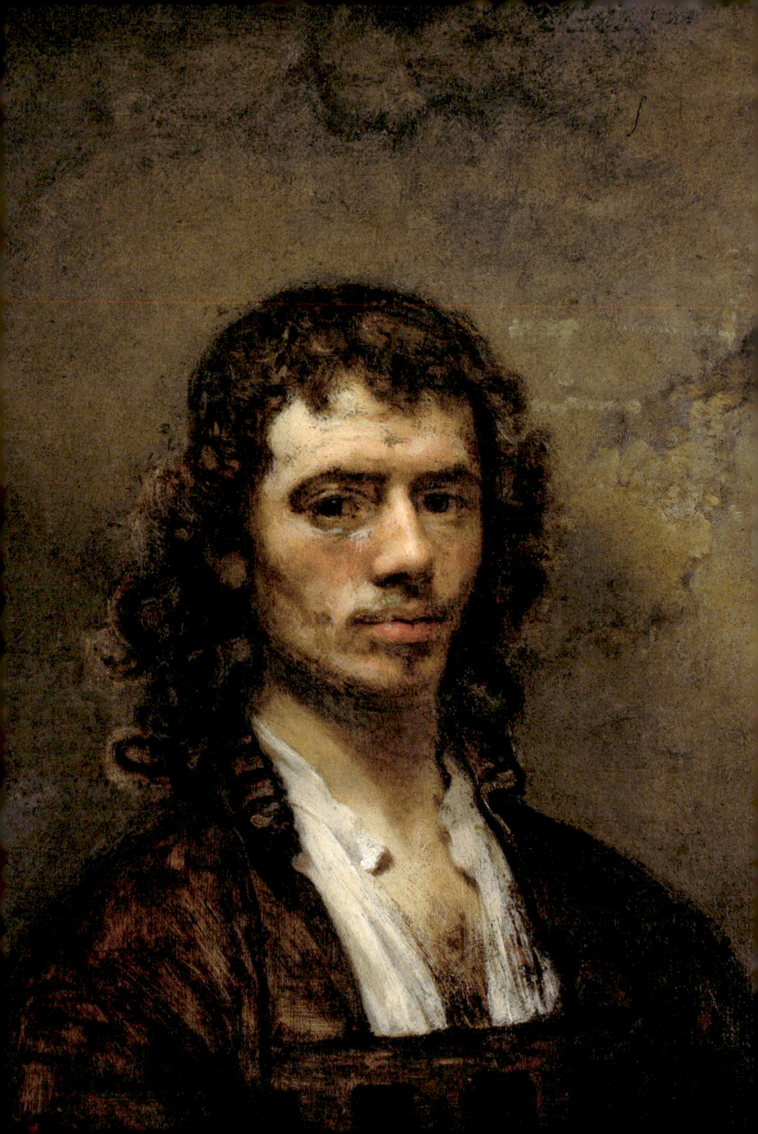

This painting from Frans Boijmans's estate was once thought to be a work by Rembrandt, but it is a self-portrait of his pupil. The oeuvre of Fabritius, who died young, is small; we know of only ten paintings.

Carel Fabritius, *Self-Portrait*, c. 1645

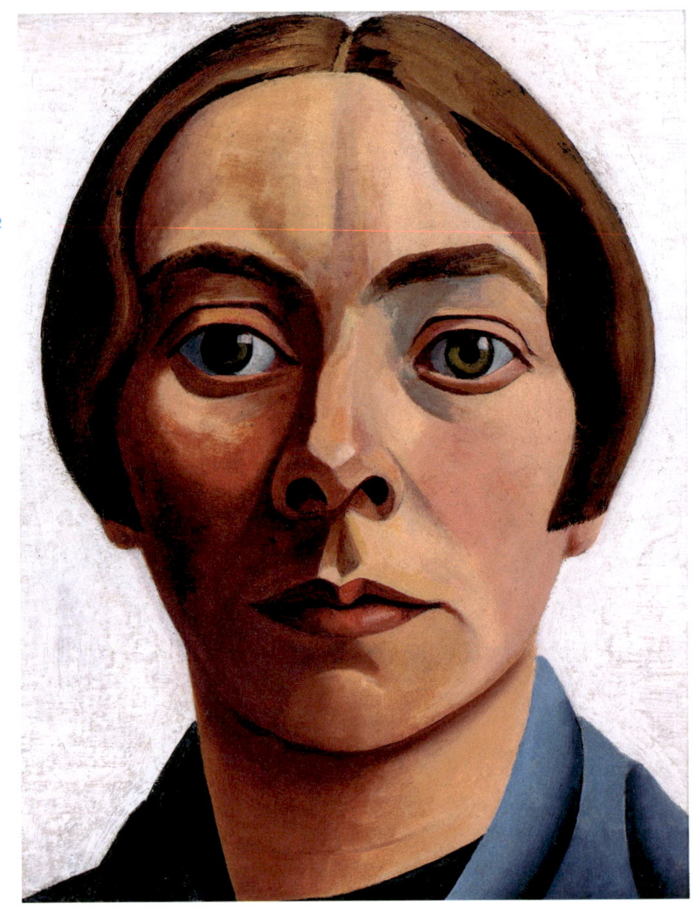

Charley Toorop, *Self-Portrait*, 1928
Tejo Remy, *You Cannot Lay Down Your Memory*, 1991 ▸

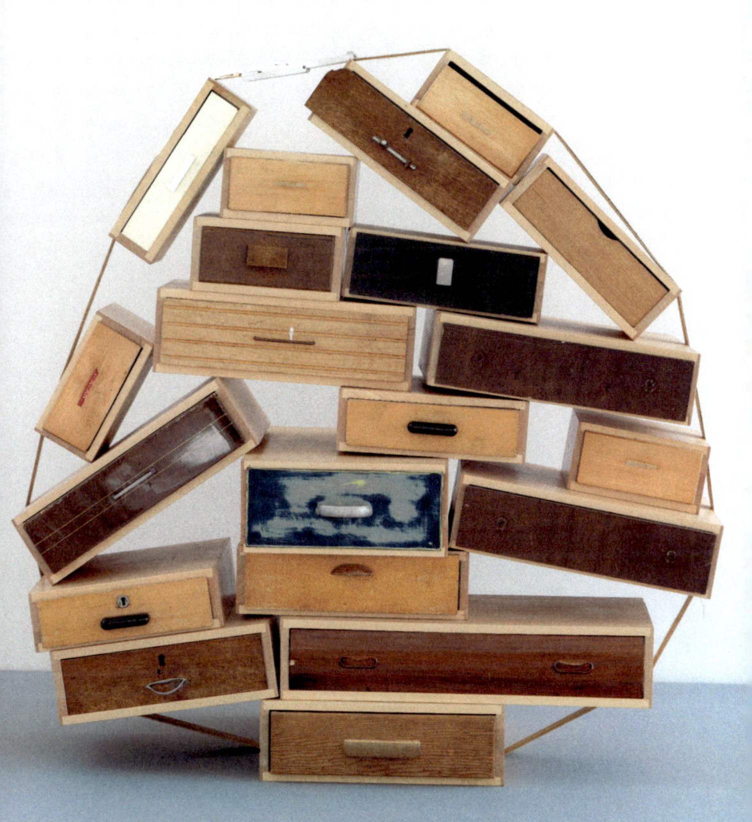

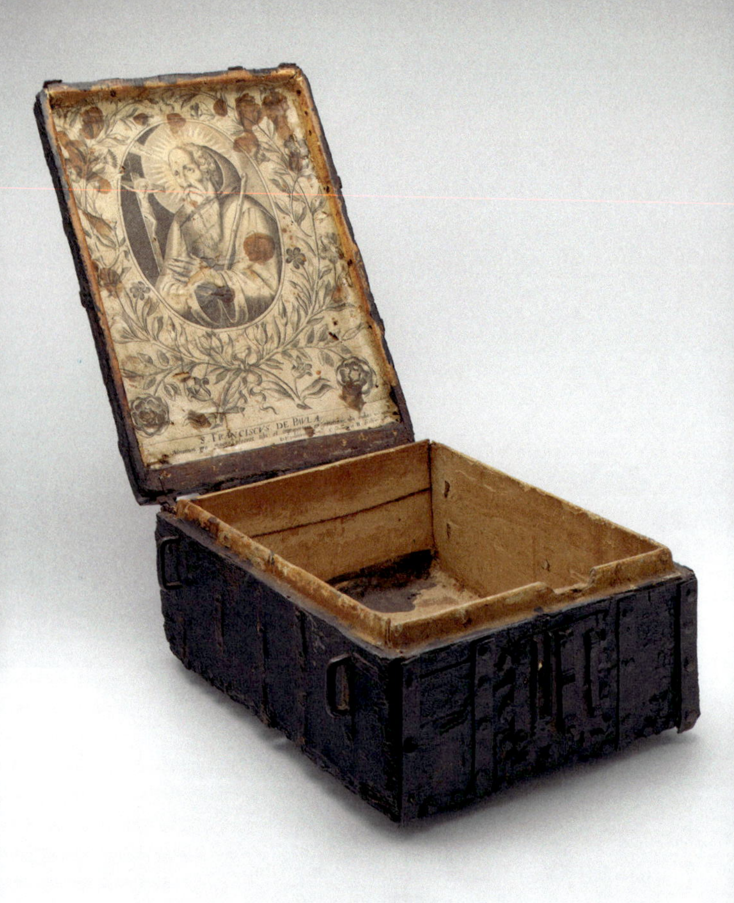
S. FRANCISCVS DE PAVLA

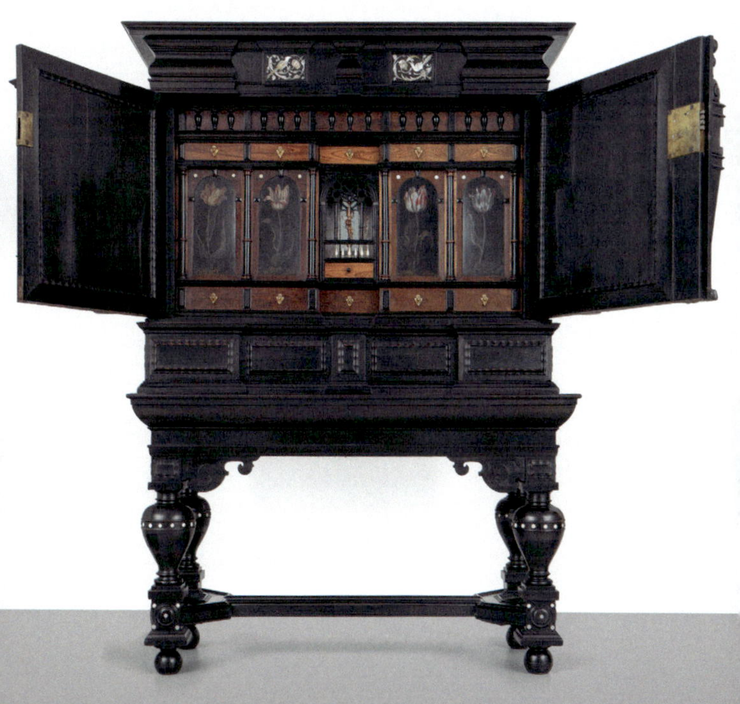

Miró made this last 'dream painting' in 1927. He was inspired by a walk beside the Seine in Paris with his friends the philosopher Georges Bataille and the writer and poet Michel Leiris.

Joan Miró, *A Painted Poem (Music, Seine, Michel, Bataille and me)*, 1927

◂ Herman Doomer, *Tulip Cabinet*, c. 1635-1650

Anonymous, David van Velthem, casket with engraving, c. 1500-1625

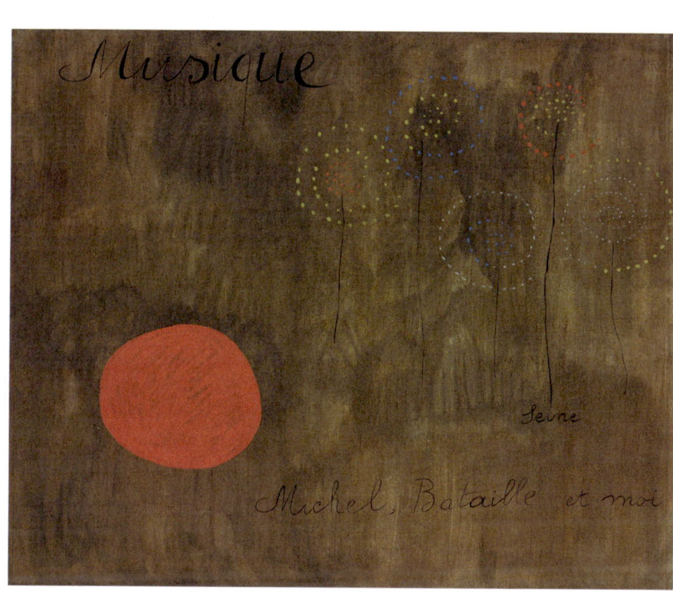
Musique
Seine
Michel, Bataille et moi

List of Works

For further information about the works of art go to
www.boijmans.nl/collectie

p. 51 Jheronimus Bosch, *The Pedlar*, c. 1500
inv. 1079 (OK), acquired with the support of the Rembrandt Association, D.G. van Beuningen, F.W. Koenigs and J.P. van der Schilden 1931

p. 54 Jacob (Jac.) Jongert, *Van Nelle for Coffee and Tea*, 1930
inv. V 1007 (KN&V), purchase 1986

p. 55 Hercules Segers, *River Valley with a Group of Houses*, c. 1625
inv. 2525 (OK), acquired with the collection of D.G. van Beuningen 1958

pp. 56-57 Johannes Hendrik Weissenbruch, *Landscape with a Windmill near Schiedam*, 1873
inv. 1964 (MK), donation Vereniging van Voorstanders der Kunst 1873

p. 59 Rembrandt van Rijn, *Titus at His Desk*, 1655
inv. ST 2, acquired with the support of the Rembrandt Association and 120 friends of the museum, loan Stichting Museum Boijmans Van Beuningen 1940

p. 60 Maurizio Cattelan, *Untitled*, 2001
inv. BRL 2002-01 a-c (MK), loan artist 2002

p. 61 Raphael, *Study for the Kneeling Infant St John in 'The Alba Madonna'*, c. 1509-1510
inv. I 110 (PK), loan Stichting Museum Boijmans Van Beuningen 1940 (former Koenigs Collection)

p. 62 Auguste Rodin, *Eve after the Fall*, 1881
inv. BEK 1330 (MK), donation J. Hudig 1899

p. 64 Cindy Sherman, *Untitled 96*, 1981
inv. MB 1982/3 (MK), purchase 1982

p. 65 Francisco Goya, *Content with Her Lot*, c. 1810-1820
inv. S 3 (PK), loan Stichting Museum Boijmans Van Beuningen 1940 (former Koenigs Collection)

p. 66 Adam van Vianen, salt, 1622
inv. MBZ 195 (KN&V), acquired with the collection of D.G. van Beuningen 1958

p. 68 Edvard Munch, *Two Girls beside an Apple Tree in Blossom*, 1905
inv. 2426 (MK), purchase 1957

p. 69 Juste de Juste, *Pyramid of Five Men*, c. 1543
inv. DN 879/451 (PK), donation Dr A.J. Domela Nieuwenhuis 1923

p. 71 Edgar Degas, *Little Fourteen-Year-Old Dancer*, 1880-1881 (1922)
inv. BEK 1239 (MK), loan Stichting Museum Boijmans Van Beuningen 1939

p. 72 Duane Hanson, *Seated Child*, 1974
inv. BEK 1529 (MK), purchase 1975

p. 73 Jean Antoine Watteau, *Study of two Young Cobblers*, c. 1715-1716
inv. F I 68 (PK), loan Stichting Museum Boijmans Van Beuningen 1940 (former Koenigs Collection)

p. 75 Peter Paul Rubens, *Achilles Educated by the Centaur Chiron*, 1630-1635
inv. 1760 a (OK), donation D.G. van Beuningen 1933

pp. 76-77 Salvador Dalí, *Couple with Their Heads Full of Clouds*, 1936
inv. 2988 a-b (MK), purchased with the support of the Stichting Museum Boijmans Van Beuningen, Rembrandt Association, Prins Bernhard Cultuurfonds, Erasmus Foundation, Stichting Bevordering van Volkskracht Rotterdam 1979

p. 78 Cady Noland, *Manson Girls 'Sit-In'*, 1993-1994
inv. 3328 (MK), purchase 1994

p. 79 Anthony van Dyck, *Saint Jerome*, 1618-1620
inv. VDV 22, loan Willem van der Vorm Foundation 1972

p. 80 René Magritte, *Not To Be Reproduced*, 1937
inv. 2939 (MK), purchase 1977

p. 82 Gilbert & George, *Queer*, 1977
inv. 2959 a-y (MK), purchase 1978

p. 83 Gerard Dou, *A Young Woman at Her Toilet*, 1667
inv. 1186 (OK), donation Henry Deterding 1936

p. 84 Jean-Honoré Fragonard, *The Intimate Conversation (La Confidence)*, c. 1778-1780
inv. F I 228 (PK), loan Stichting Museum Boijmans Van Beuningen 1940 (former Koenigs Collection)

p. 86 Emanuel de Witte, *Interior with a Woman at the Virginal*, 1665-1670
inv. 2313 (OK), loan Cultural Heritage Agency of the Netherlands 1948 (NK-collection)

p. 87 George Hendrik Breitner, *The Earring*, 1893
inv. ST 95, loan Stichting Museum Boijmans Van Beuningen 1952 (donation W.H. de Monchy and Erasmus Foundation)

p. 88 Fra Angelico, *Madonna and Child with Two Angels*, c. 1420
inv. 2555 (OK), acquired with the collection of D.G. van Beuningen 1958

p. 90 Kees van Dongen, *The Finger on the Cheek*, c. 1910
inv. ST 78, loan Stichting Museum Boijmans Van Beuningen 1949-1950

p. 91 Pablo Picasso, *Portrait of a Young Woman after Cranach the Younger*, 1958
inv. L 1959/100 (PK), purchased with the support of the Stichting Lucas van Leyden 1959

p. 92 Peter Paul Rubens, *Young Woman with Folded Hands*, c. 1629-1630
inv. V 81 (PK), loan Stichting Museum Boijmans Van Beuningen 1940 (former Koenigs Collection)

p. 93 Bernardo Cavallino, *Saint Catherine of Alexandria*, 1645-1655
inv. 2899 (OK), from the estate of Vitale Bloch 1976

p. 94 Eileen Agar, *Seated Figure*, 1956
inv. ST 528, loan Stichting Museum Boijmans Van Beuningen 2018

p. 95 Master of St Veronica, *Triptych of the Virgin and Child enthroned*, c. 1410
inv. 4232 (OK), purchased with the support of the Rembrandt Association, thanks in part to its Fonds voor Klassieke Beeldende Kunst, Themafonds Middeleeuwen en Renaissance and the annual contribution of Prins Bernhard Cultuurfonds, Mondriaan Fund, FriendsLottery, Stichting Bevordering van Volkskracht, Prins Bernhard Cultuurfonds (thanks in part to its Breeman Talle Fonds), Stichting Museum Boijmans Van Beuningen including funds from an anonymous legacy, Professor H.W. van Os and private donors who wish to remain anonymous 2018

p. 97 Leonora Carrington, *Again, the Gemini are in the Orchard*, 1947
inv. 4220 (MK), purchased with the support of the Mondriaan Fund, Rembrandt Association (thanks in part to its Desirée Lambers Fonds and its Dura Kunstfonds), FriendsLottery, Stichting Fonds Willem van Rede (Cultural Heritage Agency of the Netherlands), Stichting Museum Boijmans Van Beuningen, Prins Bernhard Cultuurfonds (thanks in part to its Breeman Talle Fonds) 2019

p. 98 Master of the Virgo inter Virgines, *The Annunciation*, 1470-1500
inv. 1568 (OK), acquired with the collection of D.G. van Beuningen 1958

p. 99 Mark Manders, *Dry Clay Head on Concrete Floor*, 2016
inv. BEK 2010 (MK), purchase with the support of a private donor via the Stichting Endowment Museum Boijmans Van Beuningen 2018

p. 100 Albrecht Dürer, *Study of Two Feet for the Apostle Paul in the Heller Altarpiece*, c. 1508
inv. MB 1958/T 24 (PK), acquired with the collection of D.G. van Beuningen 1958

p. 101 Robert Gober, *Untitled*, 1990
inv. BEK 1650 (MK), purchase 1990

p. 102 Michelangelo Buonarroti, *Studies of an Outstretched Right Forearm for the Fresco 'The Drunkenness of Noah' in the Sistine Chapel*, c. 1508-1509
inv. I 513 verso (PK), loan Stichting Museum Boijmans Van Beuningen 1940 (former Koenigs Collection)

p. 103 Man Ray, *Rayograph*, 1925
inv. 2798 a (MK), purchase 1972

p. 105 Atelier Van Lieshout, *Wombhouse*, 2004
inv. BEK 1865 a-e (MK), purchased with the support of the FriendsLottery 2011

p. 107 Geertgen tot Sint Jans, *The Glorification of the Virgin*, 1490-1495
inv. 2450 (OK), acquired with the collection of D.G. van Beuningen 1958

p. 109 Mark Rothko, *Grey, Orange on Maroon, No. 8*, 1960
inv. 2764 (MK), purchase 1970

p. 110 Bartholomeus van der Helst, *Abraham del Court and His Wife Maria de Kaersgieter*, 1654
inv. 1296 (OK), purchase 1866

p. 111 Salvador Dalí, *Mae West Lips Sofa*, 1938
inv. V 2280 (KN&V), purchased with the support of the Stichting Museum Boijmans Van Beuningen, Rembrandt Association 2003

pp. 112-113 Andy Warhol, *The Kiss (Bela Lugosi)*, 1963
inv. 2984 (MK), purchase 1979

p. 114 Giambologna, *Sleeping Nymph and Satyr*, 1580-1590
inv. BEK 1123 a (OK), acquired with the collection of D.G. van Beuningen 1958

p. 115 Claude Lorrain, *Landscape with Pan and Syrinx*, 1656
inv. F I 9 (PK), loan Stichting Museum Boijmans Van Beuningen 1940 (former Koenigs Collection)

pp. 116-117 Johan Christian Dahl, *Moonlit Landscape*, 1823
inv. 4231 (OK), purchased with the support of the FriendsLottery 2017

p. 119 Philips Koninck, *An Extensive Landscape, with a River*, 1664
inv. 1419 (OK), from the estate of F.J.O. Boijmans 1847

pp. 120-121 Yayoi Kusama, *Infinity Mirror Room – Phalli's Field (Floor Show)*, 1965 (1998)
inv. BEK 1859 a-y (MK), purchased with the support of the Stichting Fonds Willem van Rede (Cultural Heritage Agency of the Netherlands), Mondriaan Fund and FriendsLottery 2010

p. 122 Barend Cornelis Koekkoek, *Oak Forest*, 1856
inv. 1411 (OK), purchase 1866

p. 123 Daan van Golden, *Heerenlux III*, 1993
inv. Stad-S 160, purchase 1993

p. 124 Louwys Victorsz tulip vase, 1700-1725
inv. A 2240 a-b (KN&V), donation J.P. van der Schilden 1921

p. 125 Claude Monet, *Field of Poppies*, 1881
inv. 2611 (MK), acquired with the collection of D.G. van Beuningen 1958

p. 127 Vincent van Gogh, *Poplars near Nuenen*, 1885
inv. 1239 (MK), donation 26 Rotterdam friends of the arts 1903

pp. 128-129 Jim Shaw, *D'red Dwarf, B'lack Hole*, 2010
inv. 3744 a-g (MK), purchased with the support of the Rembrandt Association (thanks in part to its Titus Fonds) and the FriendsLottery 2013

p. 131 Ettore Sottsass, *Carlton*, 1981
inv. V 258 (KN&V), purchase 1984

p. 132 Jan Toorop, *The New Generation*, 1892
inv. 2337 (MK), purchase 1949

p. 133 Anonymous, balustrade, c. 1650
inv. DIV. M 3 (KN&V), purchase 1940

p. 134 Willem Jacobszoon van Heemskerk, goblet, 1688
inv. 103 (KN&V), purchase 1947

p. 136 Scholte Jansen, *Memorial Beaker Commemorating the Siege of Breda in 1637*, 1648
inv. MBZ 144 (KN&V), donation Erasmus Foundation, from the estate of Dr E. van Rijckevorsel 1935

p. 137 Anonymous, coconut goblet, 1550-1600
inv. MBZ 243 (KN&V), purchase 1969

p. 138 Guillaume Marie Edmond Bellefroid, *Thea* tea set, 1934
inv. V 1236 a-d (KN&V), purchase 1989

p. 139 Willem Kalf, *Still Life with a Ming Bowl*, c. 1660
inv. 2503 (OK), acquired with the collection of D.G. van Beuningen 1958

p. 141 Anonymous, *Three Kings Jug*, 1350-1400
inv. F 3854 (KN&V), donation Van Beuningen-de Vriese Collection 1990

pp. 142-143 Pieter Aertsen, *The Pancake Bakery*, 1560
inv. 1006 (OK), with the support of citizens and J.P. van der Schilden Bequest 1926

p. 144 Andries Copier, *Virgo*, 1937
inv. 2212 a-f (KN&V), loan Stichting Museum Boijmans Van Beuningen, purchased with the support of the Kalhorn/Timmermans Fonds 2012

p. 146 Max Beckmann, *Portrait of the Lütjens Family*, 1944
inv. 3610 (MK), purchased with the support of the Lütjens Family, FriendsLottery, Familiestichting Nolst Trenité, G.P. Verhagen-Foundation, Rotterdam City Council, Marlene Dumas, Ministry of Education, Culture and Science (OC&W), Ministry of Finance, Mondriaan Fund, Fonds 21, Stichting Bevordering van Volkskracht, Stichting Nationaal Fonds Kunstbezit, Rembrandt Association, F.J. de Visser, VSBfonds. Shared ownership Cultural Heritage Agency of the Netherlands 2009

p. 147 Jan Havicksz Steen, *'Easy Come, Easy Go'*, 1661
inv. 2527 (OK), acquired with the collection of D.G. van Beuningen 1958

p. 148 Sony Design Team, *Sony micro-tv 5-305e*, 1962
inv. V 1824 a-e (KN&V), donation Prof. Dr W.H. Crouwel 1995

p. 149 Anonymous, nautilus cup, c. 1590
inv. MBZ 185 (KN&V), loan Cultural Heritage Agency of the Netherlands 1953 (NK-collection)

p. 150 Sarah Lucas, *Bitch*, 1995
inv. BEK 1678 a-g (MK), purchase 1995

p. 151 Pieter Claesz, *Breakfast Piece*, 1636
inv. 1122 (OK), purchase 1883

p. 153 Edouard Manet, *Study Sheet with Five Plums*, 1880
inv. F II 72 (PK), loan Stichting Museum Boijmans Van Beuningen 1940 (former Koenigs Collection)

p. 154 Walter De Maria, *A Computer Which Will Solve Every Problem in the World / 3-12 Polygon*, 1984
inv. BEK 1603 a-d (MK), purchase 1984

p. 156 Piet Mondrian, *Composition with Colour Fields*, 1917
inv. 1543 (MK), donation A.P. van Hoey Smith 1928

p. 157 Gerrit Thomas Rietveld, *Zigzag Chair*, 1938
inv. V 2189 (KN&V), purchase 2001

p. 158 Marcel Breuer, *Slatted Chair Model ti 1a*, 1923
inv. V 3265 (KN&V), purchase Stichting Fonds Willem van Rede 2018 (on permanent loan from the Cultural Heritage Agency of the Netherlands)

p. 159 Willem Hendrik Gispen, *Diagonal Chair*, 1929-1930
inv. V 2131 (KN&V), donation Sara Lee Douwe Egberts 2000

p. 160 Joseph Beuys, *Ground*, 1980-1981
inv. BEK 1579 a-i (MK), purchase 1981

pp. 162-163 Bruce Nauman, *Double Steel Cage Piece*, 1974
inv. BEK 1568 1-37 (MK), purchase 1980

pp. 164-165 Alfred Sisley, *Provencher's Watermill at Moret*, 1883
inv. 3023 (MK), from the estate of A.E. van Beuningen-Charlouis 1981

p. 167 Claude Monet, *Fisherman's Cottage at Varengeville*, 1882
inv. 1544 (MK), purchase 1928

p. 168 Gustave Courbet, *The Apple Orchard of Courbet's Father in Ornans*, 1873
inv. 2591 (MK), acquired with the collection of D.G. van Beuningen 1958

p. 169 Johan Barthold Jongkind, *La Ciotat*, 1880
inv. 1378 (MK), donation G.H. Hintzen 1930

p. 171 Wieki Somers, *Bathboat*, 2005
inv. V 2463 a-b (KN&V), purchased with the support of the Mondriaan Fund 2006

p. 172 Marisol, *The Car*, 1964
inv. BEK 1493 a-c (MK), purchase 1972

p. 173 Odilon Redon, *Village Street*, c. 1875
inv. 1714 (MK), donation Mr. M.M. Valkenburg 1922

p. 174 Édouard Vuillard, *The Avenue* from *Landscapes and Interiors*, 1899
inv. MB 1953/143 (PK), purchase 1953

p. 176 Vilhelm Hammershøi, *The Balcony Room at Spurveskjul*, 1911
inv. 3750 (MK), purchased with the support of the Rembrandt Association (thanks in part to its Maljers-De Jongh Fonds), FriendsLottery and a gift from a private individual in Rotterdam 2014

p. 177 Paul Signac, *The Port of Rotterdam*, 1907
inv. ST 96, loan Stichting Museum Boijmans Van Beuningen 1952

p. 178 Pieter JanszSaenredam, *View of Saint Mary's Square and Saint Mary's Church, Utrecht*, 1662
inv. 1765 (OK), purchase 1872

p. 179 Paul Cézanne, *View of the Château Noir*, c. 1887-1890
inv. F II 212 (PK), loan Stichting Museum Boijmans Van Beuningen 1940 (former Koenigs Collection)

pp. 180-181 Jacob Maris, *View at Montigny-sur-Loing*, 1870
inv. 1489 (MK), from the estate of J.P. van der Schilden 1925

p. 183 Joseph Mendes da Costa, clock, 1900
inv. A 4761 (KN&V), purchase 1970

p. 184 Man Ray, *The Enigma of Isidore Ducasse*, 1920 (1971)
inv. BEK 1491 (MK), purchase 1972

p. 186 Hella Jongerius, *Long Neck Bottle*, 2000
inv. V 2662 (KN&V), purchase 2010

p. 188 Francis Picabia, *Egoism*, 1947-1950
inv. 3400 (MK), purchased with the support of the Mondriaan Fund 1996

p. 189 Maarten van Heemskerck, *Portrait of a Humanist*, c. 1545
inv. 1347 (OK), purchased with the support of the Rembrandt Association and D.G. van Beuningen 1936

p. 190 Lucie Rie, *Tall Slender Bottle*, c. 1960
inv. A 4020 (KN&V), purchase 1960

p. 192 Jheronimus Bosch, *The Owls' Nest*, c. 1505-1515
inv. N 175 recto (PK), loan Stichting Museum Boijmans Van Beuningen 1940 (former Koenigs Collection)

p. 193 J. Jurriaan Kok, Sam Schellink, N.V. Haagsche Plateelfabriek Rozenburg, vase, 1904
inv. A 3093 (KN&V)

p. 194 Franz Marc, *The Sheep*, 1913-1914
inv. 1575 (MK), from the estate of M. Tak van Poortvliet 1936

p. 195 Wassily Kandinsky, *Lyrical*, 1911
inv. 1430 (MK), from the estate of M. Tak van Poortvliet 1936

p. 196 Oskar Kokoschka, *The Mandrill*, 1926
inv. 2338 (MK), purchase 1950

p. 198 Titian, *Boy with Dogs in a Landscape*, 1565-1576
inv. 2569 (OK), acquired with the collection of D.G. van Beuningen 1958

p. 199 Anonymous, aquamanile, 1200-1300
inv. KB 61 (KN&V), donation Mr. J.W. Frederiks Collection 1994

p. 200 Anonymous, batter tub, 1475-1525
inv. F 9680 (KN&V), purchase 2006

p. 201 Fra Bartolommeo, *Studies for Bystanders in the 'Madonna della Misericordia'*, c. 1515
inv. I 563 M 3 verso (PK), loan Stichting Museum Boijmans Van Beuningen 1940 (former Koenigs Collection)

p. 202 Erhard Schön, *Lansquenet with Helper*, c. 1530
inv. MB 2010/1 L (PK), purchased with the support of the Stichting Lucas van Leyden, Mondriaan Fund, Rembrandt Association, VSBfonds 2010

p. 204 Rembrandt van Rijn, *Study for one of the Syndics, Volkert Jansz*, c. 1662
inv. R 133 (PK), loan Stichting Museum Boijmans Van Beuningen 1940 (former Koenigs Collection)

p. 206 Vincent van Gogh, *Portrait of Armand Roulin*, 1888
inv. 2608 (MK), acquired with the collection of D.G. van Beuningen 1958

p. 207 Maarten van Heemskerck, *Portrait of a Young Student*, 1531
inv. 1797 (OK), purchase 1864

p. 208 Jan Cornelisz Vermeyen, *Portrait of Muley Ahmed*, c. 1535-1536
inv. L 1959/51 (PK), purchased with the support of the Stichting Lucas van Leyden 1959

p. 209 Pyke Koch, *The Shooting Gallery*, 1931
inv. 1425 (MK), donation Friends of the Museum 1931

p. 210 Arnold van Maeler, *Saint Leonard*, c. 1480
inv. KB 63 (KN&V), donation Mr. J.W. Frederiks Collection 2000

p. 211 Honoré Daumier, *Pleading Lawyer ('L'argument décisif')*, c. 1860-1870
inv. F II 170 (PK), loan Stichting Museum Boijmans Van Beuningen 1940 (former Koenigs Collection)

p. 212 Barthélémy d'Eyck, *Isaiah*, 1442-1445
inv. 2463 recto (OK), acquired with the collection of D.G. van Beuningen 1958

pp. 216-217 Anonymous, *The Norfolk Triptych*, 1415-1420
inv. 2466 (OK), acquired with the collection of D.G. van Beuningen 1958

pp. 218-219 Donald Judd, *Untitled*, 1984
inv. BEK 1632 a-z (MK), purchase with the support of the Rembrandt Association 1987

p. 221 Pieter Bruegel (I), *The Tower of Babel*, c. 1568
inv. 2443 (OK), acquired with the collection of D.G. van Beuningen 1958

pp. 222-223 Paul Noble, *Ye Olde Ruin*, 2003-2004
inv. MB 2005/T 3 a-q (PK), purchased with the support of the Stichting Museum Boijmans Van Beuningen, Mondriaan Fund, Stichting Van Beuningen/Peterich-fonds 2005

p. 225 Gio Ponti, Piero Fornasetti, *Bureau Architettura*, 1960-1965
inv. V 2433 a (KN&V), purchase Stichting Fonds Willem van Rede 2006 (on permanent loan from the Cultural Heritage Agency of the Netherlands)

p. 226 Claes Oldenburg, Coosje van Bruggen, *Screwarch*, 1982
inv. BEK 1589 a-j (MK), purchase 1982

p. 227 Ugo Rondinone, *Breathe, Walk, Die*, 2014
inv. BEK 1974 a-n (MK), purchased with the support of the FriendsLottery 2016

p. 228-229 Theo Colenbrander, *Cathedral*, 1922
inv. V 913 a 1-e 2 (KN&V), loan Stichting Museum Boijmans Van Beuningen 1956

p. 230 Giovanni Battista Piranesi, *The Smoking Fire*, 1761
inv. L 1952/33 (PK), purchased with the support of the Stichting Lucas van Leyden 1952

p. 231 Anselm Kiefer, *Notung*, 1973
inv. 2975 (MK), purchase 1978

p. 233 Joachim Patinir, *Landscape with the Destruction of Sodom and Gomorrah*, c. 1520
inv. 2312 (OK), loan Cultural Heritage Agency of the Netherlands 1948 (former Koenigs Collection)

p. 234 Jean-Michel Basquiat, *Kings of Egypt II*, 1982
inv. 3686 (MK), loan Stichting Museum Boijmans Van Beuningen, donation Hans Sonnenberg 2012

p. 235 Christopher Wool, *Untitled*, 1988
inv. 3204 (MK), purchase 1989

pp. 236-237 Cornelis van Dalem, *Landscape with the Dawn of Civilisation*, 1560-1570
inv. 3363 (OK), purchased with the support of the Stichting Museum Boijmans Van Beuningen, Rembrandt Association, Stichting Elise Mathilde Fonds, Erasmus Foundation, Familiestichting Nolst Trenité, Van Ommeren-De Voogt Stichting, G.Ph. Verhagen-Foundation, Stichting Van Wijngaarden-Boot, Ministerie van OCW, VSBfonds 1996

p. 238 Matti Suuronen, *Futuro*, 1968
inv. BEK 1766 a 1-c 7 (MK), purchased with the support of the FriendsLottery 2007

p. 239 Lee Bontecou, *Untitled*, 1960
inv. BEK 1495 (MK), purchase 1972

p. 240 Olafur Eliasson, *Notion motion*, 2005
inv. BEK 1742 a-b (MK), donation Han Nefkens H+F Mecenaat 2005

p. 242 René Magritte, *The Living Mirror*, 1928
inv. 3825 (MK), purchased with the support of the Stichting Museum Boijmans Van Beuningen, Rembrandt Association (thanks in part to its Dura Kunstfonds), Mondriaan Fund, Stichting Fonds Willem van Rede (Cultural Heritage Agency of the Netherlands), Prins Bernhard Cultuurfonds (thanks in part to its Breeman Talle Fonds), FriendsLottery and private individuals 2015

p. 243 Jacob Isaacksz van Ruisdael, *A Cornfield, in the Background the Zuiderzee*, c. 1660
inv. 1742 (OK), from the estate of F.J.O. Boijmans 1847

p. 244 Yves Tanguy, *Landscape with Pink Clouds*, 1928
inv. 3577 (MK), purchased with the support of the Stichting Museum Boijmans Van Beuningen, FriendsLottery, Rembrandt Association, Mondriaan Fund, VSBfonds, Prins Bernhard Cultuurfonds Zuid-Holland and Breeman Talle Fonds, and also with the support of several private individuals and businesses who provided funds during a benefit gala dinner (28 September 2007), 2007

p. 245 Camille Pissarro, *The Oise near Pontoise in Grey Weather*, 1876
inv. ST 91, loan Stichting Museum Boijmans Van Beuningen, donation Mrs E.Y. van Beek-van Hoorn Janssen 1951

p. 247 Paul Cézanne, *Landscape near Aix with the Tour de César*, 1895
inv. VDV 95, loan Willem van der Vorm Foundation 1998 (former Koenigs Collection)

p. 248 Viktor&Rolf, *Look 18, Van Gogh Girls, Haute Couture Collection*, spring/summer 2015
inv. DTM 295 a-e (KN&V), purchased with the support of Han Nefkens Fashion on the Edge 2015

p. 249 Lucas van Leyden, *Potiphar's Wife Displays Joseph's Garment*, c. 1512
inv. 2455 (OK), acquired with the collection of D.G. van Beuningen 1958

p. 250 Anonymous, dish, 1729
inv. A 5114 (KN&V), purchase 1978

p. 253 Pieter Bruegel (I), *One of the Seven Virtues: Caritas (Charity)*, 1559
inv. N 18 (PK), loan Stichting Museum Boijmans Van Beuningen 1940 (former Koenigs Collection)

p. 254 David Claerbout, *White House*, 2006, video, 13 hrs. 27 min. 53 sec.
inv. 66, loan Stichting Museum Boijmans Van Beuningen 2006 (collection Stichting Van Beuningen/Peterich-fonds)

pp. 256-257 Joseph Anton Koch, *Dante's Inferno*, 1825
inv. DN 327/224 (PK), donation Dr A.J. Domela Nieuwenhuis 1923

p. 259 Jan van Eyck, *The Three Marys at the Tomb*, 1425-1435
inv. 2449 (OK), acquired with the collection of D.G. van Beuningen 1958; the restoration of this painting in 2012 was made possible by Nedspice

p. 260 Max Ernst, *The Couple*, 1923
inv. 2708 (MK), purchase 1966

p. 261 George Segal, *Couple at the Stairs*, 1964
inv. BEK 1453 a-d (MK), purchase 1970

p. 263 Francis Bacon, *Man in Blue I*, 1954
inv. 2700 (MK), purchase 1965

p. 265 Bas Jan Ader, *I'm Too Sad To Tell You*, 1970
inv. 3277 (MK), purchase 1992

pp. 266-267 Jean-Baptiste de Champaigne, Nicolas de Plattemontagne, *Double Portrait of the Two Artists*, 1654
inv. 1120 (OK), donation heirs D. Vis Blokhuyzen 1870

p. 269 Hubert Robert, *The Artist in His Studio*, 1763-1765
inv. 2586 (OK), acquired with the collection of D.G. van Beuningen 1958

p. 270 Carel Fabritius, *Self-Portrait*, c. 1645
inv. 1205 (OK), from the estate of F.J.O. Boijmans 1847

p. 272 Charley Toorop, *Self-Portrait*, 1928
inv. 3590 (MK), purchased with the support of the FriendsLottery 2008

p. 273 Tejo Remy, *You Cannot Lay Down Your Memory*, 1991
inv. V 1677 a-u (KN&V), purchase 1992

p. 274 Anonymous, David van Velthem, casket with engraving, c. 1500-1625
inv. L 2009/1 a-b (PK), purchased with the support of the Stichting Lucas van Leyden 2009

p. 275 Herman Doomer, *Tulip Cabinet*, c. 1635-1650
inv. DIV. M 17 a-d (KN&V), acquired with the collection of D.G. van Beuningen 1958

p. 277 Joan Miró, *A Painted Poem (Music, Seine, Michel, Bataille and me)*, 1927
inv. 4295 (MK), purchase with support of: Rembrandt Association (made possible thanks to the contribution of its Nationaal Fonds Kunstbezit, its Dura Kunstfonds, its Innorosa Fonds, its Themafonds Moderne Kunst and the annual contribution of the Prins Bernhard Cultuurfonds), Museaal Aankoopfonds, Mondriaan Fund, Stichting Museum Boijmans Van Beuningen, FriendsLottery, Stichting Bevordering van Volkskracht, G.Ph. Verhagen-Foundation, Kring van Eyck, Boijmans Business Club and Boijmans Corporate Members, Stichting Elise Mathilde Fonds, Erasmusfoundation and several private donors, 2022

Photography
Studio Buitenhof
Ernie Butts
Peter Cox
Ossip van Duivenbode

Bob Goedewaagen
Tom Haartsen
Erik & Petra Hesmerg
Aad Hoogendoorn
Rik Klein Gotink
Jannes Linders
Attilio Maranzano
Ernst Moritz
Lotte Stekelenburg
Studio Tromp

Selection and texts
Peter van der Coelen
Alexandra van Dongen
Albert Elen
Sjarel Ex
Saskia van Kampen-Prein
Annemartine van Kesteren
Sandra Kisters
Friso Lammertse
Mienke Simon Thomas
Francesco Stocchi

Editing
Sandra Kisters
Esmee Postma
Sabine Terra

Translation
Lynne Richards

Production
Sabine Terra

Design
Tessa van der Waals

Separations and printing
robstolk® amsterdam

Binding
Boekbinderij Van Mierlo

With thanks to
Hanneke de Man

ISBN 978-90-6918-328-2

This book is also published in Dutch
ISBN 978-90-6918-325-1

Publisher
Museum Boijmans Van Beuningen
PO Box 2277
3000 CG Rotterdam
T +31 (0)10 4419400
info@boijmans.nl
www.boijmans.nl

museum boijmans van beuningen

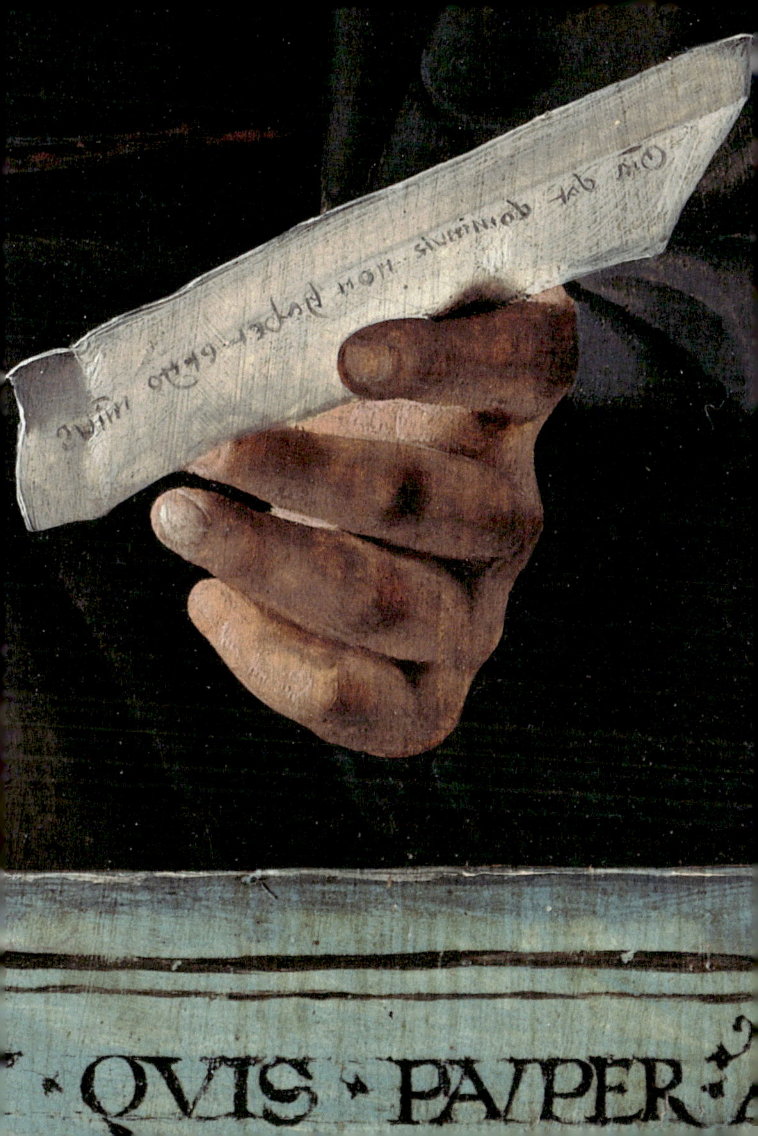
QVIS PAVPER

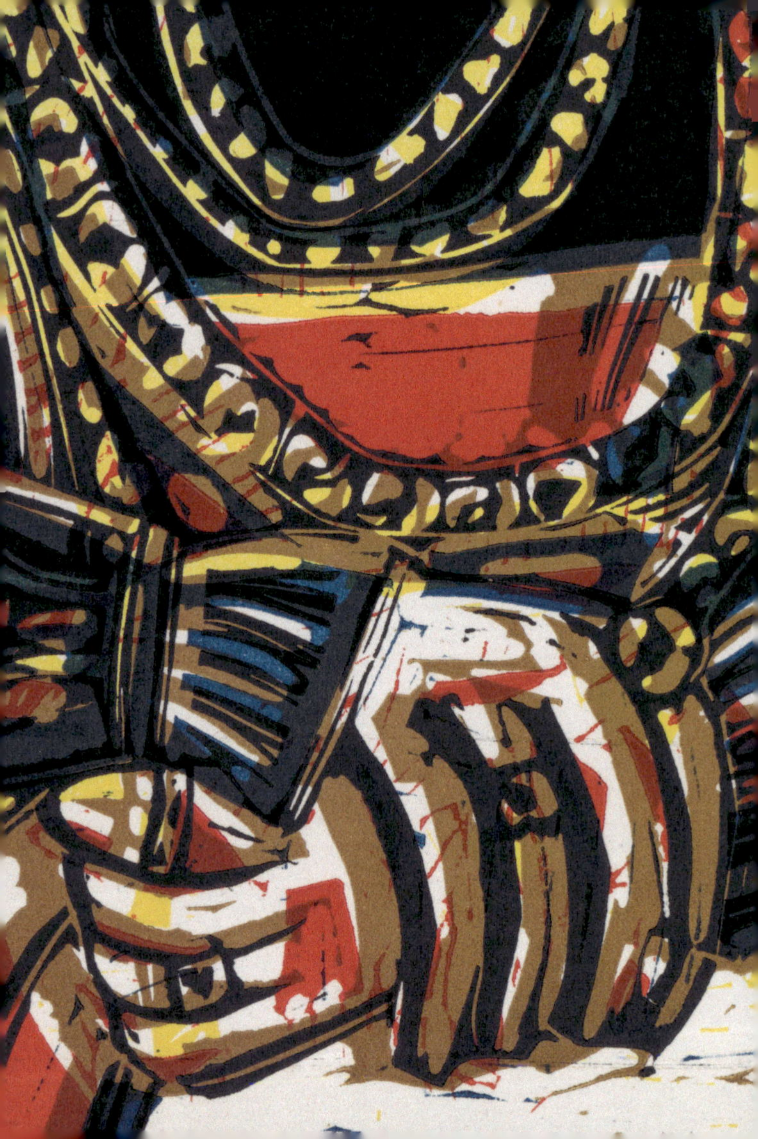

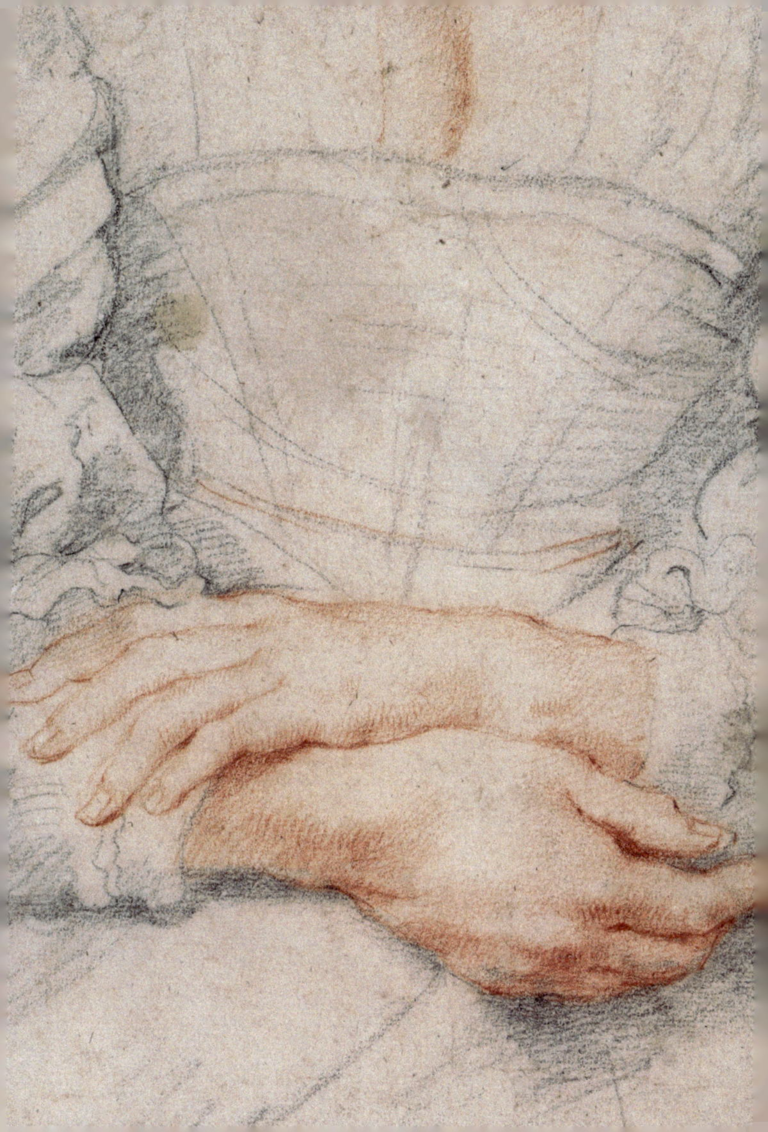

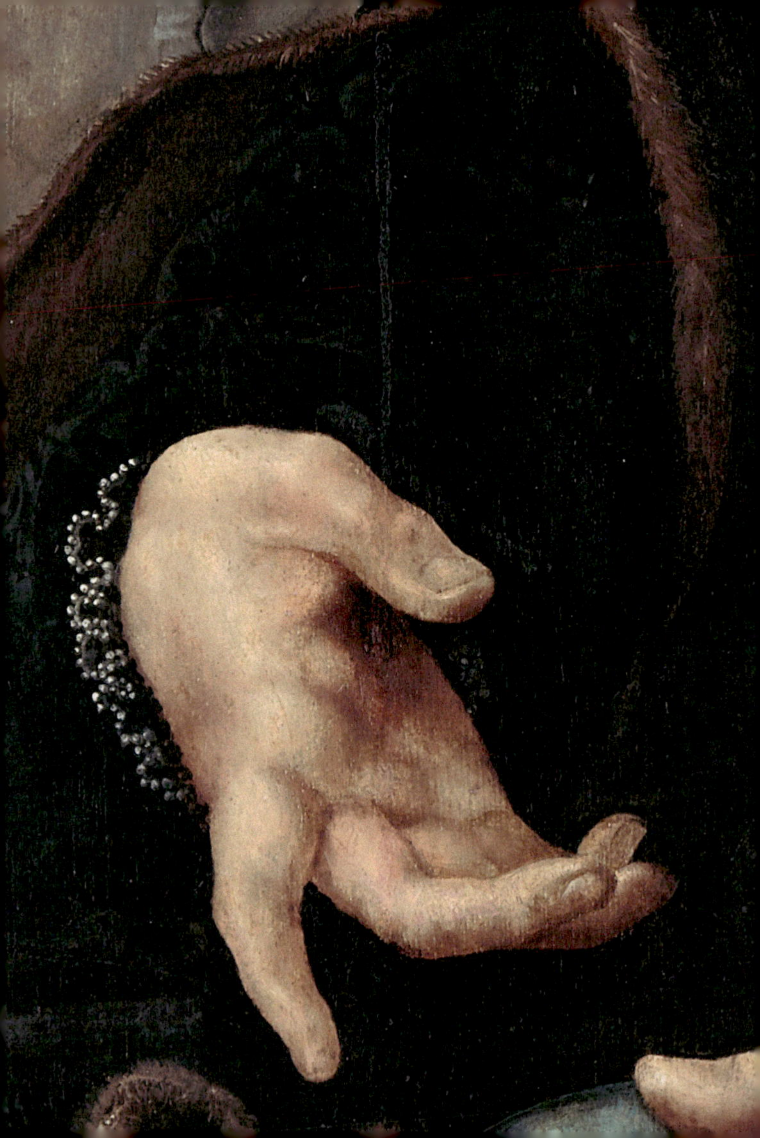

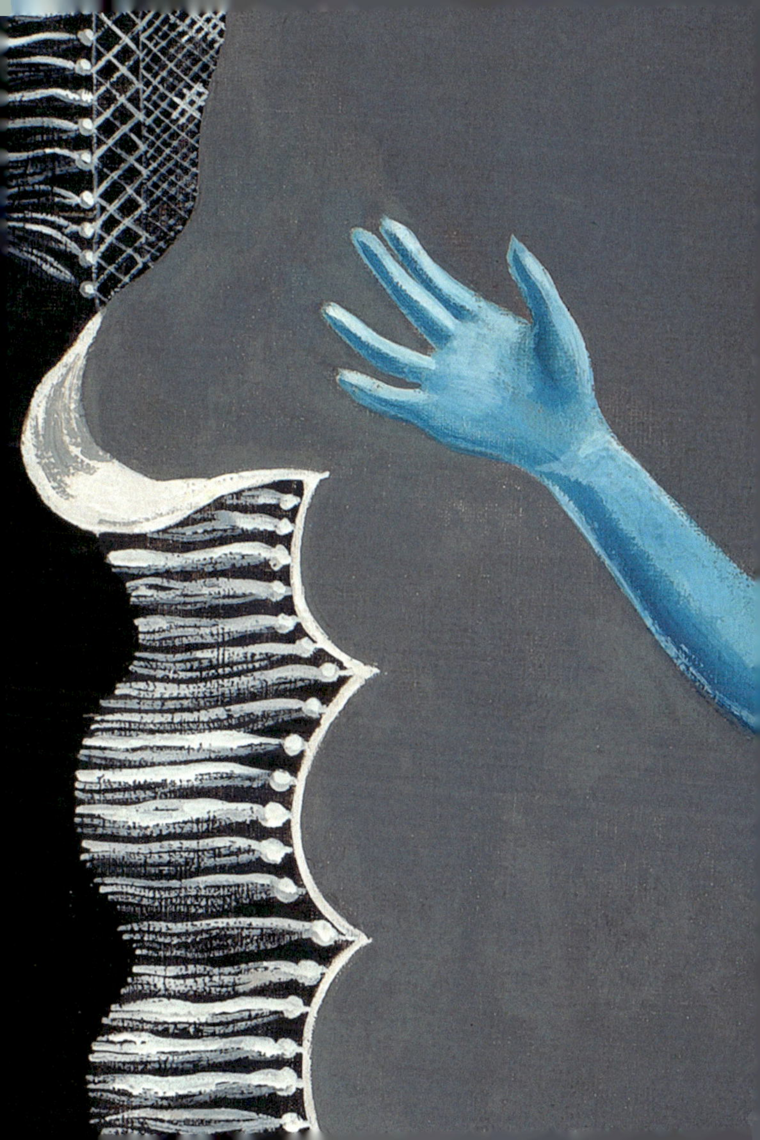

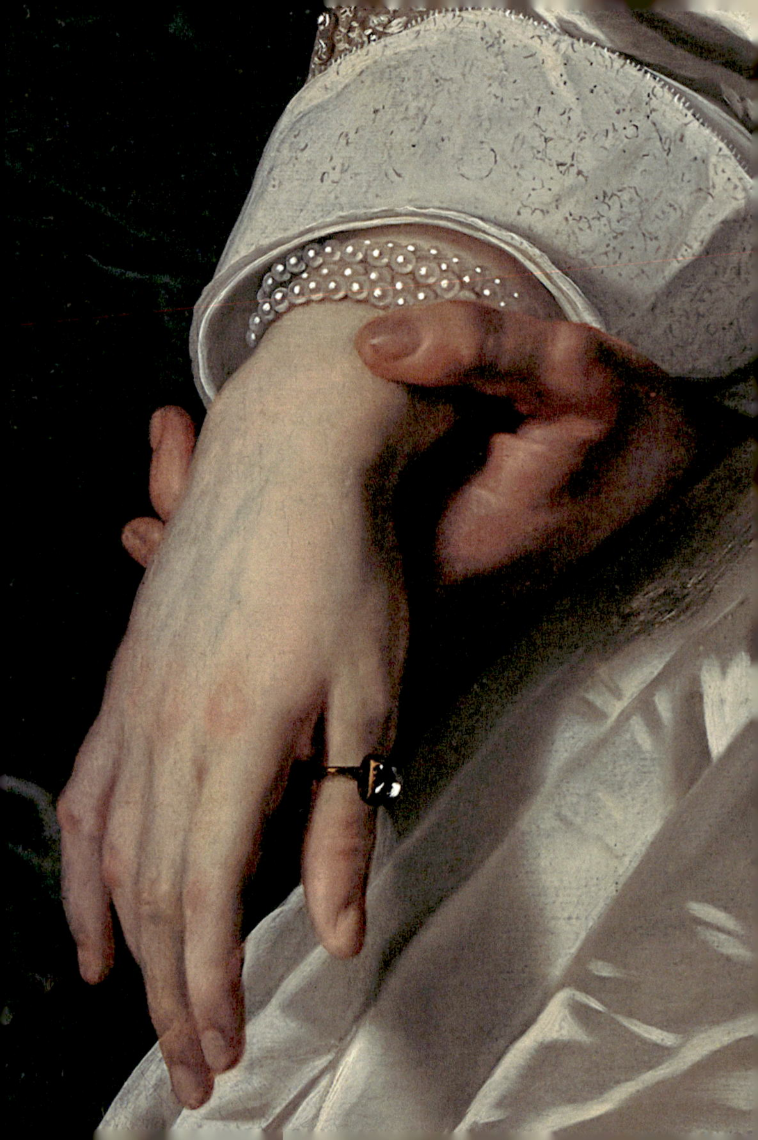

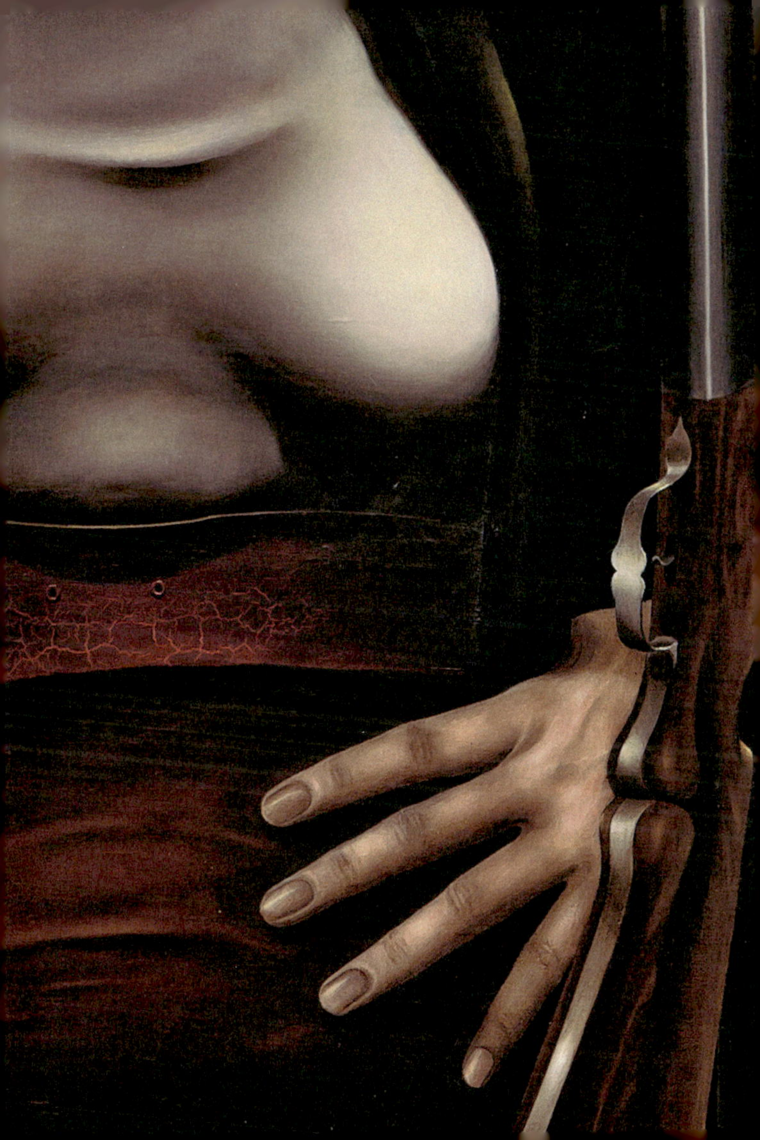

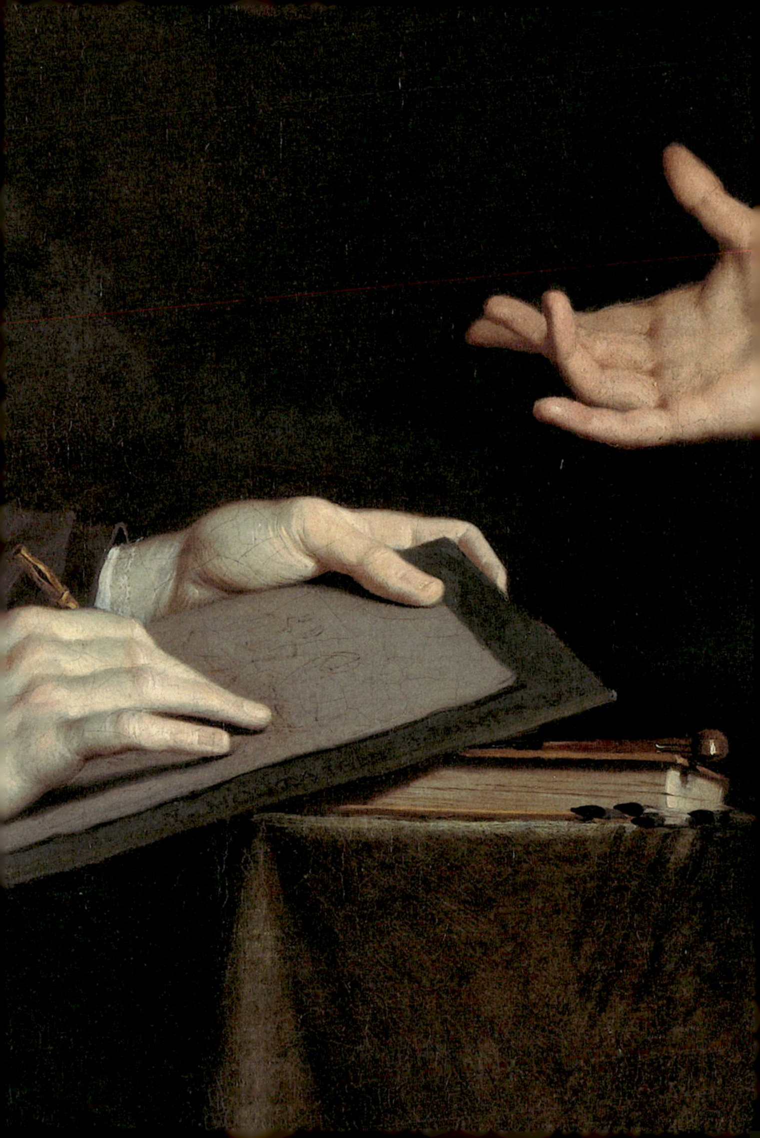

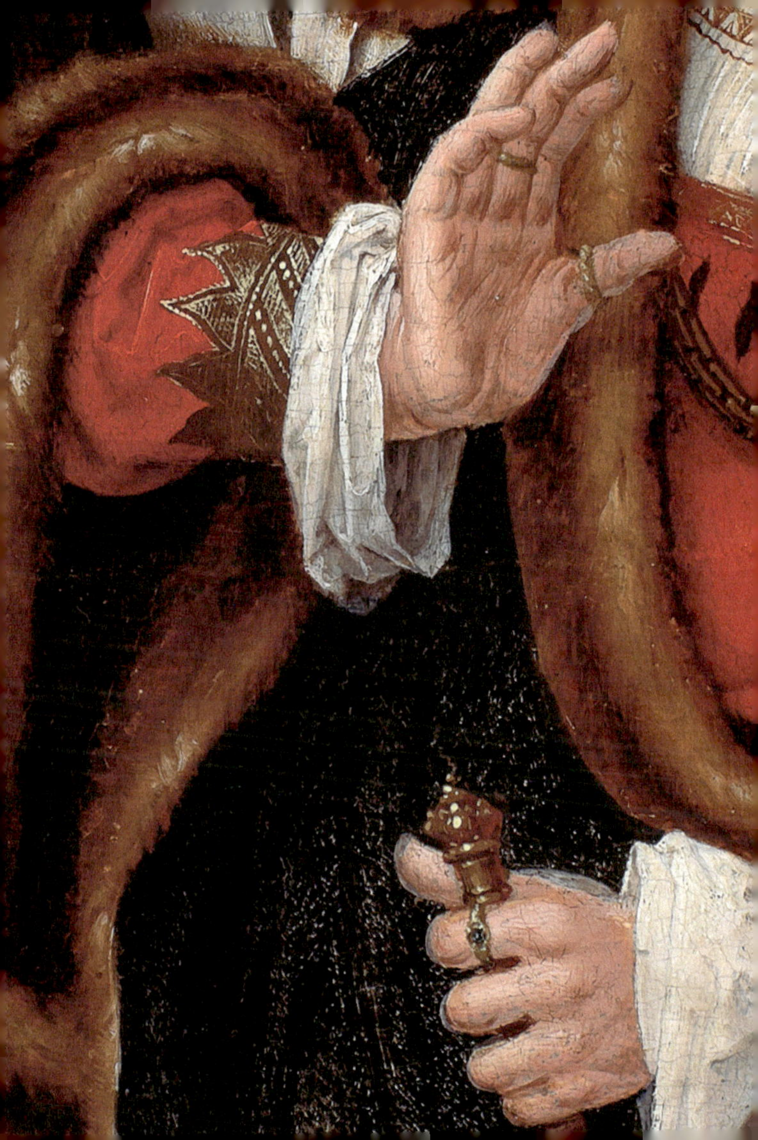

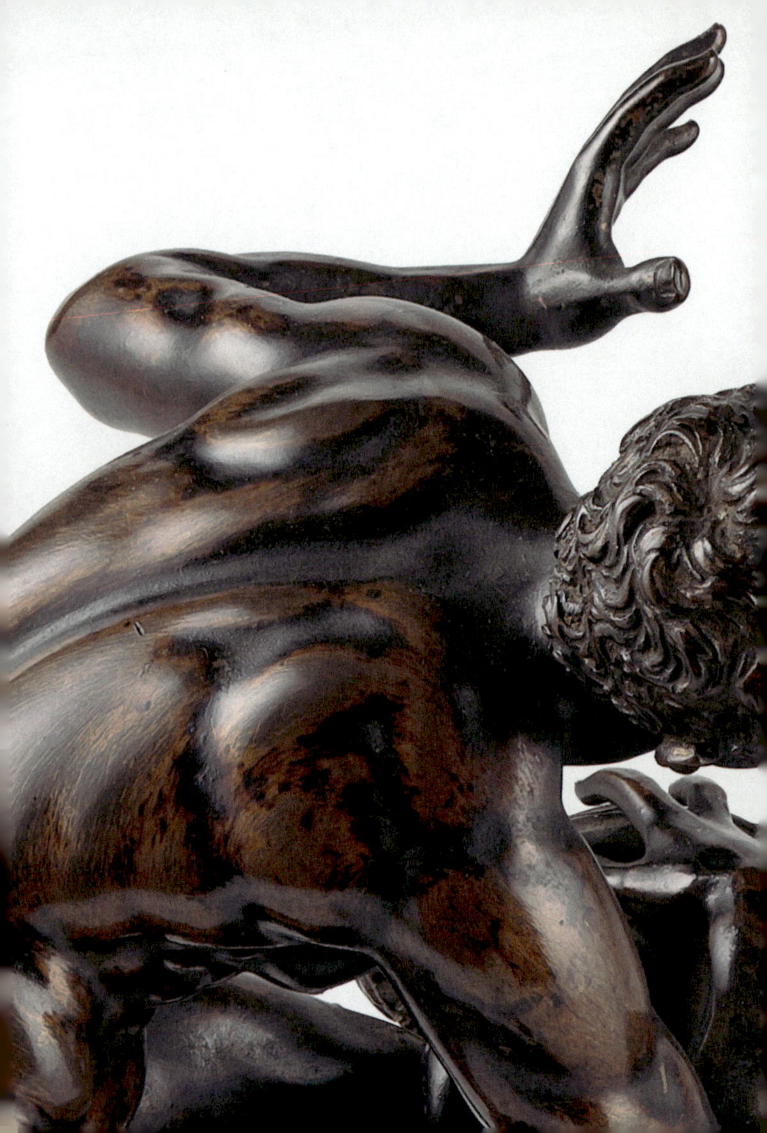

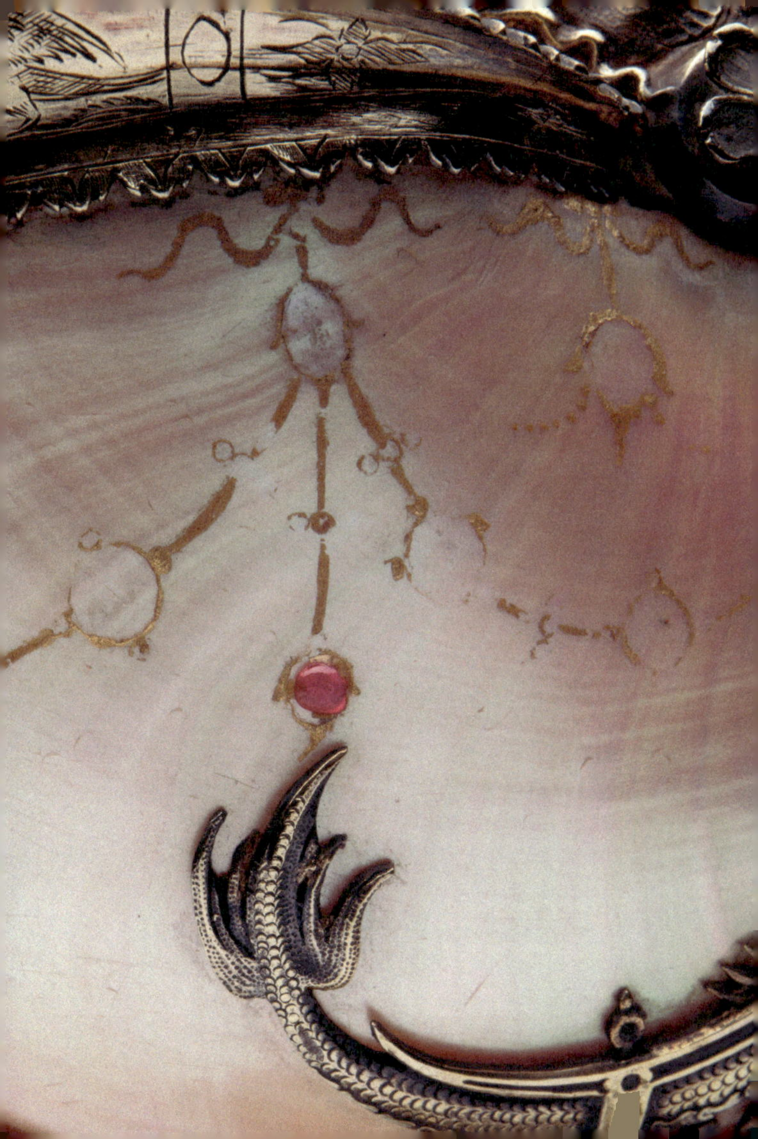

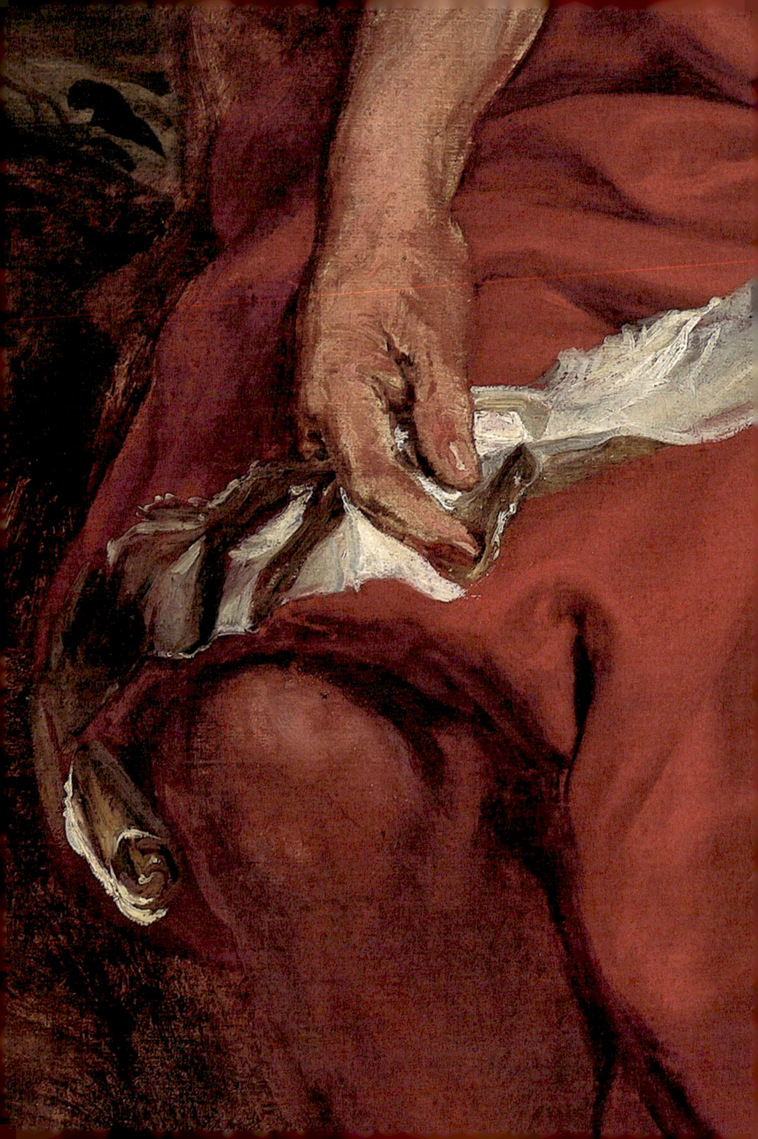

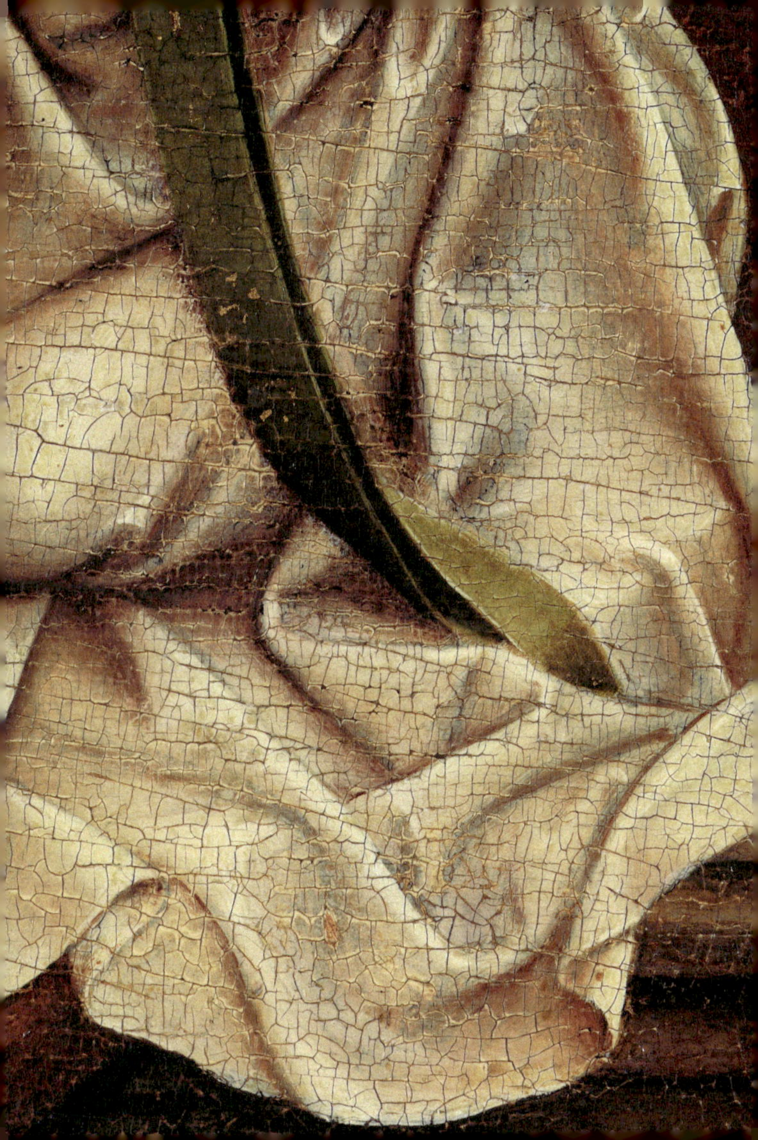

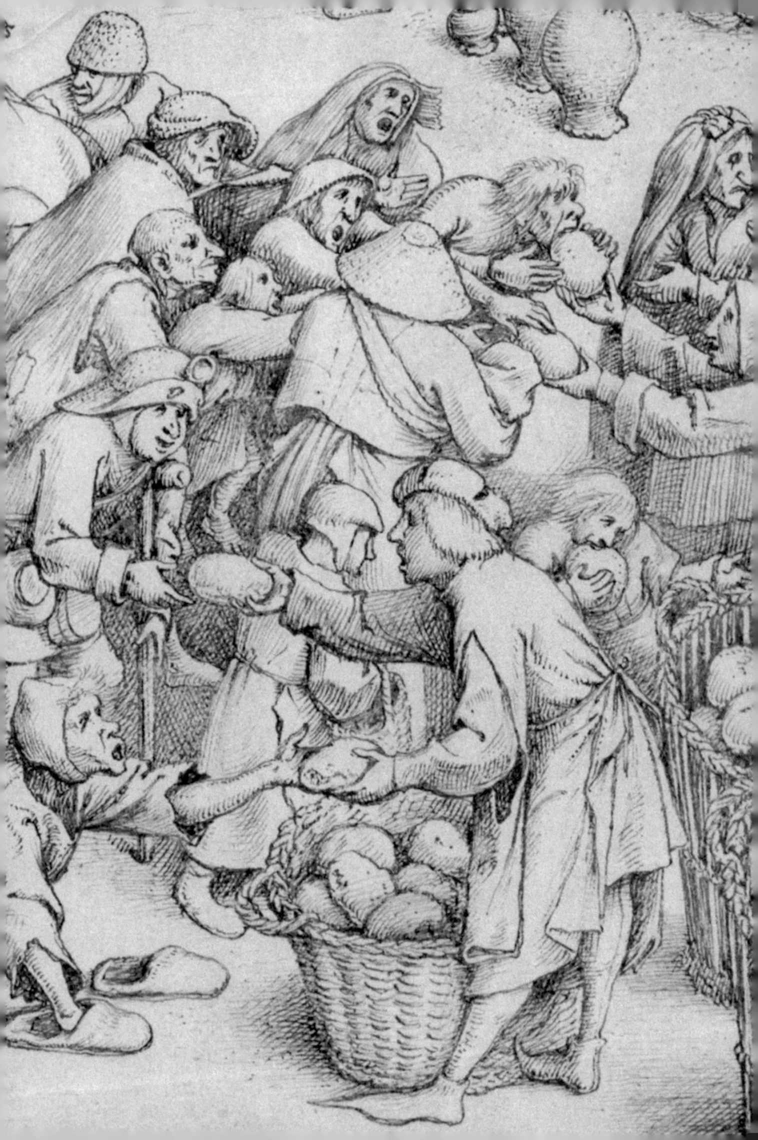

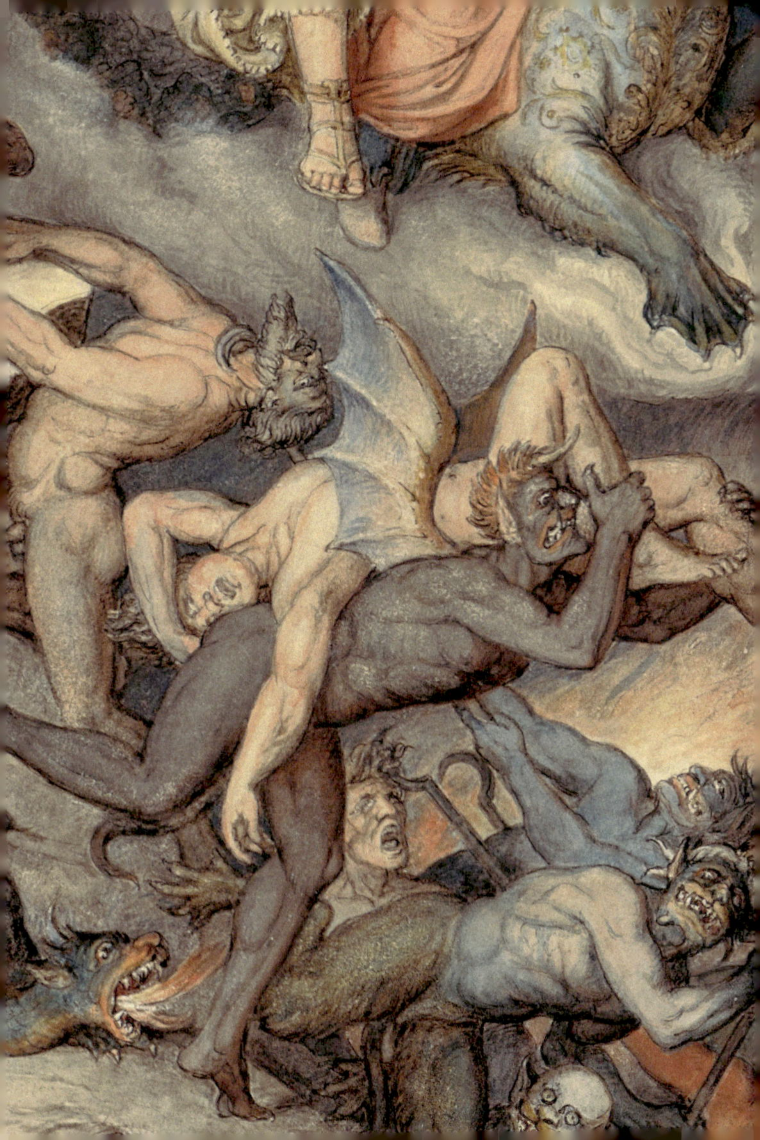

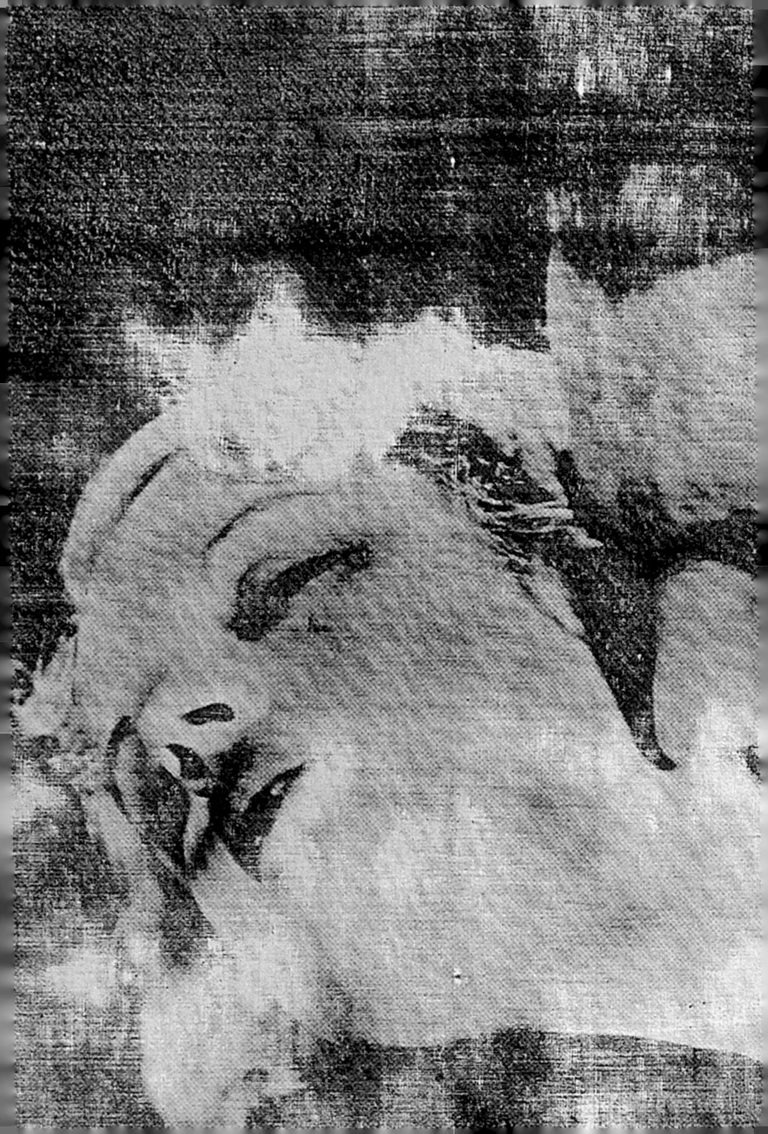

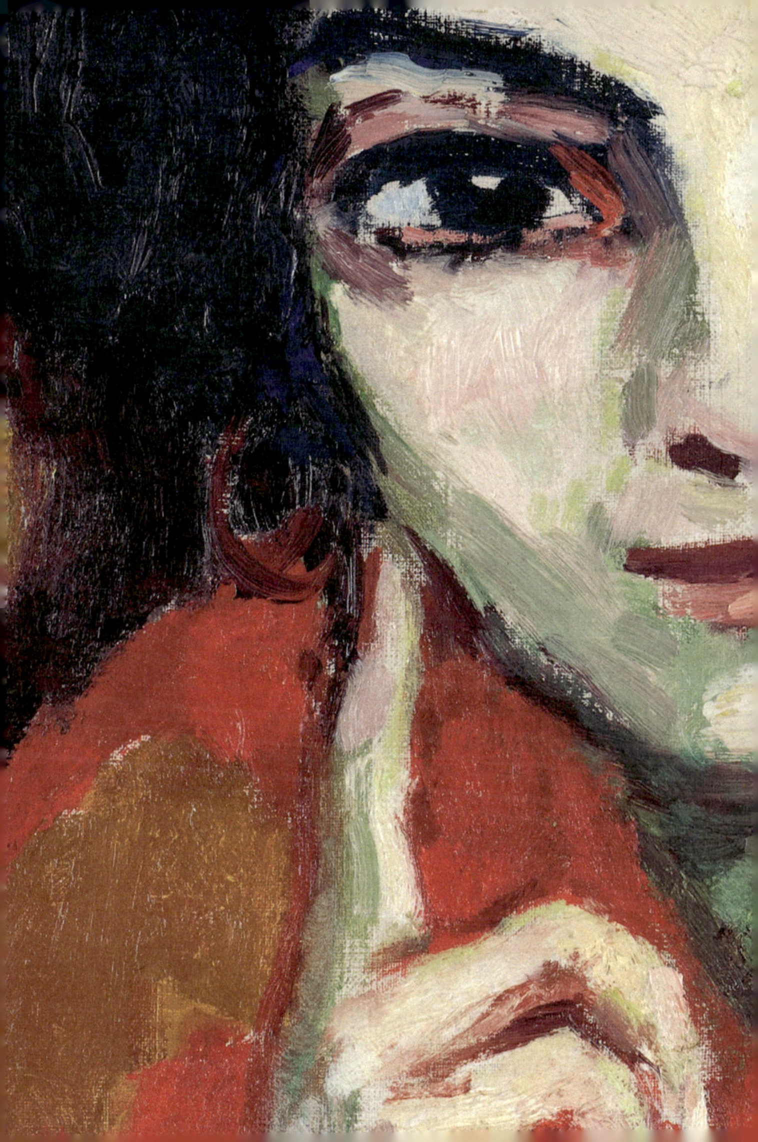

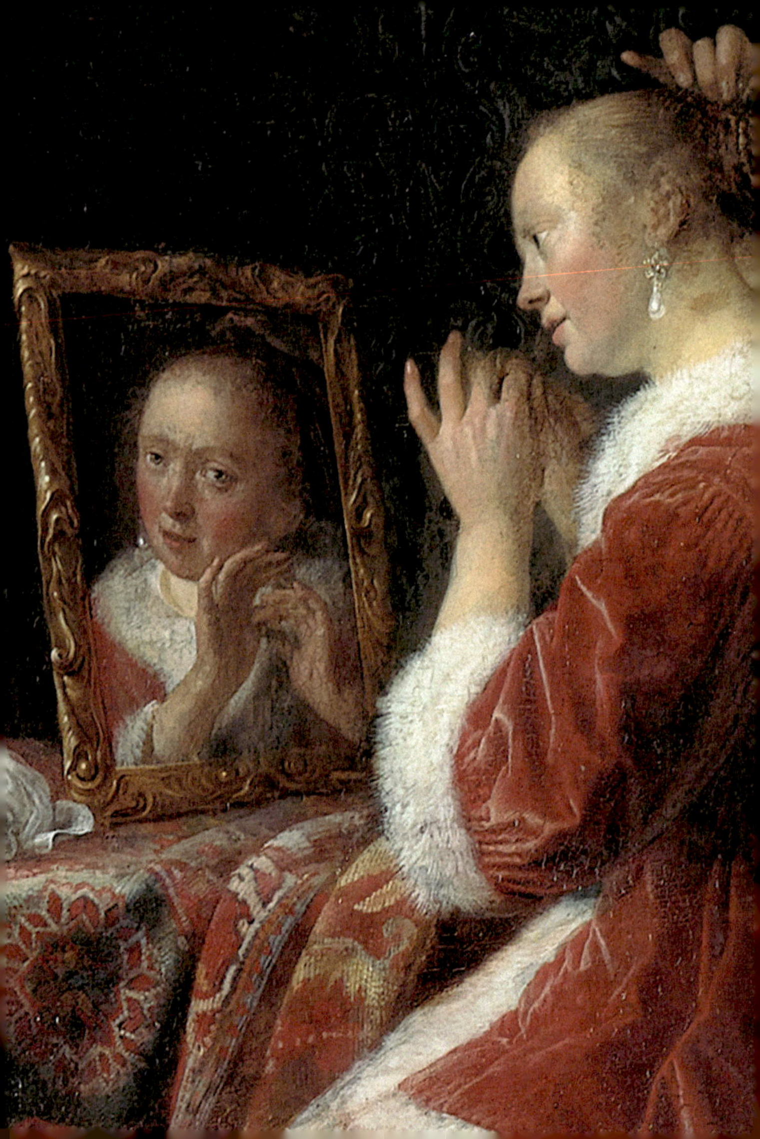

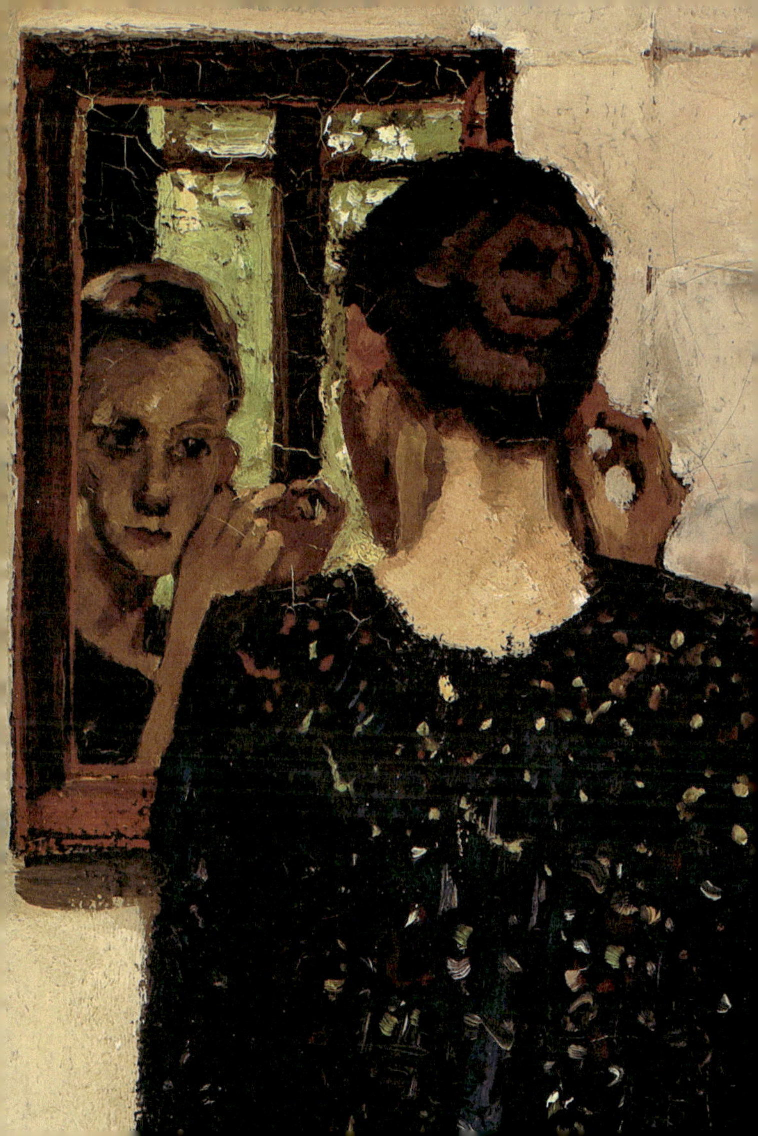

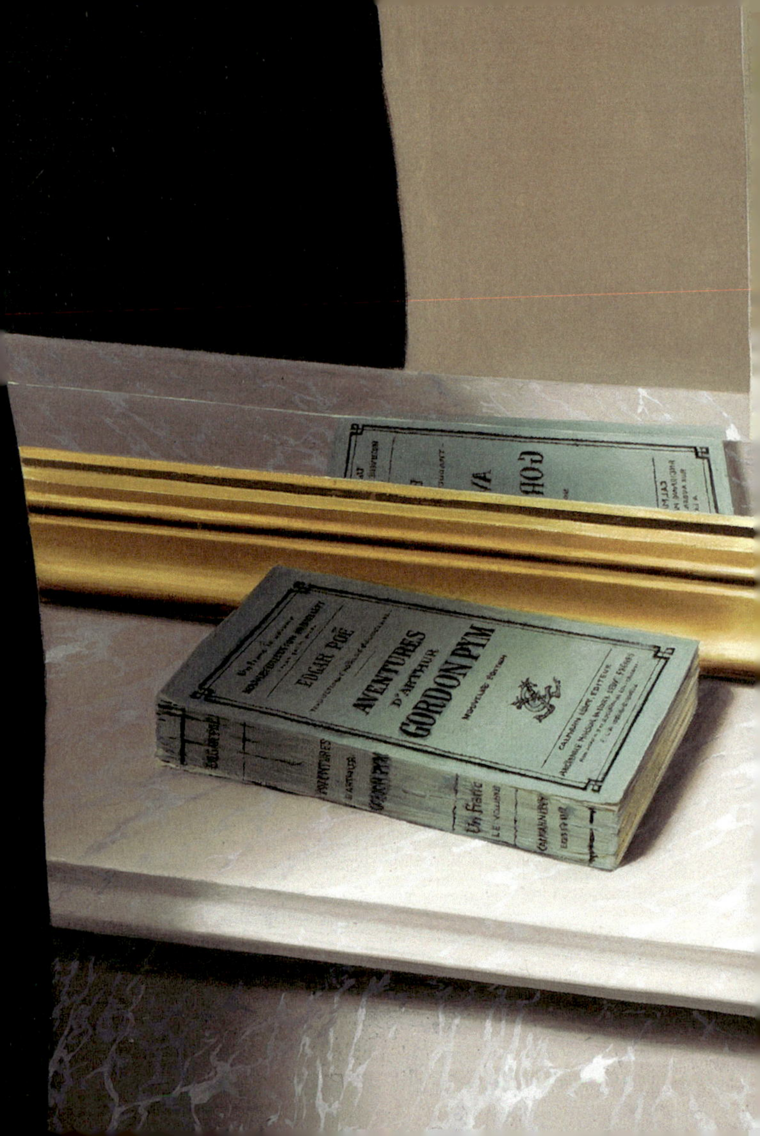

EDGAR POË
AVENTURES
D'ARTHUR
GORDON PYM
EDGAR POË
AVENTURES
D'ARTHUR
GORDON PYM
Un Franc
LE VOLUME

CROWN
COPYRIGH

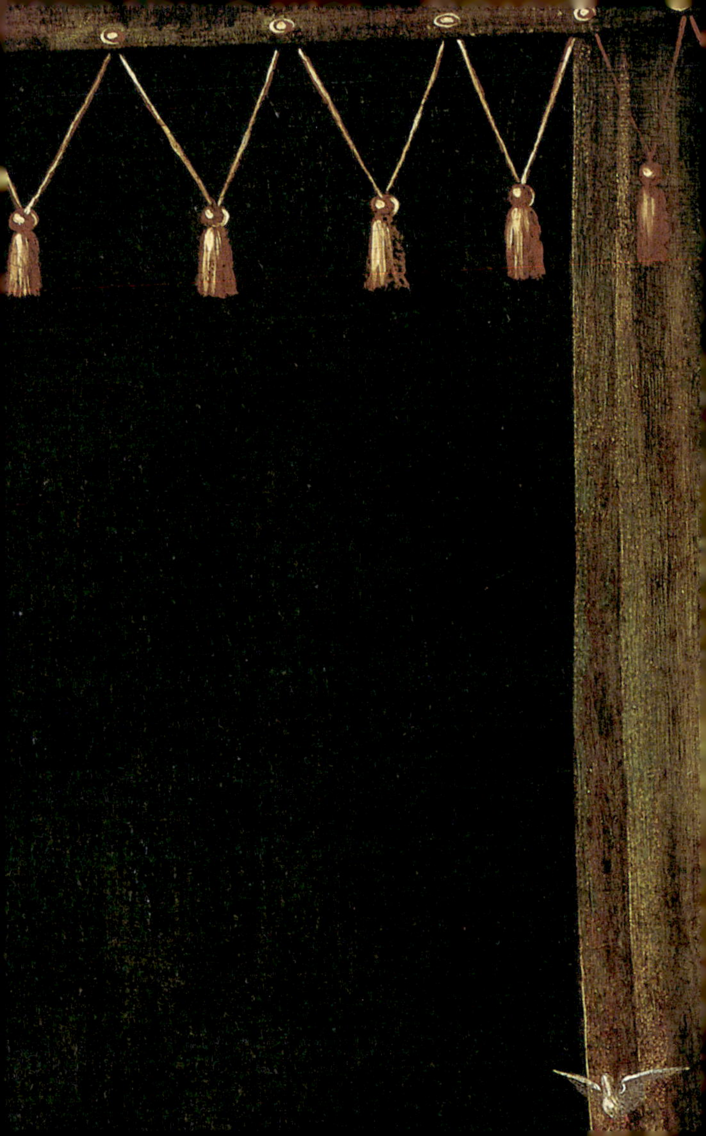